You're the Boss

You're the Boss

K. K. Wallace

Contemporary Books, Inc.
Chicago

Library of Congress Cataloging in Publication Data

Wallace, K. K.
    You're the boss.

    Includes index.
    1. Organization.   2. Success.   3. Vocational guidance.
I. Title.   II. Title: You are the boss.
HD31.W25   1982   650.1'4   81-69627
ISBN 0-8092-5839-0   AACR2

Published by Contemporary Books, Inc.
180 North Michigan Avenue, Chicago, Illinois 60601
Manufactured in the United States of America
Library of Congress Catalog Card Number: 81-69627
International Standard Book Number: 0-8092-5839-0

Published simultaneously in Canada by
Beaverbooks, Ltd.
150 Lesmill Road
Don Mills, Ontario M3B 2T5
Canada

Contents

Introduction

All of us in the working world are being thrust, kicking and screaming, into a critical new arena created by economic pressures and by management's new wave of expectation that employees participate in finding ways to help their organizations survive. Productivity, profitability, and tapping the resource that lies in knowledgeable workers are active goals of management.

Competition for jobs in the '80s and as we move into the twenty-first century is taking shape as the keenest ever experienced.

How we as individuals survive on the job hangs on two basics: a better understanding of how the business environment operates and an understanding of the human relationships involved, particularly in boss–subordinate relationships.

Now, more than ever, one factor above all others may determine how well we ultimately succeed in our jobs. That factor is how well we relate to our bosses.

As management increasingly mandates employee participation and better utilization of employees' talents, the boss becomes the funnel through which must pass our every idea, effort, plan, raise, or advancement.

As never before, we need to know how we can gain the boss's confidence and increase opportunities to exercise the kind of initiative that helps us get ahead. We need to know how to analyze what the boss thinks about us. Indeed, we *must* know how to package our ideas—or complaints—in order to be heard. We must become more adept at building in payoffs for the boss that let us reap rewards in turn. We must learn techniques for gaining agreements between ourselves and the boss on the scope of our jobs and the realization of our potentials.

This book presents realistic guidelines in boss–subordinate relationships that can help each of us find our way toward promotion and monetary or personal job fulfillment.

BOSS—THE COMMON DENOMINATOR

Anyone—man, woman, or mule—who has ever held a job finds himself or herself at one time or another confronting some kind of problem with the boss.

Because of the importance of this relationship, we can't afford to have an inadequate knowledge of the things that affect it. As an organizational consultant working to improve boss–subordinate relationships in every stratum of nearly every type of organization, I get the on-the-line truth from both camps: from bosses I hear what's wrong with subordinates, and from employees what would be different if they were the boss.

Sample laments heard over and over:

- "Why can't the boss criticize my mistakes without making me feel like *I'm* a mistake."
- "The boss stands over us to police everything we do. I sometimes wonder when he'll start going to the john with us."
- "My boss? The whole department cheers when he is out of the plant, and we get more work done."
- "He's moody—I never know whether to say good morning or keep my mouth shut."
- "My boss is two-faced. Consequently, we have a constant uproar in the department."
- "I will never get a promotion as long as that SOB is the boss."
- "The boss never buys my ideas."

Boss–subordinate relationships are much the same regardless of the type or size of the organization. I have drawn extensively, but by no means exclusively, on experiences in client companies, among which are banks, universities, food and meat processors, glass and chemical manufacturers, supermarkets, and insurance companies.

While actual names and organizations in case histories used in this book have been left out or otherwise disguised to protect the innocent (and the not-so-innocent), all examples are based on composites of real people and events played out from factory floor to steno pool to board room.

QUESTIONING ASSUMPTIONS

Each chapter title begins with an assumption commonly held by thousands of individuals; for example:

- If at first you don't succeed, try, try again.
- Take the job now; worry about the boss later.
- It's who you know, not what you know, that counts.

Countless people I talk to roadblock their careers because they cling to such worn ideas and refuse to question whether some of the assumptions they labor under might be false. Using faulty assumptions as chapter titles points out these mistaken beliefs and the need for looking at every aspect of the job with attitudes suitable for the modern work world.

REMOVING SEXUAL AND OTHER HANG-UPS

To get the most out of this book, it is important at the outset to remove the obstacles of our own prejudices and faulty assumptions:

- *If you are a man and a case is about a woman—and vice versa of course—there is nothing in it for you.* Hogwash! The principles are the same for men or women, and the reward goes to those who are able to recognize it.
- *The experience of persons in industries, companies, or*

jobs other than your own have nothing to do with you.
Balderdash! Other settings can provide us with a
learning experience. And what may not be a problem
today *may* be your problem tomorrow. There are
enough similarities in the experiences of others to offer
lots of insights into your own situation. Reading about
someone else in a job or industry removed from your
own also provides objectivity that you may not be able
to apply to a situation in which you are directly or
emotionally involved.

• *I refuse to think of myself as a subordinate, and I hate
  the word* boss. (On this point, you may be in trouble,
  since that word probably appears no less than fifty
  thousand times in this text.) Nuts! You must keep in
  mind that boss–subordinate describes nothing more
  than a dependent relationship in business. It has nothing to do with titles or forms of address. Even the
  chairman of the board has the stockholders as boss.
  Though they may not be referred to as such, the
  chairman operates by the principles of the boss–
  subordinate relationship—if he or she intends to remain
  on the board.

A REVOLUTION IN THE OFFING

More and more in companies that I work with, top management is coming to realize that it is no more important than the
rank and file. I see trends developing in which companies will
invest in the kind of organizational overhaul that allows, yea,
demands, employee participation in management. I predict that
management will increasingly change its attitude that workers do
and managers think, thus creating greater balance between boss
and subordinates and their individual needs.

Is this the beginning of a revolution in the work place? I
would rather think that it is the dawn of a new freedom and
responsibility for each of us.

We can use that responsibility to improve our lot through the most positive actions open to us: managing the boss and changing ourselves.

You can begin by recognizing that there are times when you will know best, times when your boss will know best, and times when you both will have to abide by company policy, regardless of who—if anyone—knows best. This book is designed to give you insights into the difference and ideas on what to do about it.

You're the Boss

1

Faulty Assumption One

TAKE THE JOB; WORRY ABOUT THE BOSS LATER

*"If I'd known what a loser my
boss was when I took the job,
you can believe I wouldn't be in
the mess I am in today."*

*Female, 28
industrial relations area
major food processing company*

I work for money—mostly. It's a fair assumption that you do,
too, and that most of us seem to have money myopia. We are
far more concerned about getting and spending our paycheck
than about who we have to please to keep receiving it.

Whether you're on the job, applying for a job, or considering
a transfer to another job, it is important to realize the impact
your immediate boss or supervisor can have on your paycheck.
This includes whether or not you will get a fatter one and even
ultimately whether your career goes up, down, or just stagnates.

In fact, we could translate *job trouble*—including no-advance-
in-pay trouble—as *boss trouble* and be accurate nine times out
of ten. Yet most of us accept positions with very little thought
given to who or what the boss is and what makes him or her
tick. Few individuals bother to find out anything specific about
their boss's background even when they have the chance, much
to their regret later on.

1

FORESIGHT BUILDS REWARDS

Foresight is to the outcome of a job what foreplay is to sex. Without it you are likely to suffer these consequences:

Feeling frustration. Most job frustration stems from a faulty relationship with the boss, frequently from causes that give clear warning signals before you take a job.

Failure to get the most out of the situation. All employees— be they entry level, hourly, first-line, supervisors, or middle and top management—can help themselves immensely by understanding their immediate bosses and how those bosses can help or hinder their progress in the organization.

Experiencing faulty intercourse with fellow workers. Your boss and his or her relationship or problems with others will affect your ability to get your job done.

Take the case of one woman—let's call her Suzanne—who related her experience to me in the course of my work with her company. She held a position in the industrial relations area of a major food processing firm. At the time we first talked she had been working there for three years and was ready to quit the job, even though she had considered it her big opportunity at the outset.

Suzanne's boss had made enemies of key managers with whom she had to work, and they in turn would not cooperate with *her* because they didn't want her boss to look good. This, in turn, made it almost impossible for Suzanne to perform her duties.

Part of the problem was the boss's personality. He antagonized and embarrassed too many powerful people. For example, he blurted out to the manager of sales training during an executive meeting that "most sales training isn't worth a plug nickel and yours is worth less." He congratulated the personnel manager on his new promotion by asking, "Was it worth marrying the old man's daughter?" And he greeted the president's new assistant—a former college professor—by saying loudly in the presence of others, "At your age, it's about time you started to gain some real world experience."

It was small consolation to Suzanne to realize that a man who puts down others in public usually isn't satisfied with himself and won't be with anyone else, or that he made everyone else's business his own because he really had so little of his own to attend to.

Herein lay the rub. Suzanne's department consisted only of her boss, who was in his mid-fifties, herself, and a secretary. The department supposedly had been created to carry out work on a special project (for which Suzanne had been hired), but was in reality an interim pasture for her boss before the company could offer him early retirement without setting off fear and trembling throughout the managerial ranks. By the time I talked to her again she was bitter, and with reason: he finally had been let out, and the department, along with her job, had been eliminated.

But Suzanne put her finger on the problem herself: "From the very beginning I should have asked more questions, tough questions, about my boss. You know, the company flew me in twice for interviews and I never once got to meet him."

CHOOSE YOUR TRUTHS CAREFULLY

If I had been advising Suzanne, I would have given her some of my golden rules of boss casing. Most of them have at their base the bit of advice passed along to me by my grandmother, who was a buyer in the retail trade long before women entered this business in force: "Be sure to choose your truths carefully, and don't get smart too late." Not by any means inclusive, these suggestions head the list.

- Insist on interviews as high up the company ladder as possible and get as much information as you give.
- Ferret out some tidbits about the company on your own instead of relying on what the company tells you.
- Force yourself to see, hear, and analyze everything instead of letting yourself select only those things you want to see and hear. (Joining a company is, after all,

more similar to an arranged marriage than a love
match.)

- Don't assume that the prospective employer has your
best interests at heart or even abides by the codes,
conventions, and customs of fair play.
- Common sense, mother wit, and intuition should be
employed at all times.

HOW TO FLUSH OUT INFORMATION IN THE JOB HUNT

If Suzanne had been smart, how might she have handled
things to her advantage? There are options open to all of us that
can help us get a better handle on a prospective job.

*Prior to an interview, request the names and titles of those
persons you will be meeting with.* In Suzanne's case, she should
have phoned the recruiter with whom she had her first job
appointment on the pretext that she would like to familiarize
herself with the names and positions ahead of time.

This is a tactic I use frequently when lining up meetings at
which I sell my consulting services, to ensure that the *right*
people will be present. It lets you, as a new recruit, know if you
need to seek additional interviews, and it can show the prospective company that you are thorough and will be well prepared
for meetings ahead of time. And you have nothing to lose,
because no one should be insulted by such a request. (If anyone
is insulted, that would tell you something, too!)

Ask to talk to other people in the company. If you are being
brought in for the interview at the company's expense, as
Suzanne was, you can always argue that it might be to the
company's advantage for you to see as many people as possible.
After all, they will want to get the most mileage from their
investment in you.

For those of you who get to an interview under your own
steam, it works well to stress the desire to learn more about the
company's business and how you fit into the overall picture. You
really do need to learn more about the duties of interfacing
departments if you are to function effectively. If the recruiter

hems and haws, you can bet you're about to be offered a nothing job! (And if up front you find that the position is one that will keep your light under a bushel basket, you can be sure that once you accept it, management will pile a couple of bricks on top to be sure it stays there.)

Snoop at the library, read between the lines of the annual report, and ask, ask, ask. Do all these things to get the names of the people you should be talking with and to find out some relevant facts about the company. Take the librarian into your confidence. Don't try to sift through the mountains of reference materials all by yourself. Let the librarian lead you by the hand to save precious time. For instance, if Suzanne had made a trip to the library (many libraries now index the local daily newspapers), she would have found that her prospective company had been severely criticized in a business page article for its poor record in hiring women for management positions. In the article, she also would have come across the name of the vice-president of industrial relations, who headed the area where she would be working. (Numerous weekly and monthly publications in this country are rarely found on your local newsstand but are indexed by product line, service, and industry in such resource journals as *Standard Periodical Directory, Ulrich's International Periodical Directory,* and *Writer's Market.*)

Annual reports also name some of the persons you may wish to contact for a brief interview. In addition, they give some idea of the structure of the department in which you will be working and who reports to whom. If the library doesn't have a copy of the firm's annual report on file, you usually can obtain one by writing to the company in care of the personnel or public relations department. Smaller companies often don't spend big bucks on a glossy annual report. But don't despair. Other key indexes to reference for information on the organization's products, field locations, financial figures, and names of key executives are *Moody's Industrial, Dun & Bradstreet, Standard & Poors,* the *Thomas Register,* and by no means last, the local chamber of commerce business directories or periodicals.

(Detailed financial data can be obtained by reading a copy of the 10-K report submitted by large organizations to the Securities and Exchange Commission. Formal requests should be addressed to The Securities and Exchange Commission, 219 South Dearborn, Room 1204, Chicago, IL 60604. Only those firms that meet one of the three criteria outlined in the Security and Exchange Act of 1934 are required to fill out form 10-K. These criteria will not be listed here but can be acquired easily at the aforementioned address. Make note of the fact that small companies are not compelled legally to complete this report; to my knowledge, none volunteer to do so.)

Don't forget to read between the lines in these resource materials. How many pages does the annual report allot to a discussion of your prospective department, for instance? You may find it has only a one-paragraph mention, while others receive a two-column spread. Read the whole report to get a handle on the type of employees the company hires with the particular skills you have to offer and the apparent opportunities there may be for career advancement.

And don't just look at the pictures (as a great number of stockholders can be counted on to do); analyze them carefully. Have most of the top bananas reached a ripe old age? Or is there life with the company at forty-five or even thirty-five? Had Suzanne kept a head count of the number of women between the glossy covers of Company X's annual report and taken a hard look at the level of their jobs, she would have turned up an interesting fact: an adroit photographer had turned a clerk typist into a regular Walter Mitty. The same woman appeared as a supervisor on the assembly line, an engineer inspecting plant equipment, a biologist (white coat, no gloves) chatting with two male colleagues, and a chemist looking meaningfully at a test tube.

Pump the switchboard operator. The best approach to getting names to set up interviews is to call the switchboard operator in those small to medium-sized firms that have a central system. Often she (and face it, it invariably is a "she") will know the person's name and complete title and can even spell it for you. In larger companies, you generally reach a particular department or division, but someone there usually can be pumped for information.

When using this technique, always remember honesty is *not* the best policy. Think of a good reason ahead of time why you need someone's name, such as: "My name is Jane Matheson (give an alias); I represent (insert here the name of a community service group, a trade association, or a nonprofit organization composed of area businesses) and wish to obtain the name of your department head for an important mailing we are sending out to executives in the area (never infer that you are sending out a survey or anything the executive might need to complete!)." Male recruits should have a sister, mother, sweetheart, or female impersonator make the call. Women give out a lot of information to other women. In fact, it has been my experience that women ask far fewer questions concerning why you want a particular executive's name. Nonetheless, make it a practice to get off the line fast; never chat.

The grapevine can yield perspective on a boss. Many people rely on the grapevine. Keep your ears open in company cafeterias (a surprising number of which are still accessible to outsiders). Gate-crash trade association meetings or play it safe by registering as a guest. These organizations are always looking for new members. Be sure to sign up for evening meetings. As a rule people talk more after having a few drinks. Join the boss's club; frequent the same barber or hairdresser.

Other people I've known look for anyone wearing a uniform. Their rationale is that these individuals are frequently in a position to observe more than they are observed and are the smartest, most savvy source for knowing what's really going on.

Don't forget former subordinates or the person that held the job before you came along. I once knew an executive director of a prestigious institution whose former public relations directors could have filled a stadium. This fraternity was a gold mine of information for anyone foolish enough to consider the job.

Although current subordinates could provide revealing information about your prospective boss, it should always be remembered that they may have ulterior motives. Many currently on the payroll may fear that the boss will get wind of anything they tell you (after all, they don't know you), or they may fear the consequences of your being hired at all. (You could be competition for them.)

In Suzanne's case both the recruiter and the secretary of her boss-to-be had misled her about the candidates trying for the job. Each had reasons for not wanting Suzanne to turn down the job.

HOW TO GET INFORMATION
WHEN YOU'RE THE INTERVIEWEE

The recruiter who handled Suzanne's initial interview used a very common ploy: applying pressure through the specter of several competitors for the position and thus implying that unless she made up her mind quickly, the job was going, going, gone. This accomplished several things at once:

- She was successfully detoured from dickering about salary.
- She allowed herself to be manipulated into taking the job through fear of losing out more than through the feeling that it was the right career decision for her.
- She was diverted from asking questions about the job and the boss, which the recruiter would have found difficult to answer satisfactorily.

Calling their bluff. The quickest way to establish whether an interviewer is bluffing about competition for the same job is to ask, "What do you consider to be my strengths and weaknesses compared to the other candidates you are considering for this position?" You might also politely point out that you have another job offer or prospect, providing that you do, and that it may be better for you to accept that position if your skills are not the ones the company is looking for and which your competition may possess.

It is also valuable to know and remember that at many job

levels (and certainly this was Suzanne's case) positions are left open for months and sometimes for a year or more. That is one of the essential facts that should be a part of anyone's information gathering about a job.

In Suzanne's case the stiff competition turned out to be:

- A forty-two-year-old man whose longest length of service with any given employer had run two full years.
- A twenty-year-old, working on her degree in psychology, who appeared for her interview in a backless sundress and included with her resume a photo of herself as "Miss Bikini of Beta Beta Phi."
- A hotshot graduate of a prestigious eastern university whose employment demands could only have been met by slotting him into the CEO's spot.

WHAT AN INTERVIEW SHOULD TELL YOU

If Suzanne had requested and received an interview with the person who was to be her boss, she would have averted much of her problem. When a meeting wasn't offered, she should have requested one. If he had been too busy or on a trip out of town, at the very least she might have capitalized on that as a legitimate reason for seeking another interview (perhaps with his boss, the V-P of industrial relations). Sometimes this even allows a broader range of specific questions than she might have felt comfortable asking in a face-to-face interview with the person who was to be her immediate superior.

In such an interview you might ask the prospective boss these questions:

1. *"How did you get started in the business?"*
This is a perfectly appropriate question. It puts people at ease and allows them to talk about their favorite subject.

2. *"In what capacity did you work before attaining your current position?"*

This sheds light on the company's reporting chain and gives some important background on what it takes to be promoted in the firm. Suzanne would have discovered that, to be a serious candidate for promotion to any top slot in her division, she would have had to hold a law degree. The V-P of industrial relations, Suzanne's boss's boss, was a lawyer. He had made a name for himself by settling labor disputes quickly before they erupted into open warfare. Obviously, she was hired with no intention of letting her go anywhere.

3. *"What are your key responsibilities? What changes have you introduced since coming aboard?"*

This line of questioning spotlights the tradition-bound boss quickly. It also gives you some idea of whether or not he or she is deadwood or cut off for some reason from the main action.

4. *"When was the department formed (or how long has it been in existence), and what purpose does it fulfill?"*

Had Suzanne asked this question, it would have revealed that her boss was probably a *floater,* a term sometimes applied to early retirement candidates or those who are deadwood and being phased out gradually by assigning them to perform spot jobs in various areas of the company. This is second only to having been assigned the task of writing the company history.

5. *"What do you consider the most pressing concerns you wish to see the department address in the next five years?"*

If the goals are something like a personal copying machine in every office or covered parking, forget it, unless that's your idea of career growth. If solid goals are named, ask what programs he or she has under way to address them. And follow up by asking the following question.

6. *"What role do you perceive me playing in the implementation of these programs?"*

If that seems too cheeky for your personal taste, substitute "the department" or "the staff" for "me."

Don't hesitate to pose these and similar questions to your prospective boss or others. Obtaining answers to these types of questions will help you define what your boss's role has been in the past, what it's likely to be in the future, and where you fit in (if at all). Don't wait until you've taken the job to find out whether your boss is the wet-behind-the-ears son of the company president; someone promoted from the line who continues to look backward rather than forward; a hotshot brought in from outside the organization by a headhunter whose ancestors include survivors of the Donner Pass, or someone like Suzanne's boss with a penchant for making enemies.

READING TICKS, BLINKS, AND STARES

There are subtle, sometimes very revealing answers to glean from the manner in which the boss responds to the foregoing questions.

Be polite, but don't be passive. Ask those questions that are more serious and sensitive in nature after the interview is well under way.

Watch for gaps of time in the prospective boss's career. Try to determine if this is just forgetfulness or if the person may be hiding something.

Ask each question quickly but clearly. Maintain constant eye contact. Should any query cause silence, an attempt to skirt the issue, or confusion, don't reword the question (since the prospective boss may wish to infer that you didn't make yourself clear) but move on to the next one.

In the event that you have a very cool customer who doesn't visibly flinch at any probe, look instead for a few hooded blinks of the eye. If the eye blinks, doesn't reopen, and is accompanied by slow, deep breathing, terminate the interview.

THE HIGHER YOU ARE, THE HARDER YOU FALL

If you are considering taking that big step forward to the top, make sure you won't slip backwards. Check out your prospective boss first before saying yes, even if you are seeking a high level position. Many former presidents of large corporations, whose tenure lasted less than a year due to "personal differences" with the chairman, will attest to the importance of taking this step. (The old man really didn't want to step down and relinquish operating control.)

The higher up the corporate ladder an individual climbs, the bigger the paychecks, the plusher the offices. But don't overlook the personal gamble by taking a seat at the wrong board table. Keep in mind how difficult it will be to pull up stakes and locate another. Find out who your boss is up front and don't play musical chairs.

YOUR BILL OF RIGHTS

- Every job seeker is entitled to know who the boss is going to be and to get a chance to talk with that person before taking the job.
- If your prospective boss can ask what types of jobs you've held in the past, you can pose the same question.
- You have a right to get enough information to determine if the job description provided by the personnel department will bear any resemblance to the actual duties. Regardless of what personnel tells you, whether or not you get to do the job for which you are hired is left entirely to your boss!
- If your prospective boss wants to know where you wish to be in five years, ask to see or hear future plans for the department and where your boss expects to be in five years.
- If your boss wants to see your track record, it's okay to ask him or her to run a few laps for you!

2
Faulty Assumption Two

THE BEST BOSSES ARE MADE, NOT BORN

> *"My boss was never going anywhere. It was him or me. I figured the only way out—short of killing him—was to get him a job offer by selling him to the competition."*
>
> *Male, 32*
> *marketing department*
> *research division petroleum company*

One of my favorite fairy tales as a child was *Cinderella*. It's a safe assumption that most of us best remember the happy ending in which Prince Charming sweeps Cinderella off her feet and bestows on her the perks of royalty, while we tend to forget her life of drudgery amid the pots and pans and the slings and arrows of her ugly stepmother and stepsisters. But you can also bet that, like real-life Cinderellas (and fellas) who are promoted into the ethers of the corporate or business kingdom, *she* didn't forget the hard lumps endured to get where she was. The years of struggle have a way of taking their toll on minds and bodies.

Happy endings notwithstanding, how do you suppose Cinderella fared as a royal highness? A realistic scenario is that when she got to the royal kitchens and had to assume the role of boss over those responsible for putting the royal burnish on the copper pans or sweeping up the princely hearth, she found herself feeling pretty uncomfortable. No doubt, instead of investing time to learn and perform her new duties in court dalliance and intrigue, she may even have found herself grabbing a polishing cloth and showing the scullery maids how things were to be done in the kitchen.

Those who come up through the ranks frequently remain haunted by the past: *they never want to go back, but they often are afraid to break away, to relinquish what they know best and feel most comfortable with.*

PROBLEMS WITH THE SELF-MADE BOSS

It might be argued that the "made" boss, the so-called self-made man or woman, really knows what you're going through on the job and can relate better to your problems because he or she has been there.

Ideally, that is so. But put away your fairy tales.

Too often the attitude of the boss promoted through the ranks can cause myriad problems for a subordinate. This kind of boss may exhibit one or all of the following traits.

The do-it-all trait. This type of boss may constantly watch your every move or actually perform your job for you. This is particularly true of the bosses who held the exact job in the past. If their way was good enough for them, it is good enough for you. Some may use their new clout to make sure. After all, how would it look if others did the job better than they had?

The know-it-all trait. This boss may be dictatorial and downright undemocratic, turning know-how into know-it-all. And it won't do you any good to bring up his or her humble beginnings. In fact, that's one of the surest ways to cut your own throat. Can't you just see someone reminding Cinderella that she used to be a kitchen maid?

The take-it-all trait. This person may be totally unsympathetic to your needs and career aspirations. Remember, as long as you're his or her subordinate you pose no threat. What's more, these kinds of bosses often don't believe anyone truly is capable of taking over. They, and they alone, are indispensable for every job.

To live through the problems created by any of these traits, it helps to understand where such bosses are coming from. There are even ways to turn this knowledge to your advantage.

YOU MAY BRING OVERSUPERVISION ON YOURSELF

When you get right down to it, the self-made boss is often insecure. This can be imagined or it can be caused by a lack of belief in his or her own abilities. It can also be a real situation that has nothing to do with you—when the boss's job is on the line or his performance is in question by others.

When, as a result, this type of boss won't let go or turn over the job, the subordinate's typical reaction is to sing the "Over-bossin' Blues" rather than to look at how his or her own actions—or inaction—hook the boss's feelings of insecurity or threaten an already precarious position.

It is necessary to examine yourself critically:

- Why do you think the boss doesn't delegate to you, or watches your every move?
- Could any of your actions—or inaction—be contributing to your boss's insecurity?

You just may find that you need supervision! You may also come to the realization that the boss is sincerely helping out or lending assistance.

Where neither is the case, you can take preventive steps that make it unnecessary for your boss to oversupervise.

Step 1:
Start by Understanding Your Own Subordinates

First make a list of all the things your own subordinates do that cause you to worry about their work or to feel uncertain about how well the job or project is progressing.

Next, write down specific instances when your subordinates made you feel anxious and compelled to check their performance.

Ask yourself whether any of your actions—or inaction—may rouse the same uneasiness in your boss, or if you may be mimicking some of the behavior that causes you to feel uneasy about others when the shoe is on the other foot and you are the boss.

Step 2:
Keep Track of Conversations You Have with Your Boss

Be careful to list all the times your boss says: "I'll have to get right on that for you." "Let me look into the situation for you." "I'm sure something can be done about that problem." "Let me think about it." These phrases should clue you in to the fact that you do not appear to your boss to be fully capable of making your own on-the-job decisions.

In fact, your boss may be hovering over you and watching your every move because you actually ask for that kind of treatment without realizing it. Or you may bring so many problems to your boss's attention that he or she really begins to get worried about your ability to handle the work load in your department.

Step 3:
Note Frequency and Reasons for Your Boss's Visits

Make mental notes or, better yet, record the time, date, and number of visits your boss makes to your department. The reason may surprise you. *Your boss may feel left out in the dark* about all kinds of things, and that's what keeps him or her hovering over you.

All sorts of textbooks strongly recommend delegation of tasks. They stress that the manager must (and will) set up appropriate follow-up mechanisms to track assignments handed over (and even those palmed off) to subordinates.

Don't fall into the trap of believing that this follow-up will necessarily happen. There are lots of gaps between theory and implementation. For instance, *management by exception,* or MBE, has become a buzzword. (Buzzwords are those words that sound self-evident. They *seem* to explain themselves. But in fact they frequently come into use for ideas that everyone thinks they know about but couldn't explain if their lives depended on it.)

MBE is supposedly a system through which "deviation limits" (self-evident, right?) are established between the boss and subordinates to allow some flexibility in the performance of tasks. However, these limits are seldom written down; instead, they are left in a kind of twilight zone or are just "understood." The trouble is, no one really understands, and the boss who most needs to know must frequently resort to ferreting out information on his or her own.

Step 4:
Record the Boss's References to Being Professional

Pick up on what the boss says about why others are hired or are considered professional: "Miss Martin is certainly professional in her dress." "Mac is a real pro." "You can always tell the professionals from the schlocks."

Nine times out of ten, "being professional" means to your boss that you *show* that you are on top of the job.

Last year I interviewed several public relations firms to determine which one to hire. I had to consider as unprofessional the firms at which my contact failed to call me back in a reasonable time, and they were dropped from the list. Your boss may similarly have standards of professionalism by which he judges performance, whether he says so or not.

HOW YOU CAN CAST OFF THE TENTACLES OF THE SELF-MADE BOSS

Remember that, if your boss is a self-made man or woman, the odds are high that he or she got there by being resourceful and by exhibiting self-reliance. Such people admire and consciously or unconsciously seek this trait in others. The fundamental way to deal with this kind of boss really lies in developing yourself through observing this rule.

Cardinal Rule:
Learn to Lean on Yourself

Be sure to follow these tips:

- Don't lean on your boss so much.
- Be strong.
- Develop your own forward movement.
- Be self-reliant.

The next time you face a ticklish situation, pretend your boss has just left town and isn't there to tell you what to do. You have no one to run to, no shoulder to cry on or shift the burden to. You have only yourself to rely on. Think what you should do to resolve the situation and why. Some corollaries to the Cardinal Rule will help you do just that.

Cardinal Rule Corollary:
Learn What's Important and What Isn't Before You Take It
to the Boss

Before approaching your boss always consider whether the matter is worthy of his or her attention. I am not suggesting that you withhold information, take on more responsibility than you should, or go around your boss. I am suggesting that you shoot less from the lip and firmly determine whether or not your boss is the proper target. Some situations need to be discussed with your boss, but many do not. A well-developed sense of priorities and good timing are marks of the successful.

If your boss is always harried, or is prone to the unwanted rescue of subordinates, don't add fuel to the fire by provoking his or her involvement and supervision where it really isn't necessary. This is particularly advisable during the first year of your boss's new promotion. Everyone who is promoted goes through a period of adjustment.

Cardinal Rule Corollary:
Understand Exactly How the Boss Reacts to or Handles Pressure

Learn to understand some of the pressures the boss may be under and learn to handle things you can to decrease that pressure rather than adding to it. Also, be supportive of the boss.

Don't just sit back and complain like a secretary I recently talked with. She had a new boss who was appointed regional manager for a firm that manufactures and leases tractor trailers. The secretary was put off by the new boss because he was extremely harried, she said. (The root cause of being harried is generally pressure to prove yourself, which she didn't understand.) She was also biased in favor of the older bosses, who, she noted, seemed calmer and easier to work with.

Shortly after the new man came on board, the secretary informed him that the office lease was soon to expire and the developers would need three months' notice of intention to renew. When I talked to her she was complaining that her boss had yet to do anything about the lease.

It was obvious to me that this was a task she could have handled herself. But that aside, when I inquired whether she had again reminded her boss of the now quickly approaching deadline, her answer was, "No, I already told him about it." As if the poor man didn't have another thing on his mind!

She was certainly setting herself up for a real loss of confidence in her abilities and even in her motives, which could easily backfire.

Cardinal Rule Corollary:
Analyze the Questions the Boss Typically Asks You

Make special note of the type of information your boss requests when he or she happens to drop by. (Special note: If the information is illegal, scatological, or immoral, you may need to keep your own confidential record for your own protection.) If it is pretty predictable, determine how you can provide the data—ideally before it's asked for—to set the boss's mind at ease.

A good salesperson is aware of the types of questions prospects may ask or types of information they may seek, and is prepared to provide it. This frequently makes the critical difference in getting a sale. Apply this technique to your boss and provide data you know he or she will request.

Some of the information bosses may request in their quest for clarification may not be appropriate for a written report—or, indeed, even an oral one. For instance, in a supermarket chain the head of security had to report to a suspiciously over-curious boss.

The security head's boss always wanted clarification—with the most explicit details—of any employees who were caught "doing it" (in the boss's words) on the premises. In fact, he was called twice to go over the details of the couple caught in the walk-in meat freezer. But even when all were behaving themselves, the boss suspected hanky-panky, made accusations, and had the security chief continuously checking and reporting. (A defamation of character suit eventually was filed by one young woman.)

RECOGNIZING WHEN THE SELF-MADE BOSS BECOMES A ROADBLOCK: A CASE OF SHIFTING GEARS

Many a self-made boss who makes it to a top position in a company is afflicted with a fear-generated madness I call "top domino paranoia." Whether the affliction is caused by the strenuous climb to the top or just some difficulty in adjusting to the rare ethers of the new altitude is undetermined.

The main symptom of this disease is the use of craftiness and deceit, which this kind of person feels justified in using to pursue and protect his or her power and position.

The problems generated by this kind of person have a ripple effect, with pressures of all kinds being passed along through the ranks. Such a boss becomes a major roadblock in the career path of subordinates.

Recently a young woman set up an appointment to talk to me about her boss. Kim, as I'll call her, was a supervisor in a large insurance company who reported to a department head. We'll call him Ben. He was in charge of loans and cash values. When we talked she had had it with him. As she put it, "He just doesn't trust me to do anything. I have to show him every single piece of paper that leaves that department. I'm not an assistant manager; I'm a high paid clerk."

Kim had never recognized that the problem did not originate with Ben. He merely was carrying out orders from his own boss, who had major operating responsibilities and several departments reporting to him.

We'll call this executive Marshall. It was he who required every item leaving Ben's department to go out under Ben's signature. Since there were literally hundreds of cash surrenders in a typical week, on top of regular correspondence, it was not unusual for Ben to sign his name more than a thousand times to that many documents.

Busy work? Right. But this was precisely the kind of work Marshall wanted Ben to perform. He reasoned that as long as Ben (and the other department heads) stayed occupied with this load of duties, it was less likely that he (or the rest) would ever become a threat to Marshall's position.

Marshall had reached the top one step at a time, struggling and straining and outlasting others. (In fact, in several instances he got promoted because he was the only one left to take the job. Insurance companies frequently have rather high turnover, so many of the promotion goodies go to those who have hung in there the longest.) Now, nobody, but nobody, was going to take Marshall's power away from him—especially if he had anything to say or do about it. Marshall, therefore, took great pains to keep his department heads as tightly confined to rigid duties as they were in the little boxes on the organizational chart, at least until he was ready to let them out.

This is typical of many individuals who, after years of waiting and working to get ahead, feel extremely threatened by the ambitions of subordinates.

At my suggestion, Kim first applied the self-analysis test to see if she was doing things that kept Ben from giving her more challenging tasks. Finding no serious deficiencies, Kim started taking stock of her situation and became aware of several warning signs.

Warning sign number one. Ben's job, when you got right down to it, was just that of a higher paid clerk than her own. Did Kim really want to set her aspirations on that job?

Warning sign number two. Marshall had manipulated hirings and firings to remove logical stepping-stones to his job. Kim would never have Ben's job because Marshall had him blocked.

Warning sign number three. Ben had worked nearly 2½ years without even taking a vacation or receiving more than a gratuitous raise. Nor was he powerful enough to get raises for Kim and her subordinates.

As a result of her analysis, Kim realized that her career, for all practical purposes, was roadblocked.

With a better understanding of her own strengths, Kim shifted career goals to get around the roadblock of Marshall and Ben. She returned to school, while remaining at her undemanding job, and eventually was able to transfer to the investments division.

Gear-Shifting Recommendations

A regular review of any job allows you a chance to do preventive repairs before major trouble develops.

A necessary detour around a roadblock in the career path often forces you onto exciting or new roads of opportunity where you wouldn't otherwise venture.

HOW TO SPOT TROUBLE WITH THE SELF-MADE BOSS AND WHAT TO DO ABOUT IT

I certainly do not wish to infer that all self-made men and women exhibit the foibles or near paranoia of some of the types portrayed in these pages. But there are enough of these bosses running around that it behooves you to be aware of the problems and to be able to spot the most glaring trouble signs.

My own career might well have been different if I had not done that very thing several years ago when I participated in an executive training program. I spent six months going from department to department, learning about the company. One month was spent in the sales promotion area. The manager, Roy, was a younger version of Marshall. He tipped his hand after only a few discussions regarding different promotional campaigns the company had under way.

During these briefings he used the terms *my* and *mine* consistently, even though I knew very well he had three hard-working colleagues and a go-getter secretary working for him. But as far as the outside world was concerned, the impression he gave was that he produced the work single-handedly.

Looking through several files the secretary pulled for my orientation revealed another significant fact. Every proposal and all correspondence went out over Roy's signature and on his letterhead, regardless of who originated it. (The situation was quite different from that of Ben. In this case Roy was signing his name for his own benefit.)

When anything came up about the contribution of his subordinates, Roy was quick to point out that they had a lot to learn.

As a participant in this training program, we were told that it was possible to join any of the departments we worked in if the respective manager was receptive. Needless to say, even though Roy was willing, I was not.

Actually, I learned quite a lot from this experience that has been reinforced through the years. Ferreting out clues to potential trouble may take a little detective work, but it's well worth the effort.

Clue number one. The subordinates in the department have a long tenure under your prospective boss. With some allowances for those perfect companies where subordinates live happily ever after in the same position, this may mean one of several things:

- They are all has-beens no one else will take on.
- The skills gained in this department are not transferable elsewhere.
- The boss (first-line supervisor, department head, or vice-president) has set up a good line of defense and blocks everyone.

Clue number two. On the other hand, be wary if turnover is high. Given the nature of things, it's likely that there's a fox in the hen house when too many chickens fly the coop.

Clue number three. The prospective boss's career path holds too many or too few positions. This is a sure indicator of your promotion chances.

Ask any prospective boss to outline his or her career path. Be careful to note the boss's seniority versus number of positions held. Has this boss held five positions in thirty years or just two? (Since trying to figure out exactly what this means on this information alone is about as precise as reading tea leaves, go on to a more accurate indicator.)

Try to discover his or her feelings about past jobs as well as the current one. (One prospective boss with whom I interviewed made the following statement about his current job: "It has taken me all my life to find something I'm good at and this is it.")

From the territorial tone of his voice and the look in his eye, I decided to pass. I knew taking a job under him would have been a dead end for me, since he looked to be in perfect health and longevity, no doubt, ran in his family. On the other hand, if the person always seems to be rising in the company with a subordinate taking the open position, chances are the boss is a good risk.

Clue number four. Subordinates have nothing but nice things to say about the boss.

If you will be a supervisor or department manager with subordinates reporting to you, ask to interview some of these people to get a feel for morale.

Remember that many people still live by their mothers' rule: "If you can't think of something nice to say, say nothing at all." If this happens, read between the lines, so to speak. Does your intuition tell you that they aren't telling all? Do they start to say something and then seem to pull back? Could it be that they are afraid to tell the truth? Do they make a jab in the form of a joke and then say, "I was only joking"? (This is a sure sign that there might be some underlying truth to what they say.)

Clue number five. The position has been vacant a short time and you are being pressured to accept.

As grade levels increase, so should the search time. If it doesn't, you may be correct in assuming that the title doesn't really match the job responsibilities or the actual duties you will be performing, or that the position was held before by a glorified "gopher" who is sorely missed. A truth in advertising suit probably would require the ad to read: "Wanted: Sucker."

Clue number six. When asked about the strengths and weaknesses of your predecessor, the boss focuses on the weaknesses.

If you are replacing someone, ask your prospective boss to state the strengths and weaknesses of the individual you may be replacing. Which characteristics would your prospective boss like to see emulated?

Beware of the boss who focuses primarily on the weaknesses of former subordinates. One boss of a large firm talked at great length about the poor eyesight of one of his subordinates and how he constantly had to help her proof copy. I found this all very curious as a reason for dismissal. I subsequently learned the young woman's infirmity to be nothing more or less, poor thing, than that she wore glasses. I then didn't have to go very far to learn that the boss frequently made passes. If you rebuffed him, you weren't long for that department.

Clue number seven. The prospective boss can't name three key contributions or accomplishments made by the person who has just left.

Persons like Roy or Marshall, who go out of their way to be indispensable, will draw a complete blank when asked such a question.

The indispensable boss rarely delegates any major projects or responsibilities to subordinates.

This kind of boss usually gives the excuse that subordinates aren't experienced enough to handle this or that task. This way the impression is created that the ship would not possibly stay on course without the boss at the helm.

It is axiomatic that you will neither gain experience nor go anywhere under the thumb of this type of boss.

PLAYING DAVID TO THE BOSS'S GOLIATH

You may already find yourself reporting to a boss who has made himself or herself indispensable. In order to protect yourself, and even to achieve a modicum of control, you can load a few stones into your slingshot.

Smooth Stone Number One:
Never Compete Openly with the Boss

One of my friends had a boss who was both superterritorial and in the process of making himself indispensable. He came out ahead in the end by not only *not* competing openly with the boss but actually by being overly supportive. In this way he turned the tables on him.

Jay joined the research division of a large midwestern petroleum company that was gearing up to develop a whole group of petroleum-based products. He joined a relatively new department that was formed to market their innovations. He was excited because he felt that he was on the ground floor of an important new venture that offered a glowing future.

His boss's operating style, however, was to try to keep

everyone feeling anxious, ignorant, and guilty. He created friction among the PhDs and scientists on the research staff. He constantly put in his two cents about everything, including laboratory experiments, and played one person against the other. He kept the technical staff separated from the clients, demanding only their briefings to keep himself on solid ground.

As for Jay, he learned quickly why his boss had chosen him. He thought Jay would be useful to him without posing any threat. He had correctly perceived that Jay was enormously capable and also willing to work hard.

Jay's predecessor had attempted to make presentations that fell within his area of expertise to prospects. The boss saw this as an attempt to steal his thunder and to acquire part of his territory.

After less than a year this would-be interloper got the axe. (Note: This brief tenure should have set off warning signals in Jay's head.)

Jay did, however, perceive the threat posed to the boss by his predecessor and took great pains to dispel any suspicion of a potential threat from him.

How did he accomplish this? Since his boss liked being in the limelight, Jay provided beaucoup kilowatts of backup power:

- He lined up numerous speaking engagements through trade associations whose member companies could be potential clients.
- He got his boss newspaper interviews and TV coverage locally and in cities where he was going to be giving speeches.
- He wrote his speeches and penned articles for trade publications under his name (and made sure multiple copies were available when they were published).
- He even kept a scrapbook for him that was filled with his "accomplishments."

By now you must be thinking Jay was out of his mind. Wrong. Absolutely wrong. All indispensable people generally are insecure at core, and in their heart of hearts they feel unloved and incapable of gaining appreciation at their full worth from others.

Jay tore a page from the book of his predecessor and very, very wisely chose never to compete with his boss on the same turf. However, Jay had other things in mind.

Smooth Stone Number Two:
Never Appear Aggressively Ambitious

It may never have entered Jay's boss's head that he had career aspirations of his own. He was totally preoccupied with his own situation.

Jay accepted this. Talking career goals with such a boss would have been a waste of time because he certainly wasn't suddenly going to turn into the helpful boss; and it might even have proved dangerous by awakening his latent fears.

Instead, Jay adopted an overt hands-off approach to anything he claimed as his. He was also circumspect about his association with others in the division.

If you work for this kind of boss, it is very tempting to go elsewhere to seek encouragement and support. But that leaves you open to misinterpretation of your motives.

It is critical to build relationships elsewhere, but they need to be positive, career-oriented ones, not ones based on complaints about the boss. You also need to be very low-key about it.

Obviously Jay's department needed closer ties to and support of the scientific research staff. Jay achieved what he could in this direction, but not openly. To have done so would have targeted him directly in the boss's cross hairs.

Smooth Stone Number Three:
Make Your Own Opportunities

Bosses like Jay's almost always leave you stranded, sometimes totally on your own. If you are going to get anywhere, you must develop a strategy to move yourself forward.

- Self-made bosses often have had to rely so much on themselves that it's impossible for them to trust another soul. Self-sufficiency has become a virtue. They never want to admit dependency on anyone.
- Few will give adequate direction to subordinates. They strive to keep them feeling anxious, ignorant, and guilty—which keeps them a bit off balance, and lets the boss keep the upper hand.
- Tasks delegated to underlings often are mundane or routine.

Jay was never sure exactly when he hit on the idea that was to become his salvation. I think it went back to an evening when he looked up over an after-work glass of beer and mumbled miserably: "He'll never give up that job. If something doesn't happen, I'm stuck. Why can't we just make some people disappear?"

Since killing him was obviously out of the question, killing him with *kindness* was obviously the next best solution. Jay contends that he came up with the idea by very objectively analyzing his boss. He concluded that his boss was motivated almost entirely by his monstrous ego and that the best way to proceed was to use that ego as the weapon to effect his boss's demise. Jay set only one goal. It was a long shot and one he dared not share with anyone. *He would sell his boss to the competition.*

Although no one who worked with the division believed the image Jay was creating for his boss through the media, outsiders were taking notice. He compiled a list of executives with petroleum and chemical companies and organizations with large research facilities. As a "service," he saw to it that summaries of his boss's speeches and copies of "his" articles were mailed to these individuals. (Do not think for one minute that his mailing list was composed of personnel directors. Jay knew they couldn't make this kind of hiring decision.)

His boss did get an offer from one of the competing companies, and he subsequently left to join it. Jay could never be 100 percent certain, but he was pretty sure he had made this happen.

Jay didn't immediately step into that job, but he was eventually promoted there.

As an interesting postscript, Jay later heard that his former boss had apparently taken his management style with him to the next job. But at his new company, when he interfered in such matters as the selection of the chief research scientist's secretary, he was "pressured" to resign.

3

Faulty Assumption Three

I'D NEVER BE ASKED TO DO THAT

*"I'm a college graduate. I took
an entry-level secretarial job to
get my foot in the door with a
company that promotes from
within. Anxious to please, I
made the mistake of becoming
the boss's office domestic. After
five years I'm still going
nowhere."*

*Female, 26
secretary
insurance firm*

*"By God, don't these girls ever
realize they aren't the only ones
that get stuck with menial jobs?
I remember when I worked for
the old man who started this
company. He even had me go
out and buy his suspenders."*

*Male, 55
vice-president
marketing services
insurance firm*

Surprisingly, one of the biggest on-the-job problems for many
people involves handling assignments they consider beneath
them, contrary to their job description, or downright menial.
There has been a great deal of carping via the popular press
about the boss who saddles his secretary with domestic duties
such as picking up his dry cleaning or pouring coffee. Is this
thoughtlessness on the part of the boss? Does it have to do with
some demeaning way the boss views the employee and her job?
Would he be less objective in considering promoting this handy
office domestic to a better career position when that might mean
he could no longer expect to receive her non-job services? Or are
other things involved altogether?

31

An almost classic illustration of the limiting attitude implied by this chapter's faulty assumption—"I'd never be asked to do that!"—is the story of Ann, a secretary in a large insurance firm.

Ann took an entry-level position out of desperation when she couldn't find any other job, even though she had a BA in art history.

When I talked to Ann I was conducting management training sessions, during which I talk to both the boss and the subordinate to get a complete picture of any existing problems. Ann was well into what I call the "bitch, bitch, bitch" stage, in which the person seldom sees even one positive factor in the job. Her major complaint centered on the statement, "I'm a college graduate and Mr. Mac expects me to be his domestic—get his coffee, bring him this, bring him that. And last week he asked me to pick up his personal cleaning. I had my eye on moving into a job that opened up in the claims division. I can't prove it, but I know he gave me a bad recommendation because he wants to keep me here to run errands. In five years I've never gotten more than piddling raises. I only make $750 a month and I'm a college graduate."

Mac's side of things point up a very different situation. When I talked to him, some of Ann's complaints had gotten back to him through coworkers and he seemed genuinely hurt. His reaction to her allegation that he turned her into a domestic was, "I asked her to pick up cleaning twice when I had to go out of town on company business. Did she bother to tell you that I've done her a couple of favors? I let her use the health club, even though it's frowned on. And I pulled some strings to get her indoor parking."

Ann's accusations that her boss had blocked her promotion were equally ill-founded. The claims manager had selected someone with more competence, more knowledge of the business, and more get-up-and-go.

This certainly was confirmed by what Mac went on to tell me: "Ann has really disappointed me. She never tackles or does anything more than she absolutely has to. For example, several weeks ago the claims manager was in my office when he heard his phone ringing. After counting ten rings he excused himself to run to get it, tripped over an extension cord, knocked over a plant on my desk, and got the phone in time to see the light go out. He asked Ann at the next desk why she didn't get it when his secretary was gone and her response was, 'She didn't ask me to.'"

Before you get steamed up about your own boss's idiosyncrasies or those I-never-thought-I'd-be-asked-to-do-that situations, think about the following questions.

- Do perfect bosses exist? And could you cope with one if they did? Or would perfection, too, become a fault?
- Are your job expectations completely clear in your mind?
- What does having a job mean to you?
- Do you know with certainty what your boss's expectations are of your job?
- Have you a clear job description? Has anyone ever looked at it or discussed it with you? Do you do only what you think you're paid to do?
- What does it take to get ahead in this day and age?
- Can you expect any rewards for going the extra mile? Any trade-offs for favors or payoffs for taking on those grungy jobs?

THERE ARE TWO SIDES TO EVERY STORY: YOUR SIDE AND THE BOSS'S SIDE

Echoes are like good friends—both have a tendency to tell you what you want to hear. So the next time you gripe about your boss, imagine giving him or her equal time.

It's important to consider what might be the boss's view of your record. Are you perfection personified? Could anything possibly be wrong with your performance? What complaints might your boss justifiably voice about you?

To get you started on this appraisal, I have compiled an arbitration checklist with a few choice comments picked up in my work that have led to solutions of problems between bosses and subordinates.

ARBITRATION CHECKLIST

The Plaintiff
(Write in your name)

1. I have to run all day for my boss to get this and that. I should come to work in my track shoes.

2. My boss is tradition-bound; everything has to be done his way or no way.

3. His pets get their choice of the best projects. I get the dregs.

The Defendant
(Write in your boss's name)

1. If she were organized, she wouldn't have to keep retracing her steps and would make better use of her time and mine.

2. Maybe if that lamebrain would find out why we have procedures and how effective they are for us, she'd have less to gripe about.

3. Everyone in the department has to learn the ropes. School's out. I'm not going to risk losing an important customer by letting her fly solo before I see how she performs on a practice run.

(You're on your own from here. For every deficiency you see in your boss, write down what might be your boss's side of the story.)

4. _____   4. _____
   _____   _____
   _____   _____

5. _____   5. _____
   _____   _____
   _____   _____

ONLY A GOOSE SHOULD NEED GOOSING

If our friend Ann had written her arbitration list fairly, she might have concluded that Mac didn't recommend her to the claims manager for the new job *because Mac didn't want to jeopardize his relationship by recommending a lemon.* He did not bad-mouth her or block her chances, but he had no basis on which to make a recommendation because of her demonstrated lack of initiative.

In the five years she had reported to him, in Mac's words, "he'd always had to goose her" to get her regular work done. She would do exactly what she was told to do and no more.

Sound like anyone you know? I have met countless Anns in countless organizations and businesses in countless fields of endeavor. The minute they finish with a task their boss has given them they sit back and wait for the next one. Or worse yet, they break out a novel to read, daydream, or stay on the telephone with friends. Most of this type tell me their work is boring, tedious, and far beneath them. They feel put upon to perform the tasks their boss requests of them or, indeed, even to do what the company pays them to do! They commonly blame their boss for getting in their way or holding them back. Before they complain further, I have them ask themselves this question: Who else would want you—or have you—and why?

HOW TO GET AHEAD ON THE JOB

Fact number one: To get ahead, you must use your head. Your head is not just up there for ornamentation. Learn about the business. You will never be able to provide genuine assistance to your boss until you do. If your boss can count on you, the odds are in your favor that the reverse will also be true. The more help and support you provide for your boss, the more likely he or she will do the same for you.

Fact number two: To get ahead, move ahead. Get the job done. Be dependable. You may feel you're the only one with job frustrations. But remember your boss has superiors, too. Your boss's boss wants the work done and isn't likely to listen to the excuse from your boss that his or her work isn't done because yours isn't. Your boss may withhold larger, more complex assignments because you haven't shown the organizational ability, skills, or temperament to complete smaller ones.

Fact number three: To get ahead, don't expect a pat on the head. Have you really *earned* your boss's trust and confidence? Remember, your boss isn't one of your grade school teachers, who will tutor you patiently after hours or give you a makeup test if you have the flu. The work has to get out, and your boss doesn't want to run high risks by giving work to a subordinate who (a) requires constant coaching to be able to handle it, or (b) constant encouragement to take on a task.

Fact number four: To get ahead, be able to keep your head while others lose theirs. Your boss's attitude toward you is shaped by conflicting feelings of dependency and insecurity— dependency on you to get a particular job accomplished and the insecurity or risk to himself or herself in having to explain to an even bigger boss why a task hasn't been done. You may have to *prove* yourself time and again, especially when things are most trying. Only then is your boss likely to feel secure enough to hand you those juicy plums of reward, i.e., special assignments, promotions, raises, or merit increases.

DISCOVER YOUR BOSS'S EXPECTATIONS

Ask Not What Your Boss Can Do for You; Ask What You Can Do for Your Boss

First, learn to verbalize. The best way to learn what your boss expects of you is to ask (and thus avoid the I'd-never-be-asked-to-do-that syndrome). Pitch out the crystal ball and don't rely on the mumbo jumbo of college textbooks, which tell you that this is your boss's responsibility. Your boss may not be up on this theory or may be too busy to think about it. Don't delay; initiate these discussions yourself.

Only through these face-to-face talks (more than one is usually required) can you begin to understand what your boss expects of you and what degree of independence you should or should not be exercising in the performance of your duties.

Avoid just muddling through or making assumptions (I'd never be asked to do that!) on what the boss expects. And ignore the advice of personnel counselors who show you a copy of your job description and say that the things listed are what you will be paid to do. (What you will be paid to do is please the boss, to whom you are bound by the purse strings—believe me.)

For example, according to Ann's job description, one of her primary functions and responsibilities was to *initiate correspondence on routine matters.* This little one-liner—typical of many listings on job descriptions—is open to interpretation. To some, this phrase may mean no more than slitting open envelopes on incoming mail and getting it to the right recipient. To others it would mean they were to draft letters for their boss's signature. In both cases the interpretations might be wrong.

To Ann's boss, this phrase meant she should (a) annotate letters with a yellow marker and underline key points, dates, and names in the body of the correspondence (a task she frequently neglected, particularly on letters of more than one page); and (b) attach copies of any previous correspondence pertaining to the incoming letter and pull related documents or files with information pertinent to answering requests set forth by the correspondent. (After five years, she knew it was Mac's habit to ask for those very things, yet she never got them on her own.)

It is significant that at no time had either Ann or Mac specifically related her job description to his expectations.

Don't Be a Cretin of Habit; Your Way May Not Be Perfect

Clinging to habit patterns, prejudices, and outmoded behavior often proves to be the sheerest form of idiocy in today's business world. Just because ways of doing things proved useful once, or once upon a time, is no guarantee that they will continue to serve you when a situation or environment is different. Just as the time has come for some ideas, the time is past for others. Let's look, for instance, at Mac's past.

None of Mac's former secretaries had a bachelor's degree, and some were not even well-qualified secretaries. For a long time the company had hired non-career oriented secretaries at low wages. Over the years, Mac had grown accustomed to those who were not too competent, but made it up by doing nice things for him. When Ann didn't live up to his expectations of a college graduate, he fell back into his old habits rather than demand or push her to perform. This was an attitude Mac could ill afford, because he needed a secretary who could free him to meet career pressures of his own.

Ann's past shows a different problem. She never got over the culture shock of leaving college and entering the nine-to-five world. Rather than returning to an old pattern, like Mac, she never adopted a new one to suit her new lifestyle.

Many employers kid themselves by assuming college creates great thinkers. Too frequently professors spoon-feed their students with multiple-choice tests created straight from their lectures, so no one has to open a textbook all semester. Then the employers look at a student's grade point average as an indicator of future career success. Unfortunately, as often as not, high grades are earned not so much by those who are initiators as those who are followers.

Ann looked on the job like she was working for a grade. Doing enough to get by and maintaining a C average, she thought, would be acceptable enough to get her a paycheck. And Ann rated Mac an easy boss. Like a professor without a course syllabus, he gave her no written job description and his verbal demands were often forgotten in the press of business.

Imitating Peers Is Foolish
Unless the Boss Approves of Their Behavior

Whether you're being broken in on a job by someone or

learning the ropes for yourself, take particular care to assess the abilities of your teacher or role models.

Ann learned a few tricks of the trade from her peers, all of them costly to her career future. Would you recommend promoting someone who does or has done the following?

- Locked your desk with the keys in it.
- Paints her nails and sets her hair at her desk, yet refuses to eat her lunch there in a pinch to watch the phones.
- Forgot to tell you an important meeting had been rescheduled for the day before.
- Spends an average of an hour a day on the phone with her boyfriend.
- Lost all your speech cards for a presentation you were expected to give to the board in fifteen minutes.

Ann moaned about not being paid what she was worth. She may have been right. She was probably worth a lot less.

Don't Be Haunted by the Ghost of Subordinates Past, Even if They Were Perfect in the Boss's Eyes

One of the most deadly dampers on the spirit of a new employee is comparison—be it negative or positive—to the person who had your job before you. Whether the boss says, "Mary always remembered that I like cream in my coffee" or "Mary never remembered to put cream in my coffee," whether he claims, "Neville always stayed late" or "Neville never stayed late," you feel pressured by the specter of your predecessor. Are you flagging to the boss's attention that you may be too eager a beaver, or does your staying late indicate some failure to get the job done?

It is important that you discover all you can about your predecessor and determine what the relationship between your predecessor and the boss really was. These things can make a great deal of difference, affecting your peace of mind, if nothing else. For instance, your boss may be accustomed to staying late to proof letters because his secretary needed a refresher course in grammar and spelling. On the other hand, she may have been an English teacher who went on to bigger and better things.

If your boss is accustomed to responding in a certain way to any person holding your title, based on interactions with past subordinates, it will behoove you to find out what that experience was like. Only then do you have a chance to set about overcoming your boss's perceptions.

GOING THE EXTRA MILE ON YOUR JOB
MAY REAP REWARDS

Don't sweat the small stuff. That's my motto. I have seen successful people live by it and survive in the corporate jungle year after year.

The boss in my first job expected me to chauffeur him to the airport and pick him up for business trips because I lived close by ("I'd never be asked to do that!"). Then he would put through a travel expense voucher with $25 in taxi fares and neglect to pay me back for my gas.

On the other hand, in the interest of fair play, he was frequently annoyed by, but infrequently brought up, my habit of leaving used paper cups and Kleenex tucked into the conference room chair. Nevertheless, we cooperated and got along.

My conclusion was that, when handled carefully, it was possible to turn the faulty assumption "I'd never be asked to do that!" into a correct assumption: "If the boss expects you to kiss his ass, then you may be able to demand equal time."

THE SWEET SMELL OF SUCCESS

There are individuals who have allowed themselves to be used and even abused and have survived to get their just rewards—short of dying and going to heaven.

This rags to riches story proves my point.

Heroine: Jean
Rags: $9,000 a year salary
Riches: $48,000 a year salary, plus perks and bonuses and still more room for growth

Jean is currently the director of corporate services, the first woman to hold that title in her company. She is responsible for a multimillion-dollar coupon redemption center and a large print shop facility along with an assortment of smaller departments.

STEPS TO SUCCESS

Be a Willing Volunteer

Originally Jean was hired as an assistant supervisor of computing and clerical services. Not only was there a heavy load of work, but this job had numerous tedious tasks as well. Yet when the editor of the in-house magazine decided to run a series of historical pieces on the company and called for a volunteer to sort through volumes of historical records, Jean took on the job as a favor. In the process of performing this task, Jean learned a great deal about the company and the power base of many bosses within it.

She began listening more carefully to the chairman's speeches at the shareholders' meetings (sometimes worth the price of a few shares of stock) and faithfully read the chairman's column in the newsletter. From these she learned that the chairman planned to triple sales of the company's major product lines. Jean thought it stood to reason that the company would need more production capacity. The vice-president of engineering and director of corporate services would be in charge of meeting this challenge. So she went where the action would be and took a horizontal transfer to become his secretary.

Use Your Job Description as a Base, Not an Edict

Once in her new position, Jean acquired a copy of her job description as well as that of her boss. Then she kept a diary of her own duties, her boss's, and those of support personnel in the area. (This technique is far more effective for learning the true nature of your boss's work, since high-level executives are given a great deal of discretion in carrying out their duties. A job description might list only two or three vague statements under principal functional responsibilities. Take the CEO, for instance. That job description generally contains but one line: insures the future growth of the company. These generalities are not very helpful in defining the actual scope of your boss's duties and where you fit in.)

After several months, Jean broke her job duties into two categories: those she would keep and those she could delegate to less skilled clerks in the area.

Next, from her diary, she listed all the activities her boss performed. As she proceeded through this list, she recorded how capable she was of handling each item. She rated herself on each activity, as follows:

- Definitely can handle it now, am already skillful, performing the task.
- Need a little more training before becoming truly proficient.
- Have potential, but need a great deal more training and study to feel at ease working alone.
- Probably will always be weak and have difficulty performing this duty.

Jean knew that she could not charge in to her boss, suggesting changes right and left. It would be slow going, perhaps taking years. While she went slowly, she held to her game plan. Her first efforts were a series of powwows, at least two every quarter, to reevaluate her duties. Prior to these meetings she carefully prepared herself:

1. If she intended to ask her boss to let her handle certain portions of his job on her own, she would consider what his fears might be and was prepared to allay them.
2. She always asked herself what the boss might expect in terms of net results from the change and was prepared to meet them.

This groundwork made it easier for her to get a decision from her boss during each session instead of being put on hold while he tried to anticipate what trouble the change might bring.

To do what Jean did, mentally visualize a balanced scale. On your side, list your needs. Balance them on your boss's side with his or her needs. For instance:

Yours	*The Boss's*
Money	Performance
Responsibility	Accountability
Prestige	Discipline

If your boss lets you fulfill certain needs of your own, you can bet he or she wants certain things in return. Be prepared to negotiate.

When Jean wasn't yet capable of assuming certain duties on her own, she followed this course of action:

1. She sought her boss's advice regarding what courses she might take and what books would be helpful to read.
2. She followed through and signed up for several courses in statistics to increase her understanding of certain functions performed in the coupon redemption system.
3. She read the books the boss suggested.

Throughout a seven-year period, Jean kept her boss abreast of her accomplishments and the status of various assignments delegated to her. At all times she was careful to be well prepared so that the time they spent together was productive.

Jean never took her boss's time for granted. She never assumed he would automatically see things her way. She believed her success (as with most successful people) hinged on her ability to think things through and to keep herself busy, not relying on others to do it for her. She knew it was her responsibility to move herself ahead; there are no fairy godmothers in the business world.

Expect the Unexpected

Jean always made sure she scheduled meetings with her boss early in the morning, when her boss was normally at his fittest.

Lest you assume that Jean's relationship with the vice-president was all smooth sailing, let me share a vital statistic with you. There are more than 13 million alcoholics in this country. Many of them remain functional and in positions of responsibility while still actively drinking. Jean's boss was one of them.

Life with an alcoholic—regardless of how functional—at home or in the office presents difficulties on a daily basis. Many afternoons Jean covered for her boss if he'd had too many martinis during a business lunch. She went so far as to lie for him (I'd never be asked to do that!), rescheduling meetings on the excuse that the boss was ill. She sometimes took the blame for a scheduling foul-up herself. Or she'd tell her boss's superiors he had worked late the night before and consequently wouldn't be in until 10:30 or 11:30 A.M. Several times she drove her boss home (I'd never be asked to do that!) to keep him from killing himself or someone else. She consoled his wife over the phone, frequently late at night or on weekends. None of these things were duties listed in her job description.

When her boss finally admitted to himself that he was an alcoholic and requested a three-month leave of absence to seek help, Jean kept things running smoothly in the interim—at no increase in pay, of course. (I'd never be expected to do that!).

A few months after her boss's return he was promoted to head a new company the corporation had acquired. (Some firms are enlightened.) Before he left, he named Jean director of corporate services.

4

Faulty Assumption Four

IF YOU'VE GOT IT, FLAUNT IT

> *"The minute Pam took over that job she started straightening things out. God, that was a rotten situation with those district managers. The real ringleader in that group was banking all the checks collected and turned in by the sales reps in her own bank account. Then she delayed orders so she didn't have to turn the money in to the company right away and made a bundle by collecting the interest. Pam figured it might amount to several thousand dollars a year. When she asked to see the books, that's when they went after her . . . began their campaign to discredit her."*
>
> *Female, 37*
> *sales training director*
> *cosmetics company*

People who receive promotions often are shocked by the treatment they receive from others. Suddenly individuals who never before gave them the time of day speak heartily. On the other hand, former coworkers with whom they shared lunch and laughs after work over a few beers give them the cold shoulder.

No matter how much harder you've worked than others, no matter how well your credentials stack up against those of the competition, there is nothing like a promotion to prick the sleeping green-eyed monster of jealousy into furious action. Its weapons are legion:

- envious stares
- discomforting glares
- backbiting
- bad-mouthing
- rumormongering
- spurious innuendo
- rude remarks
- blatant untruths
- accusations

The irony of all this is that the "monster" somehow feels justified in lashing out because *you* are the cause of it all. You supposedly are flaunting your good fortune.

If you don't learn to handle these things you may find your career threatened.

Don't give anyone real ammunition to use against you.

With the backing of your boss and the support of co-workers—fit in or risk having to get out.

Don't let yourself be drawn into confrontation—learn to roll with the punches.

LEARN THE NEUTRALIZING EFFECT OF HUMOR

When you get hit with one of the green-eyed monster's barbs you can draw yourself up in indignation or you can learn to laugh a little at yourself and at the situation. Regardless of the seriousness of the implications, you can usually water down the effect with humor.

I will never forget a former lunchtime buddy who approached me after my promotion had been posted on the bulletin board and asked me nervily if I was the reason for my boss's divorce.

My standard comeback is always, "If I had been to bed with every man I've been accused of shacking up with, I wouldn't have the energy—or time—to do anything else."

Unfortunately, most innuendoes are based on situations that can be misinterpreted at face value. Denial or an explanation only makes things worse.

At the time my boss was fifty-nine and I was in my early twenties. Often we had to travel together and entertain clients. As a woman executive, given my age and the caliber of the company, I was highly visible. And I knew I was originally hired for my looks as well as my brains. The chairman, never immune to feminine charms, liked having someone to show off to other executives. The fact that I had something upstairs (higher than my chest) was an added plus.

I fondly remember receiving a phone call late one Friday afternoon from the vice-chairman, who asked me to drop off some brochures. He was going to speak before a group of top business leaders in Barbados and thought he might have an opportunity to use them to drum up a little business. Since it was after the last mail pickup I gathered up the materials and hopped an elevator to the top floor.

As it turned out, the chairman was in the vice-chairman's office and both were feeling little pain due to a few TGIF (Thank God it's Friday) drinks. Just as I was handing the brochures to the vice-chairman's secretary, who gave me her usual frozen, disdainful stare, the chairman walked over close to me and said, "Kay, you got great legs." I responded by laughing and said, "Yours aren't bad either." Both men were grinning from ear to ear as I turned to leave.

The next Monday *my* boss said it had come to his attention that the chairman thought I dressed far too sexily. This was obviously not what the old man thought at all. Nor was it true. The source of that rumor could be laid without doubt at the door of the vice-chairman's prim and proper secretary.

I took this turn of events with a grain of salt. I made a silent resolve to stick to doing my job and doing it well, despite the occasional detractor.

Observation number one: Subordinates who put out more effort wind up getting ahead. Rather than face up to this, many other people protect their own egos and cover their deficiencies by cutting the doers down.

LEARN TO FIT IN OR RISK HAVING TO GET OUT

It's true that the newly promoted can be afflicted with a near-missionary zeal. As a result, they go barreling into a new job, changing everything right and left. They flex their new muscle and flaunt their new authority. They may even treat coworkers like a bunch of bumbling buffoons. (Even if they *are,* it's wise to cool it.) What a way to guarantee that your life will be miserable. Those around you will see to it!

Observation number two: If you stir up a hornet's nest and prove you don't fit in, your boss isn't likely to fire everybody else. You're the one who is very likely going to be told to leave, even if you find evidence of wrongdoing.

I define *fitting in* in a very special and narrow sense. I do not mean accommodating until you are completely blended into the situation. Nor do I mean to preserve the status quo. Rather, I mean it to suggest being *adaptable* to a situation, working *with* the grain, not against it.

Take the case of Pam. In a nutshell, as the result of her promotion and her determination to right wrongs, she became a threat to her peers. It was Pam who got the ax. And it wasn't fair.

Pam was a go-getter. She joined a cosmetics company as a

representative selling door-to-door. Neither sleet, nor rain, and particularly not snow kept her from customers. People stay in when it snows and consequently buy more then, she always says.

For three years running, she earned a diamond pin in recognition of her outstanding record as top salesperson. In spite of her success, Pam longed to be a district manager.

But there were certain strings attached. Pam was given the "opportunity" to show what she could do over the summer months by substituting for six of the district managers, as each rotated off for vacation. It was a nightmare of work. She faced myriad problems. For example, the books were not kept up to date. The district managers whose work she performed in the summer months were quite forgetful when it came to recording the names of reps they hired. Therefore, it was questionable whether major sections of the city were being covered. Pam's response was to hire more reps.

Another problem was that the customers' orders were not sent in at the appropriate times. Pam found out why there were so many customer complaints. Two order cycles were used. District managers were assigned A weeks (the first and third weeks of the month) or B weeks (the second and fourth weeks of any given month). As far as Pam could tell, many district managers were sending their orders to the home office in the wrong cycle, which eventually came to the attention of the regional director through Pam's only confidant in the company—the training director.

The mistakes and the poor records were deliberate moves. The manner in which the books were kept made it quite difficult to track the number of people who were sales representatives and the subsequent collections being made. All the small checks collected by the reps were turned in and cashed by the district managers. They would itemize all orders and send in one large check to headquarters. The confusion concerning the cycle billing was intended to keep certain cash in greedy little hands a little longer. The real ringleader earned a pretty penny yearly in interest by delaying orders. (And Pam originally thought she was just a dumb blonde.)

Pam began agitating to see the books and to get the system straightened out. Several district managers refused to hand over their books to her. That's when the campaign to discredit Pam began in earnest. First there were rumors that Pam didn't pay for samples like everyone else. Then they started a slur campaign about how all the new reps Pam hired left as fast as they came on board, with the implication that Pam was a poor manager. If the regional director had bothered to seek out the truth from the reps hired by Pam, he would have discovered that they not only adored her but each one turned in higher sales in her first month with the company than had any previous new recruits.

But the regional director was oblivious to everything save one fact: Pam didn't fit in. He could not afford to fire twelve district managers. He could not endure the constant bickering and backbiting. As far as he was concerned, Pam could return to being a sales rep again if she chose to do so, or she could walk.

LEARN HOW TO BIDE YOUR TIME

In many organizations the primary responsibility to train a new staff member rests with the person who previously held the job (assuming he or she is still around), or a person in a like position—not the new person's boss. So, upon accepting any new job or promotion, keep this in mind:

Observation number three: You need your peers more than they need you.

A middle-aged woman I know, called Josey, kept this fact uppermost in her mind during her breaking-in period. She had been a secretary for years and didn't want to muff her first big promotion.

Josey took over the position of transportation administrator at a significant increase in pay, and handles the external freight audit system for a major food processing company. The transportation administrator reviews all the shipping and transit bills paid for by the traffic managers within the company's different plants. All these bills—with the exception of those associated with the shipment of raw ingredients subject to long-term contracts and those totaling $20 or less for UPS or Federal Express services—are sent to outside auditors for review.

These auditors run a double check to make sure the merchandise received wasn't classified improperly, resulting in the company being charged a higher rate for transit of product or materials. Trucking lines and railroads are allowed to charge specific tariffs or rates after receiving approval of the Interstate Commerce Commission to impose surcharges during the year to cover or offset fuel price increases that cut into their profits. If a traffic manager paid more than was necessary, the auditor handling the claim gets 40 to 50 percent of whatever is recovered off the top. The opposite can also happen, with the company ending up owing money to the carrier.

Josey was shifted to the traffic department of her company to take over the traffic administrator position when it was vacated by the promotion of a forty-year veteran with the firm, whom I'll call Ethel. No one was overly fond of Ethel, but they were well indoctrinated to her way of doing things. And Josey was smart enough to recognize the importance of remaining somewhat laid back when it came to introducing certain procedural changes.

Observation number four: Don't rush in where angels fear to tread. Determine slowly and carefully the best time and way to introduce procedural changes if you're under the eagle eye of the person who set them up in the first place.

During Josey's orientation on the job it became clear that the department was very disorganized. As Josey picked up scuttlebutt from coworkers, she also found that Ethel's business acumen left a great deal to be desired. Several problems surfaced immediately.

Minor matters like pitching folder upon folder of charts of outdated materials—some from plants which had long since closed their doors—Josey took care of herself. But she decided it was critical to bring those problems that could cause real trouble to her boss's attention. The first of these had to do with freight bills.

> *Ethel's method:* Wait until at least 100 freight bills accumulate before sending them off to the auditors.
>
> *The problem:* The auditors must find errors within a certain time period or the company loses the right to claim money owed it through overpayment to carriers.
>
> *Josey's realization:* With this procedure it was highly probable that many bills would go beyond the statute of limitation, making it illegal to collect. Why put the company at risk of negotiating a settlement with a carrier, a procedure which could take up to five or six years? Ethel's system made no sense to Josey at all.
>
> *Her boss's reaction:* "Who in the world told her to do that?" (This gives you some idea of how long the problem existed.)
>
> *Josey's solution:* She quietly changed the procedure. Now she separates all bills by plant, inserts them in separate envelopes with an identification number, and at the end of the month shoots them off to one of the outside auditors.

The second problem Josey brought to her boss came to light when Josey discovered in a box marked "miscellaneous" a whole stack of auditor's notes going back some six years. None of these notes gave any indication of having been paid or otherwise handled.

When Josey brought this matter to her boss's attention, she and her boss wrote out a fifteen-page report and submitted it along with these notes to the auditors in charge. Luckily, the majority of these freight bills had been collected. But there were several pending and of vital importance to various billings in litigation. Others Josey needed to know about for a series of special reports upper management wanted on the status of several accounts. Ethel evidently had filed them in the catch-all and forgotten them.

Ethel's "miscellaneous" box contained yet another skeleton: grievances filed by traffic managers of operating divisions whose accounts did not receive a credit when carriers paid.

Ethel's system: When a check was received from a carrier, Ethel would send it to accounting but neglect to make a journal entry.

The problem: Traffic managers whose accounts were charged received no credit, even though the company was reimbursed. Ethel ignored the complaint calls and dumped any formal grievances mailed to Corporate into her favorite "file."

Josey's solution: Now when Josey sends a check received from carriers to the cashier in accounting, it is accompanied by a "remittance advice" form, which she developed. This form notes the proper account to be credited. When Josey gets the information back from the cashier after the deposit, she prepares the journal entries so each traffic manager is credited properly.

How did Ethel take all these changes? About as you would expect the wicked stepmother to react. She was jealous and sick to death of hearing everyone comment about how nice the files looked since Josey took over and how great Josey was doing.

Josey's first big challenge from Ethel came when a special report Josey had prepared was returned to her by the distribution department. The person who sent it back thought Ethel was still in charge, so it fell into her hands.

Observation number five: If you take over someone else's job, be sure to pass the word along to others. Save yourself the embarrassment (or worse) of having something wind up in the wrong hands.

Josey had simply neglected to calculate freight rates plus the surcharge increases per pound and had only figured the poundage of finished goods shipped, which was serious but not devastating. From Ethel's reaction, however, you might have thought this minor error had cost the stockholders a $2-per-share loss. In a voice loud enough for all the departments to hear, Ethel told Josey that there was no reason for this to have happened. She said she had discussed this report with Josey fully, which she had not, and that if Josey was going to stay on the job she had "better get more organized."

Josey nearly bit off the end of her tongue but replied politely, "You're quite right, Ethel." She was not about to give Ethel any real ammunition to use against her. Josey was simply biding her time until her training with Ethel was finished and, to put it bluntly, she didn't need her anymore.

Josey's method was to take precautions to correct minor problems without bringing these matters to the attention of her boss. Running to him with every little thing might have made him uncertain about her ability to handle the job.

She also shared with her boss problems in which her own neck was on the line, problems that were hotbeds of trouble, and ones in which he needed to take the primary responsibility of solving. If Josey had instituted changes without his knowledge, someone might have asked questions about why he had allowed the situation to develop in the first place.

Finally, Josey fit in by working with the grain rather than against it. She refused to be drawn into any confrontation with Ethel and rolled with the punches as long as it was necessary.

LEARN TO LOOK BEFORE YOU LEAP

There is another very compelling reason for not barreling into a new job, making changes right and left: *You may be dead wrong.*

A new secretary who was something of a take-full-charge type and wanted to make some points on her job decided to make changes in certain office procedures. Her job included summarizing the time records of six public relations account executives covering some twenty or more client accounts on which all executives might log some time during any month's period. To save herself time, she drew up a system that would have resulted in each executive having a separate log for each client. Precious time would have been lost as executives tried to locate the right logbook for a particular client in order to record the number of minutes spent on its business.

This cumbersome solution to *her* work (unbillable time) would have ended up costing the firm a fantastic loss in billable time, to say nothing of the exasperation of the account people.

Flaunting what you think you know may be the quickest way to prove you really don't know it.

THE RÉSUMÉ: WHERE FLAUNTING YOURSELF MAY CUT YOUR OWN THROAT

Nowhere is the tendency to flaunt yourself so fatal as it is on the résumé you present in applying for a job. The majority of résumés exhibit some of the following flagrant mistakes and pitfalls, which often diminish or even cancel the chances of the job seeker rather than enhance them.

The Drown-Them-in-Detail Theory

Job seekers often work on the theory that it's best to give every detail of every job all the way back to that summer before high school when they were picking strawberries for Farmer Jones's Orchard. They drone on and on.

Observation number six: Overkill through excessive detail or history may drown the curiosity of the very person you were hoping to titillate enough to invite you to interview.

The Autobiography Theory

Loving to ski, having a trim figure and good health are wonderful things. But remember, if you are submitting your résumé in answer to an advertised job in most organizations, the primary motivation of the person reviewing the resultant résumés is to eliminate most of them. Don't give an excuse to do so out of hand. Extra information may work against you. The reviewer may simply have prejudices.

Observation number seven: Why include personal statistics such as height and weight? Let them find out when they see you. At least then you can make a case for your liabilities.

Other Pitfalls

Marital status. When giving her name on the résumé, a woman should not indicate *Ms., Miss,* or *Mrs.* To some, *Ms.* may mean you are a wild-eyed feminist. There are those who still assume that an unmarried woman of a certain age is an old maid and may be finicky or set in her ways, and others may not want to train someone who is apt to leave town to get married, so don't use *Miss* either. In the case of *Mrs.,* sometimes a reviewer assumes that with a spouse you don't really need a job. If you also list children, it may be feared that you will stay home when they get sick.

Men and women both should avoid reporting their status as divorced.

Educational excess. List no degrees higher than that required by the ad. You may be viewed as overqualified and just taking something temporarily until you can get a more suitable position. Even listing colleges attended may be a liability. For all you know, the last five people hired from your school may have turned out to be duds.

Location information. Geographic preference or attitude about travel, unless specifically requested, adds just so much unnecessary verbiage. And, who knows, you just may be cutting yourself off from something perfectly acceptable to you by stating that limitation.

Names of past or current employers. It is far better to use descriptive terms such as *Fortune 500 company, manufacturer of paper products, chemical company, national leader in agricultural products, medical research center for cancer,* and so forth. (Specifics can be given at the time of the interview.) There are many reasons for not listing past or present employers simply by name. Some companies' names will mean little to the reviewer. In addition, the reviewer may have heard that the company has just dumped a lot of its deadwood personnel and think that includes you. Or you may be called in solely so you can be asked questions about a competitor to see if that company is in trouble and thus letting employees go.

References. It is risky to use names of individuals you know within the organization. Indicating that references can be made available is preferable to listing persons who can put in a good word for you. (I will never forget one woman who, in spite of holding a PhD, listed two people on her résumé who were deceased and to whom she referred as "the late Drs." so and so!)

Hobbies, personal organizations. In general, this information is not helpful to the person weeding out applicants. Save it for an interview, and then divulge it only if asked, unless such activities can be significant to some aspect of the job applied for. (A person with too many activities may give the impression that not much time is left for work.)

The Wow 'Em Theory

Do you really think script type on hot pink paper will make your résumé stand out? It will be out, all right. This kind of cuteness is, to a reviewer, like waving a red flag at a bull.

Observation number eight: Do be sure your typewriter is in good condition and clean. Such imperfections as a filled-in *o* or *e* are distracting and may say a great deal about attitude or lack of attention to detail. Plain white paper with black ink is the easiest to read. To make a résumé somewhat different, and to add something helpful for the reviewer, you might simply clip a copy of the job advertisement to your response.

The To-See-Me-Is-to-Love-Me Theory

No matter how attractive you are, don't include a photograph of yourself. Reviewers take churlish pleasure in spindling these or dropping them in the wastebasket.

The Separate-the-Chaff-from-the-Wheat Theory

Including salary range desired is just plain dumb. In the first place, salary should be negotiated face-to-face. In the second place, you may just have placed yourself on the slave block at a bargain rate.

Since that eliminates most of what appears on résumés, what *should* they include? Most people's résumés read like job descriptions.

Key Rule: *Rather than reading a list of all the activities that have consumed your every moment while on the job, the person with the power to hire you wants to know what you have accomplished.*

BASIC ELEMENTS OF RÉSUMÉS

In general, résumés should contain the following.

Objective

This should be a brief statement of twenty or thirty words, and it should be written clearly. To be able to do so you must know what you want for yourself. No personnel manager or reviewer is going to spend time trying to figure out how he can use you after wading through the résumé. Job seekers who send out a thousand copies of their résumés find 999 of them wind up in the round file. Find out who has the final say to fill the position you want and what his or her key concerns are likely to be. Target your job objective to meet this superior's needs. Avoid using broad, flowery wording. Be succinct and clear when writing out your job objective.

Here are two samples.

Labor law attorney with responsibility for contract negotiations and wage settlements with expansive role designing effective performance appraisal systems.

This job objective is targeted at the vice-president of industrial relations, whose company has been named as defendant in several age discrimination suits by older executives. This turn of events might necessitate perfecting clear-cut performance indicators to show measurable differences in performance between managers.

> Mechanical engineer with responsibility to keep production equipment at highest operating efficiency, while reducing energy demands at peak periods.

This job objective was noted in a résumé sent to the production manager of a bakery plant after hearing employees at a local bar discussing the high-energy demands of ovens and soaring costs as key concerns of the plant superintendent.

Be realistic in your objective. Many people who haven't got it still insist on flaunting it. I am referring to unrealistic job shoppers, the type of person who wants a challenging position in management with room for advancement when the last three years have been spent working as an auto mechanic or a waiter at a fast food restaurant. For example, avoid this type of wording:

> . . . position requiring initiative, innovativeness, opportunity to move into top management.

Experience/Accomplishment Capsules

This should consist of brief, eight- to twelve-word capsules giving an overview of how your experience or knowledge has been utilized. For example:

> Establishment of short- and long-range program goals. Input to policy formulation.

Give selected examples of achievement, highlighting key words, such as *development of, creation of, initiation of, establishment of,* and so forth.

> Conception of entire merchandising plan for new designer

line of clothes, including scheduling, budget-setting, establishment of delivery system, and raw material control.

Also give an idea of how your experience or knowledge can contribute to an organization. The following written statement could be made in response to knowledge of a sales loss on the eastern seaboard within a company you want to work for full time:

Increased market share by 21 percent among industrial clients purchasing uniforms in the Northeast.

Set forth your experience in accomplishments.

SALES DIRECTOR, XYZ Chemical Co.—1982 to present (date optional)
Solely responsible for organizing sales department and realigning product shipment handling. Upgraded distribution; realized sales improvement of 25 percent in first six months.

Be brief about your education. Flaunt carefully. If your educational background includes prestigious schools (example: Phillips Exeter Academy to Yale), use only the highest degree you received. Matriculation information isn't necessary. There will be time in an interview to offer prep school background. If you are answering a job ad, use only the highest degree called for in the ad. For example:

Master of Business Administration, University of Every State.

On other information: Leave off memberships and personal information unless there is a compelling reason not to do so, or it offers an achievement contributing to a prospective job.

. . . past president of Sales Management Association for three terms, instrumental in efforts successfully exempting chemical sales from environmental tax.

Key Rule: *No matter what your occupation, using an achieve-ment orientation in your résumé can make you sound unique.*

Should you be specific when stating accomplishments? If you're applying for a job as a labor relations attorney and I am a personnel director, saying only "negotiated contracts" doesn't tell me much. Tell me instead that you settled some certain contract(s) so many days in advance of deadline, preventing a strike. Tell me you were able to get the union business commit-tee to take less in terms of benefits and salary increases. Tell me you were able to settle certain EEOC claims out of court or you were able to reduce the department's case load by such-and-such a percentage.

Should you take the credit? After all, few of us accomplish all these marvels single-handedly. Well, I can assure you, if the president of your company were looking for a job, he'd include percentage gains in sales and earnings in his achievements even though he wasn't out in the field hustling sales. Certainly, part of the credit goes to the president, no matter how far from the field he may be removed. So no one reading his résumé would condemn him for taking credit. You won't be condemned either for mentioning accomplishments on which you worked, even though others were also involved.

How long should the résumé be? The accomplishment ap-proach makes it easier to limit the résumé to one page. And it won't read like every other resume submitted by those compet-ing with you for the same job and listing their activities as if they came straight off a job description.

Should I tailor my résumé to a particular job? It often behooves you to discover particular current interests of the company to which you're applying for a job. If you have an accomplishment that fits in, certainly put it front and center. For instance, a manager seeking a new position reads an article in which a company placed great stress on people development. When he applied for a job there, he didn't simply write down that he had rapport with subordinates. He included his success in holding down the turnover rate among employees as well as the percentage of subordinates he had placed in jobs at increasingly higher levels of responsibility. This won him the job from a field of eighty-nine applicants.

Similarly, a high school counselor seeking a position in job placement at a university noted that its annual report stressed the institution's emphasis on graduates gaining good jobs so as to offset criticism that higher education doesn't prepare students for "real" jobs. When he applied he didn't just offer on his résumé, "I counseled students," but wrote that he had helped place such-and-such a percentage of high school seniors in full-time jobs. He, too, was successful in getting the position.

What if I haven't accomplished anything specifically relevant to the job? Even if you find it difficult to put your experience or knowledge into specific accomplishments—or worse yet, haven't kept track of the end results of your work—all may not be lost. If your accomplishments have been in fields unrelated to the new position you seek, you may have to rely on something more than the résumé alone. If you don't want to limit yourself to applying only to want ads, you may have to seek other ways to find an opening.

In these instances, watch for tie-in leads in trade journals, newspapers, and company publications. A tie-in is a problem you can solve.

A young woman I know noted in a banking journal that the largest bank and lending institution in her state had made a commitment to stay at its inner-city location. Its CEO was involved in every civic activity in town and made much ado (duly reported in the newspapers) about the need for revitalization of the city.

My acquaintance was working right out of college with a neighborhood group, developing an old section of town. She saw a need for loans for rehabilitation of neighborhoods if the city was ever to make a real comeback.

She drafted a simple, straightforward letter noting the problem and directed it to the CEO. She did not infer that she was seeking a job, that the banks had been remiss in not seeing this need, or that she had all the answers to the problem, just that she had a few. She sought an appointment for thirty minutes to discuss the issue. Following the interview, which was handled by a vice-president, she wrote a job description for a community development liaison officer and sought the creation of a new position for herself. She got the job.

Should Résumés Always Go to the Personnel Manager?

The personnel manager won't be the one hiring you (unless it happens to be a position under that manager's wing or one in industrial relations). But bear in mind that the personnel department is aware of a number of openings elsewhere in the company. It is always wise, even if you are going to someone else in the firm, to carbon the man or woman in charge of personnel.

Many job seekers ferret out the names of people within departments where they would like to work—people with decision-making power to hire and fire. You can nail down a job without answering a single want ad in the newspaper.

Some people get names by calling a secretary or clerk and saying, "I want to direct some mail to the vice-president or director. I wonder if you could give me the correct spelling and middle initial. Is the address still 7777 Spring Avenue? What is the zip code?" Others stop by the lobby of large companies and pick up a copy of employee publications, many of which list or mention names of powers that be in the various departments.

Can Résumés Be Sent Out Cold?

Many résumés are sent out seeking a position, not answering an ad for one. A mailing to 100 companies (addressed to specific individuals, not with the salutation "To whom it may concern," which will stir the same feelings as letters mailed to your home labeled "Occupant") may result in only two or three nibbles. Wait two weeks and send the same résumés out to the same companies. Chances are you'll get the same number of responses but from different companies. Flaunting yourself may not help, but being persistent does.

HERE I AM; AIN'T I GREAT?

Job interviewees can flaunt themselves in a number of ways. (Interviewing questions and techniques for gathering information on your prospective job and employer are covered in depth in Chapter 1.)

One of these is appearing at the interview with this attitude: "Here I am. Aren't I everything you were ever looking for?"

Prior to any interview, compile a set of materials that in some way documents your accomplishments. These should not be voluminous. A salesperson might have graphs of his or her sales results. A secretary might have sample letters or reports he or she has prepared.

The recruiter wants the candidate to talk about 80 to 90 percent of the time. Don't, however, fall into the trap of flaunting yourself and babbling on and on and on. If you're expected to talk, come with questions to learn more about the structure of the department and the temperament of your boss. Try to get the interviewer to open up and let you know more about what to expect of the job. You will also be tested through what you say to determine how well you will fit into the organization. Don't get too wrapped up in talking about yourself. Watch for signals of how you are affecting the interviewer with what you say and by your manner. Take time to listen and determine what he may be looking for.

Be careful about such seemingly innocuous questions as, "What do you typically do on Thursday?" The interviewer may be trying to judge your level of get-up-and-go. Before answering any question, consider what the person is really trying to get at. Assess the context in which the question is asked. If, for example, you had been talking about your activities in, and dedication to, any job and the "Thursday" question was popped, you wouldn't come back with something like, "I try to get everything done so Friday is a light enough day to leave early." Instead, you might say: "Thursday is a good day to take stock of where you are, to determine what's absolutely got to be wrapped up for the week. That gives you Friday to be sure it is done without building up to a crisis."

HOW TO HANDLE SKELETONS IN THE CLOSET

All of us have things in our backgrounds that could have a negative bearing on the selection process. Obviously, it doesn't pay to flaunt these skeletons, which could be the reason for leaving your last job or a gap in your work history (another good reason for using the *achievement* résumé) when you dropped out to get your personal or career bearings. Or it might be a situation that, no matter how slight your fault, will sound phony, untruthful, or too much of a protest if you explain.

Whatever the skeleton is, when it raises its ugly head during an interview, treat the subject with objectivity and nonchalance.

One tactic is to initiate discussions concerning the matter rather than wait for the prospective boss or one of his or her subordinates to force a defensive maneuver by introducing it first. Better to have thought out how you can handle a skeleton in the closet effectively than to hope to keep it in the closet.

Sometimes truth is the only way. Sometimes choosing your truths is a viable alternative. As an example, a woman said she had been asked to resign; in reality, she'd been fired due to a personality clash with a supervisor with more seniority.

This turn of events can be difficult to explain because it always leaves doubt about who really was at fault and might make an interviewer unfairly consider the interviewee to be a troublemaker. But, as a matter of fact, this woman had had two hefty pay increases during the last year, which indicated there was nothing missing from her performance. At the same time the company was expanding rapidly and there was some rumor that it might be overextended. So, in formulating an answer about why she had left the firm, she chose three truths:

- I had two significant pay raises during the past year.
- There has been a lot of speculation that the company

has overextended, which I felt might make it impossible
to sustain the increases in pay.
- My position was threatened.

Key Rule: *Lies are no better in job interviews than in much of
the rest of life. It is often necessary in job interviews to choose
one's words and truths carefully. To pretend or advise otherwise
is hypocrisy.*

5

Faulty Assumption Five

ONLY THE MILITARY OBSERVES
A CHAIN OF COMMAND

*"Arnold's allegations about Jack
were extraordinarily serious.
There was no way I could prove
a thing without destroying my
position in the process. Arnold
had pulled a real power play on
me. But he crapped out and now
he's somewhere pounding the
pavement, looking for a job."*

*Male, 39
manager, special group of
    environmental design engineers
leading box board manufacturer*

Face one important fact: most organizations (profit and non-profit) are structured along the same lines as the Army, the Navy, the Air Force, and the Marines. Businesses, just as surely as the branches of the military, have a chain of command. Ranks may not seem as clearly defined; no one wears stripes and clusters. They exist nonetheless and are separated, with each ascending rank having absolute control over the one below.

In large measure these divisions are based on the military theory that familiarity breeds contempt. Homage to rank is demanded through salute and respectful attitude (though not necessarily for the man or woman wearing the uniform). The end result in the military is order on the battlefield with troops obeying the orders of superiors without question. The chain of command in both the military and in civilian organizations and businesses is supposed to encourage greater precision in the effectiveness of an operation.

Well, if you ever served a hitch in the military, you know better. And the same goes for the business world. Too often strict adherence to this chain-of-command mentality becomes a game of covering oneself, which ends up slowing down important decisions and leading to gross inefficiency.

To illustrate, let me recount what an area sales supervisor for a major chemical company must go through to meet competitive bids. This man—here referred to as Jerry—has several salesmen reporting to him, but he makes calls on customers as well. Usually the main contact for these salesmen within a manufacturing plant is the purchasing agent. Since Jerry's company is not the only one calling on these agents, they often hear something like, "I've got another bid for the same chemicals— 100,000 pounds FOB our plant for 95¢ a pound. Yours is a nickel more. Meet the offer and maybe we can talk business." Whereupon Jerry must fill out a special form requesting permission from his company to knock 5¢ off the asking price to meet its competitor's bid.

This form is routed up the chain of command. It goes not only through Jerry's boss, who is the regional manager, but through his boss's boss, the product manager, for signature of approval. Then it continues traveling through the boss's boss's boss, the product director. At last it goes to the boss's boss's boss's boss, the director of marketing, for the final signature, at which point the process reverses itself and the permission form must make its way back down the chain of command.

Meanwhile the purchasing agent is probably buying from the competition, thus reducing the poundage this company will eventually be able to sell the customer.

Believe it or not, this little ritual is followed in this company for any request to lower prices, even for such small amounts as

$50. Now this amounts to one-tenth of a penny on the thousands of pounds of chemicals sold to even their smallest industrial customers. Yet Jerry would never dream of sending one of these request for price change forms directly to the director of marketing to save time. Taking such an action would be tantamount to breaking the chain of command. Jerry is paying homage to his boss's rank by presenting these request forms to his regional manager for initial review, just as this man pays homage to his own boss, the product manager, by going through the same motions, and so on up the chain of command.

IN MODERN CAMELOTS, PAY HOMAGE TO THE BOSS

The penalties are stiff for subordinates who attempt to outmaneuver their bosses or are even suspected of doing so. Homage to rank is demanded in business kingdoms—make no mistake.

Paying homage to one's boss has gone on since long before the days of Camelot and the later adventures of Robin Hood and Maid Marian. Only back then homage was paid by vassals (another word for subordinates) to their feudal lord for his protection. Usually this relationship was sealed through a ceremony of pennants and trumpets, in which a man would declare himself the vassal of a particular lord and proclaim his willingness to fulfill his obligations through loyal service. Holding one's lord up in reverential regard was the surest way to stay alive. Challenging your lord and master could cost you your head.

Nowadays, beheading subordinates is definitely out. Modern-day bosses are far more likely to make your life so miserable that you quit.

This is exactly what happened to a CRT (Cathode Ray Tube) operator I knew who broke the chain of command by going to the personnel department to complain about her boss and ask for a transfer. Almost immediately word got back to her own boss. He was incredibly angry that she had attempted to go around him. Within two months of this incident she gave her notice.

This woman made two tactical errors you should be aware of:

Error number one: She tried a power play on her boss, an incredibly dumb stunt to pull. (A power play is a frequent maneuver in business, politics, and diplomacy, and is derived from an offensive play in football or hockey in which mass interference is provided in a particular zone to prevent a score or make one.) Evidently, she thought this offensive maneuver around her boss would be successful because she had the personnel department to gang up and intercede in her behalf.

Error number two: She went to the personnel department for help. The personnel department cannot or will not provide mass interference on your behalf. In nine out of ten cases the only thing personnel may do for you is to have a talk with your boss and say, "Shame, shame."

Take a moment to think back to when you were first hired by your company. What did personnel really do? Personnel set up the interview, but did personnel hire you? No! Your boss hired you. All personnel did after your boss hired you was to write a confirmation letter (assuming you're a higher-grade employee) stating things such as starting salary and other goodies you could expect to receive. If you're a lower-grade employee, your boss called personnel and told them to start a file on you. And presto change-o, ala cazam, payroll put a new name into the firm's computer bank.

And who fires you? Even though personnel may carry out the dirty work and listen to you complain during that exit interview, they are only acting under orders from your *boss*.

You may not like the analogy drawn between modern-day subordinates and the vassals of feudal times. In part it chafes to think of yourself as a subordinate. It helps to remember that everybody in business has a boss to report to.

What is really important if you want to stay employed long in your current company is to recognize a fundamental truth: you are in a *dependent* relationship with your immediate boss. To refuse to recognize this fact and spend your days thinking of clever ways to get around your boss is a sure way to get hurt. The function of a boss is, after all, to supervise and to boss. Openly disobeying or trying to outflank your boss can spell real trouble and often cost you more than you gain.

This is a harsh reality many people either refuse to admit to themselves or devote little time to thinking about. Everyone in the work-a-day world is in a dependent (i.e., subordinate) position, having to account to someone (i.e., the boss) for their actions. *Individuals who get ahead* learn how to deal with the tensions this dependency produces within themselves in a constructive manner.

THE BOSS IS IN A BETTER POSITION TO CHECKMATE

Circumventing the boss is not a smart way to get a leg up in the organization. If you try, you'll probably be blocked or, worse yet, booted out on the sidewalk. The power structure in almost every business is established through fixed rules, not unlike a game of chess. Smart players in the business game don't ignore these rules any more than champion chess players do. No matter how skillful the machinations on the board, you know that the lines of power—what takes what in the game—from king to pawn remain unchanged. The queen can topple the rook and the rook the bishop and so on. Any good chess player protects his or her king from attack or the game's over, allowing the opposing player to checkmate. In chess, that's the object of the game, to checkmate or capture your opponent's king.

The movement of pieces across the chess board is guided by certain fixed rules. For example, the knight may make L-shaped movements of two squares in one row and one square in a perpendicular row over squares that may be occupied, whereas the rook has the power to move along the ranks and files across any number of unoccupied squares.

In business a subordinate's movements can be just as rigidly dictated as those of chess pieces. Breaking the rules of the game—such as breaking the chain of command—can result in your being knocked out of the game. Remember that your boss has the power to checkmate any moves you make.

To drive this important point home I will recount the story of an engineer named Arnold who worked for a company that produced box boards and packaging for several major firms across the country. Arnold was part of a small profit center, offering special engineering talent to outside organizations in the area of environmental control and energy conservation. It was a small department, which could nonetheless call on a large group of mechanical, industrial, civil, architectural, chemical, and electrical engineers for their expertise. Above Arnold was another engineer named Barry who had been appointed as the department's director.

Setting up this special profit center had been Barry's brain-child, and it had been accomplished over the pooh-poohing of the division vice-president of corporate engineering and resource conservation.

To understand the chain of command, just imagine an Indian totem pole. In this case, Arnold would be at the bottom; his own boss, Barry, would be up another rung; Jack, Barry's boss, would be at the very top.

As it turned out, there was little deep, abiding sense of kinship between Barry and his own boss, Jack. So Arnold decided the way to get to the top of the totem pole was to play two ends against the middle and deepen the chasm between the two men.

A favorite tactic Arnold tried was going out for long lunches with Jack when his own boss, Barry, was out of town on assignment. Barry was frequently out of town overseeing an important new contract he'd landed for construction of a refuse-to-energy plant operated by an electric utility company. (The plant was designed to remove metals and other useful materials and process garbage into steam to produce electricity for use in a large eastern city.)

This plant was Barry's baby, so to speak, and he had a lot riding on its success. Specifically, he hoped to get a contract with the major conglomerate that owned this particular utility company. If this came about, Barry's profit center could receive two other major contracts: one to improve the disposal of waste water within a salmon cannery, the other to design and oversee the construction of a plant to clean coal.

It was Barry's feeling that both of these potential contracts were too important to risk placing Arnold in charge. As I mentioned previously, this department was a profit center and Barry knew Jack would pull the rug out from under him in short order if they didn't stay in the black.

This did not sit too well with Arnold. He had joined the company a year before after receiving a master's in chemical engineering. He was already sick of working only on the small bread-and-butter projects Barry delegated to him. His major assignment on the job had been to recoup chemicals used in the manufacture of paper at a mill on the outskirts of town. As far as he was concerned, an engineering technician for the department could do this simple job.

Arnold's attitude amazed me when we first talked. It never occurred to him that the best way to land those juicy accounts was to perform the small jobs well, especially for a client company. This way his name would be remembered, if they required outside assistance in the future or knew of another firm that did.

Arnold mistakenly thought the best way to get Barry to relinquish some of his hold on these big accounts to him was through building up rapport with Jack. Whenever Arnold wasn't at the paper mill, he could be found visiting Jack. Jack had been somewhat removed from the center of action for some years. Nonetheless, he liked to tell stories of the headaches suffered while constructing some of the box board plants back in his day, twenty years before. Arnold would act as if he were hanging on every word Jack uttered. These jam sessions never occurred, of course, when Barry was in town. But Barry's suspicions were already aroused somewhat by the frequent absence of both of these men when he would check into the office from out of town.

Four days before Arnold was fired, those around him noted that he seemed to be on top of the world. What they didn't know was that Jack had really spilled his guts when he had been tanked up during their last lunch, giving Arnold the opening he'd hoped for.

Jack had a huge ego. In his cups he often alluded to plans for making his fortune. Arnold hadn't paid much attention to these little slips until Jack told him he was a major stockholder in a key competitive firm. This firm held designs and competed for contracts on environmentally efficient processing systems similar to those of their own divisions. And to make matters murkier, this firm had beat Barry out on several key jobs.

In fact, Barry suddenly became successful in getting contract bids accepted when Jack wasn't given the opportunity to review them. (Barry, tired of losing contracts, had taken a risk and had his first big contract reviewed by the legal department; then he shot it off by express mail while Jack was out of town. He told Jack that the prospect had set an earlier-than-expected deadline for submitting the bids, even though the actual deadline was a week later.)

Barry suspected that Jack's conservative bid advice was phony and that a conflict of interest might be involved. He had already set out making discreet inquiries.

Then Arnold waltzed in to break the news to Barry, telling him what Jack had said. Barry gave Arnold less than four hours to get out!

I'm sure at this point you are thinking that there is no justice in the world. And I can only offer what my father, a lawyer, used to point out to me: "The law is the law. It doesn't have to be just; it doesn't have to be fair; it's just the law!"

Well, Arnold hadn't broken any real laws, but he'd broken the *numero uno* law of the corporate world: "Don't break the chain of command!"

Barry wasn't stupid. He recognized that Arnold was not looking after Barry's best interests or those of the company's by sharing this juicy tidbit. Arnold was looking after his own interests and was hoping to create a full-scale war between Barry and Jack in which Arnold would emerge the victor. Arnold actually hoped that Barry would take these allegations on up the chain of command, where Jack was on better footing than Barry. If Barry had done that—lacking hard evidence, of which he had none—he just might have been finished in the organization.

Barry decided that the best course was to feign fidelity to Jack and not risk his own head on the chopping block by escalating the whole affair. Barry fired Arnold for insubordination on the basis of spreading gross lies about a supervisor. However, Barry was quick to point out what he had done and why to Jack, while looking him straight in the eye and telling him he knew he wouldn't be stupid enough to be tied up with a competitor. Jack was quick enough on the uptake to know that Barry was on to his little game. He knew that if he made one more slip he'd be out, and what's more, probably of little use to the competition.

DON'T EXPECT TRIBUNALS OF JUSTICE ON HIGH

Don't think for one minute that Arnold took this state of affairs lying down. He wrote a letter to the chairman of the board, outlining his allegations and asking for reinstatement. Upon further inquiry the chairman was assured by Barry that Arnold's charges had no substance. In this way he further cemented his position by paying homage to his own boss. And Arnold was still out.

I know a woman who was fired under similar circumstances for accusing her boss of embezzlement. A letter she wrote to the top man was routed back to her boss (now her ex-boss) with just two words on it: "Handle this." There was no way the chairman would intercede in her behalf on this kind of evidence. To do so would be breaking the chain of command in reverse. In the interest of fairness I should note that the heads of most major companies get crank letters all the time, most with groundless allegations, from dumb-dumbs who think they'll get some kind of action or revenge from going to the top. In actual fact, the top man often refuses to be bothered and routes it, virtually unread, down the chain of command to the appropriate manager for handling, which generally means putting a muzzle on the troublemaker, if still on the payroll.

THE BOSS MAY DEMAND
THAT YOU HAVE NO OTHER GODS BEFORE HIM

Obviously, in your organization you must deal with other people besides your boss to get your job done. But be very careful about how you establish relationships with others in the organization. Keep foremost in your mind how these relationships affect your boss's feelings toward you. You probably think these outside relationships help you. You may very well be right. But consider for one second. They might hurt you.

It might be wise to keep the flattering attention you direct at others low key, lest you be labeled a brownnoser or, worse, be thought to have ulterior motives such as undermining the boss. I find it fun to watch these characters operate, particularly the ones who think they are very subtle. Most of us have met people like these on the job:

- People who read the latest business journals to keep up to date but feel compelled to share this knowledge with top executives who *also* read those publications.
- Those who make note of the chairman's hobby, such as skeet shooting, and start using clay pigeons as office coasters.
- Subordinates who, though allergic to smoke, can be seen constantly carrying an unlit cigar between the index and third fingers of their right hand, just like the president.

Of course, there are many more, such as the classic case of the young man who dates the boss's boss's boss's secretary in the hopes that she will put in a good word for him. (But what if she can't think of a nice thing to say?)

This particular tactic is not limited to guys who are fresh out of school. Within one insurance firm the V-P of accounting started dating the secretary of the senior V-P of product management. This senior V-P was in charge of several departments, like actuarial pensions, research and development, but not accounting. The accounting department and its V-P reported up through the operations division to a senior V-P who had his eye on the presidency within the company. His closest competitor was the senior V-P of product management. So the senior V-P of product management viewed the romance as a dangerous foray into his territory. What did they hope to find out from his secretary?

When it became apparent that this romance was more than a passing fancy, the secretary suddenly moved into a clerical position in claims, a department under the operations division. Just as suddenly, the V-P of accounting lost interest in her, becoming quite aloof. She was of no further use to him in the claims position.

Now the secretary feels hurt and upset. Her current job pays just as much, but she doesn't have the flexibility she used to have, nor the freedom.

You may think her former boss, the senior V-P of product management, was just being paranoid and was harsh to transfer her. After all, she had a right to have a private life and he had no right to interfere. Right? Wrong!

Her affair with the V-P of accounting was, in her boss's eyes, an act of insubordination. Not only did it create a potential threat to his position, but it represented another infraction almost as important. You've heard the military regulation: officers and enlisted personnel must not fraternize. Many companies hold to this, whether the law is written or unwritten! The secretary (i.e., enlisted personnel) and the V-P who was an officer of the corporation should not have fraternized.

As I stated in the first paragraph of this chapter, one of the main reasons for structuring organizations, be they profit or nonprofit, along the lines of the military with a chain of command is the belief that familiarity breeds contempt.

PART II

6
Faulty Assumption Six

THE BOSS–SUBORDINATE RELATIONSHIP
IS AN "US VERSUS THEM" PROPOSITION

> *"Larry's attitude is screw them—*
> *the company, me, the bigger*
> *bosses. He makes a career out of*
> *breaking the rules. But I don't*
> *know how much longer I can*
> *put up with him. He's a bad*
> *example for everyone. In fact, I*
> *have more luck getting my*
> *fifteen-year-old kid to do things*
> *than I do Larry."*
>
> *Male, 43*
> *manager, process art*
> *greeting card manufacturer*

There are all types of "us versus them" contentions between bosses and subordinates. Some of it is darn near open warfare. Some of it is more subtle. Absenteeism, for instance, is of the latter variety.

As the national figures on absenteeism rise, it is time that we take a hard look at the causes. Very often a bad boss–subordinate relationship and a prevalent attitude of "screw 'em" toward the boss and the economy are at the bottom of absenteeism. "Let 'em get along without me for a day and see if things go as well!"

The all-time favorite excuse for being absent seems to be "the flu." The boss is told that the employee has picked up the Asian, swine, or the Russian variety, but during counseling interviews I've heard employees recount far more exotic varieties. Some of my favorites are:

Buck Flu: Prevalent among employees taking off on company time to interview for a new job with the competition.

Belt Flu: Most often occurs on the day following prolonged contact with the open end of a bottle containing an alcoholic beverage.

Sunshine Flu: This baffling illness strikes on particularly balmy days during the spring months. An unusually high number of sufferers return to work with an inexplicable browning of the skin resembling a suntan.

Phantom Flu: Commonly afflicts employees who write bad checks to cover their gambling debts. Requires patients to lay low for a while.

Friday/Monday Flu: This debilitating variety strikes on Fridays and Mondays. Known variously as long weekend or vacation multiplier flu.

When we begin to think in "us versus them" terms, it is helpful to realize that there are basically three major relationships in our lifetime: the first is with our parents; the second is with our mate(s); and the third is with our boss(es).

All of these relationships work best when each party accepts the *mutual* need for the other. There is no "us versus them" position *inherent* in any of these alliances. But too often this kind of standoff develops when it seems that the other person is always on the receiving end, take, take, taking, while you are on the other end, give, give, giving.

To illustrate, I will point out the perils of guerilla tactics used by a high-ranking officer of an insurance firm when he didn't get a big promotion he thought was in the bag.

WHEN YOU SET OUT TO HURT SOMEONE ELSE
YOU OFTEN END UP HURTING YOURSELF

Clarence (a fictitious name) was a divisional vice-president, one of four people, each covering a quadrant of the United States. Each division handled a complete line of insurance and all the normal functions, like underwriting and claims. Clarence was expecting to move up another notch after his boss, the executive vice-president, retired. He had, in fact, made several statements to the effect that when (note I didn't use *if*) he was in charge certain changes would be made. But he never got the chance. The executive vice-president chose one of the other divisional vice-presidents for the top slot.

It never occurred to Clarence that this man, Joe, even would be seriously considered. But, as a matter of fact, Joe had already demonstrated for six months that he could handle bigger responsibilities. Joe had taken on the management of two divisions at once while his boss searched for a replacement for another vice-president who had died suddenly. All this was apparently lost on Clarence.

At the announcement of the executive vice-president's replacement, Clarence went into a virtual state of shock, though no one else in the company seemed in the least surprised.

Although Clarence got along well with his own subordinates, none of his peers in management, nor even his own boss, could tell him a thing. Actually, Clarence often would agree to decisions made in high-level executive meetings, then go back to his office and do the exact opposite. For example: During one of my visits on site, I attended such a meeting at which they were worrying over the poor state of the economy and its impact on the small businesses that purchased policies from them. Many of their clients were trying to cut expenses by putting out policies for bid. It was decided among the group to meet competitors' challenges head-on by lowering premiums. Everyone at the table agreed. I heard Clarence say "Yes" with my own ears! Yet weeks later his division still had not cut its premiums. Whether this was done out of stubbornness or just plain orneriness isn't clear.

One thing is sure; it wasn't because Clarence was smarter than anyone else, even though he thought he had a corner on the market when it came to brains. After he didn't get the promotion he operated his division even more as a fiefdom independent of the rest of the company. He had never felt he needed help from his former boss; he certainly didn't need any from this new one.

He started right in sniping at Joe in an effort to lessen his prestige among the other divisional vice-presidents. He has been successful at getting one of these guys stirred up, but the third only straddles the fence and the fourth (Joe's replacement) isn't about to get involved with this nonsense.

What Clarence hopes to accomplish through such uproar-breeding tactics is to discredit Joe, but he's actually doing more harm to himself. People are losing respect for him even in his own division. He's bad-mouthed Joe so much about the way he manages the company that everyone tries to avoid him or no longer takes what he says seriously.

Recently I checked back with one of my contacts to hear the latest scuttlebutt on this man. My contact said, "Oh, Clarence still is in the same spot, but he doesn't have nearly the power he once had. He still takes potshots at Joe, but it just falls on deaf ears. I wish I could remember more juicy tidbits for your book, but when you hear unpleasantries you start to block them out of your mind. The rest of us often wonder what Clarence says about us behind our backs."

If Joe knows what Clarence is doing, no one has been made aware of it. The way I see it, Joe is far too smart to let Clarence provoke him or make him lose his temper. He probably is giving him just enough rope to hang himself! Clarence had better get smart and acknowledge Joe's rank, position, and experience before the floorboard under his desk chair drops down and he finds himself on the outside looking in.

He may not like Joe, but facts are facts. Joe is the boss! He should accept it. At the rate Clarence is losing credibility around that place, there would be few sad faces at his departure.

RULE BREAKERS MAKE IT TOUGH FOR EVERYONE

Nothing, but nothing, creates more hate and discontent (commonly referred to in managerial textbooks as low morale) among the troops than inconsistent application of rules and regulations. As a boss you cannot afford to let some of your subordinates get away with murder while others are expected to conform. You will lose credibility and productivity if you do.

Jim learned this the hard way as the boss of a talented artist, whom I'll call Larry. Both worked for a large greeting card manufacturer.

Actually, if you didn't believe Larry was talented, all you had to do was ask him. He considered himself God's gift to this employer. And Larry made no secret of his opinion of Jim, telling several people, "He needs me far more than I need him." Larry labeled his boss a used-up piece of deadwood with little creative talent. (This statement was patently false. Jim had already earned his stripes, after all, and shouldn't have to roll up his sleeves and do Larry's work for him.)

Larry was diligent on the job only in complaining. He seldom let up. He felt he deserved more money—recompense, I suppose, for coming in late and sneaking out early. He really deserved nothing so much as a swift kick in the seat of the pants. He spent a lot of time goofing off or putting his artistic talent to stupid uses. One prank involved drawing a dirty cartoon of a little boy and girl and then making 500 copies.

Needless to say, these cartoons turned up everywhere. Although Larry's initials weren't on the final panel, it was no mystery to anyone who had penned it. I warned Jim in a counseling session that he needed not only to give Larry a dressing down but to put him on probation as well. Larry was getting away with things no other staff member was allowed to do. The longer Jim waited to have a showdown with Larry, the greater the risk of losing the respect and morale of his other subordinates, which, after my departure from the firm, informed sources told me is exactly what happened. That, finally, was the straw that broke the camel's back, and Jim gave Larry the sack.

WHEN THE BOSS IS THE CULPRIT IN A MAKE OR BREAK RELATIONSHIP

Maintaining a good boss–subordinate relationship is just as difficult as building a good marriage. It takes two to make or break a marriage or any other kind of relationship. And it requires a lot of give and take on both sides to keep one viable.

In business, as in marriage, one partner may be more at fault than the other.

At this point I will state the obvious to bosses who are having difficulty with their troops. It might behoove you to analyze your own behavior. In too many instances when subordinates oppose a boss's authority it's due to one or a combination of the following reasons:

Inconsistency in the application of rules, discipline, or demands.

- The boss may apply one rule of conduct to one subordinate and not to others.
- The boss plays favorites.
- One subordinate (or class of subordinates) is disciplined for infractions while others do as they please.
- Poor performance may go unnoticed and others stop bothering to be conscientious.
- Demands placed on subordinates are born of caprice, whim, vagary, or freakishness, netting like performance in return.

Harassments that antagonize, pressure, or demean others.

- Cutting remarks that make subordinates feel inadequate, as if they can't do anything right.

- Snide, belittling statements that wear away at a person until they have no other recourse but to quit.
- Antagonism, pressure, and yelling that leads to subordinates making mistakes, which only causes their bosses to yell at them again.
- Creating fear in employees until they turn off their minds or play it safe just to try to make it through another day without being threatened with dismissal or being fired.
- Unwanted sexual attention; coercion to commit illegal acts.
- Open hero worship of Scrooge, Simon Legree, Captain Queeg, and others of that ilk.

Usually bosses who display these traits are scattered here and there in an organization. But I recently ran across one restaurant that had had ten different managers over an eighteen-month period, and *all* of them were lousy. That must be an all-time record.

This restaurant is one of a chain, coast to coast. If you knew what company owns this chain and supplies its management, you'd be shocked. The outlet in question is composed of approximately seventy employees, including hostesses, bartenders, waitresses, dishwashers, busboys, assemblers, a sanitation specialist, several production cooks, a secretary-bookkeeper, an assistant manager, and a manager.

I will now share the verbal account of one of the assemblers. I'll name her Jane. She stuck it out so long that she was unlucky enough to have to work under each of these ten managers. I have exercised my editorial prerogative and profiled three of the worst, focusing on their outstanding sins.

The Fourth Manager

Sexism. This manager had a real penchant for the waitresses, despite the fact that his wife was employed on the premises as secretary-bookkeeper. He would spend an average of two to three hours a day closeted in his office with one of the waitresses. He said she was giving him back rubs, but why did the door have to be locked?

As to Jane, when she spoke to the manager about a hostess job that became available, she was turned down. He informed her, "You've got a cute little ass. You'd have to wear a dress as hostess and I want to see you at work in those tight jeans."

Threats. Here is a selection of his choice comments:

- To one waitress he said, "If you don't cut down on the number of trips you make to the john, I'm having your name painted on the door!"
- To his own wife he said, "Type this letter over one more time; by now you should have it memorized."
- To one busboy he said, "You skip work one more day and I'm submitting your name to the missing person's bureau."
- To one of the bartenders he said, "Your opinions count. On the dim possibility that you ever have a good idea, I'll act on it."
- To one cook he said, "If you don't start following orders, I'm sending you with our guard dog to obedience school."
- To Jane he said, "Wear that getup to work one more time and I'm buying you a Halloween mask to match it."

"If he couldn't find a reason to nag, scold, or scream at us, he invented one," Jane said.

He was particularly fond of harassing one dishwasher. The manager would wait until this particular person had already punched out for the day and then would say that he hadn't finished all his work. He consistently asked this dishwasher to clean up more pots and pans than the other guy holding the same job. One day he asked him to stay and scrub 200 plates just after he had punched out. When he complained, the boss made his all-around favorite comment, "If you don't like working around here, you can always quit," whereupon the dishwasher obliged.

Theft. This boss had his own system for keeping the inventory at the restaurant. Although the company's policy was to serve customers only bottled or draft beer, he always ordered several cases of canned beer. He would use this for personal parties at home. He arranged to have the supplier make beer deliveries before anyone else was in and thought no one would notice. But the sanitation specialist was often at the restaurant early, cleaning the restrooms and polishing brass fixtures, and he had seen the case beer delivered several times. (He also didn't mind telling me what he had seen, when I asked him to verify Jane's account of it.)

Since most restaurant managers have authority to order food samples from various suppliers at a reduced price, the boss made a killing here, too. He would order all kinds of luncheon meats and take them home. This sometimes included whole hams, which he turned around and gave as holiday gifts. He was very generous with the company's money when he was on the receiving end, but not at salary review time for his staff.

The Seventh Manager

Laxity. According to the company policy, any employee who was written up three times in any three-month period was subject to instant dismissal. On the other hand, if you were written up only once and were good the rest of the time, you would get a clean bill of health the next quarter. This boss would never get tough with certain workers who shirked their duties. For example, one woman had been written up *six* times in *one* month, and she hadn't been fired.

This boss used the excuse that he felt sorry for her. The poor dear had not been able to shake the flu. He never gave a thought to the inconvenience or burden being placed on co-workers who had to substitute for this "sick" woman so often.

Playing favorites or pets. Corporate policy also stated that each new employee should be given a performance review at three, six, and twelve months of employment, with yearly reviews thereafter. This particular boss singled out one young dolly (a different one than the flu queen) and gave her three pay raises in five months. He got around corporate headquarters by neglecting to evaluate several other employees. In this way they wouldn't suspect that all those raises were going to just one person.

Favors. If you've ever worked in a restaurant, you already know that a weekly schedule of everyone's hours is posted by the manager. (And if you didn't know, now you've been warned.) This is a powerful weapon in the hands of some bosses. This particular one used it to get favors or other cooperation. If you didn't come across, you had your hours cut, which resulted in a loss of pay. He frequently asked Jane to make numerous trips to pick up merchandise when inventories got low. Rarely did he offer to reimburse her for gas.

The Tenth Manager

Promises. On his very first week on the job this boss talked at length with each employee. He promised them this, he promised them that. Jane couldn't believe her ears. He promised her a 75¢-an-hour raise when the most she'd ever received at one time was a raise of 25¢. He built up everyone's expectations to such a pitch that they didn't think to be curious or suspicious. The letdown came when this wonderful man nearly had his ear bitten off the next week during a drunken brawl, reeled into the restaurant, and sat down in the bar with everyone agape. He was hospitalized for alcoholism and never returned to the job. His tenure was ten whole days.

It should be noted that while all ten managers came and went, no one from on high (that is, *their* boss) pressured them to resign. The pressures of the job got to them or a greener pasture beckoned (and just perhaps a couple of them feared they might be lynched by irate employees).

Fortunately, not every one of them was totally capricious or arbitrary. Most simply lacked the experience or training for managing people.

Jane's latest boss (number eleven) isn't too bad, even though their initial relationship got off to a rocky start. He took over as the restaurant's new boss during the holiday season, which always coincides with the colds and flu season. In the first three weeks he was at the helm, Jane called in sick twice. She was genuinely ill and had been managing to drag herself into work (she certainly looked green around the gills the couple of times I saw her there). She had substituted for so many other "sick" people that she ended up having only two days off out of nineteen straight days on the job.

When she got back to work the boss started to berate her for being sick far too often. (Prior to this bout with flu Jane hadn't been out for reasons of illness for nine straight months.) At that Jane yelled, "You're crazy!" and stormed downstairs to the lockers.

Although I wouldn't recommend using this technique, it brought things to a head and the next day her boss started treating Jane with much more respect. Part of this was due to her starting things off with an apology for losing her temper. She then pointed out her actual record of few illnesses.

Further thought on her part (and a few hints from me) caused her to conclude that her boss:

- had not had time to read all the personnel files of seventy employees in three short weeks.
- had spoken out of turn since Jane was putting in a lot of extra hours substituting for others, but he himself was also working horrendous hours.
- had been venting general frustrations with the job and had just taken them out on her.

Jane learned a very valuable lesson: sometimes it pays to speak up for yourself.

Several years ago I interviewed a union steward in a supermarket chain who expressed her frustrations in this way:

"Most are afraid to talk up to a bad boss. They're afraid they'll get the dirty end of things. You know, bad shifts, even if you're a senior member of this union. I'm from the old school. I'm not trying to bilk the store. When I'm paid for eight hours I work eight hours! But if management won't follow the rules, why should we? We have to, or we get written up. Managers need to talk to us, not at us or around us. It just makes good sense. (And here's the gem.) Managing people is like a marriage. You have to give as well as take!"

7

Faulty Assumption Seven

THE BOSS IS ALL-POWERFUL

> *"Terri stood right where you are*
> *and told me her investigation*
> *had turned up a way to save the*
> *university $15,000 in the first*
> *year. Later on I as good as told*
> *her to forget it. I have never*
> *been able to tell her why, and*
> *I've yet to regain her respect."*

> *Male, 39*
> *controller*
> *private university*

Subordinates tend to overestimate the amount of authority a boss really has. They buy a hunk of frustration for themselves when they assume it's the boss's fault that things aren't going the way they would like them to. Unfortunately, many subordinates operate under the naive belief that their boss is in complete control of the work environment and thus can make things happen. This is simply not the case.

Very real constraints limit your boss's range of action, including legal, governmental, political, familial, and social constraints.

Your boss is impinged upon and pulled in many directions. As one of his or her subordinates, you are only one of many that must be heard (and sometimes endured). It is important to understand there are very real restrictions on your boss's authority to get things done, which is influenced by the complex nature of his or her organizational role.

YOUR BOSS IS AT THE MERCY
OF THE POWERS THAT BE

I don't mean to imply that every time your boss gets impossible it's the result of forces beyond his control. Heavens no! But employees can be spared a lot of grief by knowing that it isn't always their fault when the boss's behavior seems inexplicable. And if subordinates have any notions of the boss being all-powerful, they are in for a rude awakening somewhere along the line.

A classic example was the young woman I call Terri here. She was a serious person, in her mid-thirties, working in the financial office of a small private university in the East. She answered directly to the controller; I'll call him Norman. Terri handled student accounts and worked directly with students, which can certainly be hazardous duty. Terri often found herself caught in a double squeeze between the students and Township Bank (which was under contract to service certain loans, but did so ineptly). For example, new forwarding addresses of graduates were frequently not returned to the billing cycle; consequently these students were considered delinquent in their payments. In addition, Township Bank took six months or longer to place students on current status after they had previously applied for deferment. Terri therefore had to perform much additional work in counseling not only current students, but also graduates who used her as a whipping post when venting their frustrations regarding the situation.

Complaints made by Terri to representatives at Township Bank produced no results. The bank needed to update its programs but didn't want to bear these extra costs. To add insult to injury, the university got hit with additional annual service charges from Township for work the bank really wasn't performing or which Terri had to redo. So she checked out various service agencies and found one highly recommended to her by an acquaintance who used the firm. This agency also charged 12 percent less in yearly fees than Township. She figured the savings to be in the neighborhood of $15,000.

Terri presented these findings to her boss, Norman, the controller. Soon afterward he wrote out a formal proposal and attached Terri's name as well as his own to it. After all, Norman had done quite a bit of legwork himself confirming her data, and he had to assume responsibility for this project since it would have direct impact on his area. But, as it turned out, none of this extra effort paid off for either one of them.

When this report hit the desk of Norman's boss, the vice-president of finance, he was up to his ears in the financial details for the construction of a new student activity center. The board had just given its blessing to the project, which was still being kept very hush-hush, lest the all-important financing fall through. This new building, it so happened, was the university president's hot button. He saw it as the monument to his tenure that would secure him remembrance by generations to come. And, as the wheels of fortune would have it, guess what organization financed it? Township Bank, of course!

It should come as no surprise that a key university board member was also a bigwig with Township, giving him a choke chain around the president's neck. Whenever the vote by the board to approve a recommendation by the president was close, it was always the Township Bank executive who cast the pivotal vote, swinging the decision in favor of the president's proposal. (It was also this executive who acted as intermediary on a very large special endowment between the university and one of the bank's own large depositors.)

Into this situation comes Norman, who had only been at the university a short time, and his plan to oust Township. Anxious to please, he is sure his boss will back this plan in light of his prior edicts to cut costs. However, given the situation with the president *et al*, Norman's boss (trying to keep his own neck intact) decided that even a $15,000 savings wouldn't be worth much to him (and much less the president) if it risked making this important banker unhappy.

Norman considered taking Terri into his confidence. But she was such a straight arrow that he was afraid she might unfrock them all, and he had nightmares of facing Mike Wallace on "60 Minutes" and caving in. Consequently Norman gave no explanation of the reasons that the recommendation had to be temporarily tabled, but told her to be patient . . . he would personally watch it.

Four years later Terri's plan was finally put into practice. But it didn't happen until after the president and the Township Bank executive lost power after a quorum of the board forced them out. Please remember that even though Norman was the controller—a relatively high position within the university—he was powerless to even hire a new service organization until these two power brokers were handed their walking papers. Things simply had to wait until the political climate was ripe before reopening the issue of Norman's and Terri's proposal.

Your boss may have to wait for others to depart this world for heaven, hell, or the greener pastures of the competition before setting out to win certain battles for you.

YOUR BIG BOSS MAY BE SMALL FRY TO SOMEBODY ELSE

I am at heart a realist. Therefore, I feel strongly that it is in your best interest to understand that much of your boss's power is contingent on other people and does not flow from the title he or she holds. Relationships outside the company as well as within dictate how effective your boss will be and consequently how effective you will be.

It helps to know that issues of personality and style become much more important when a person becomes a boss. How he or she relates to people whose words carry weight in the organization becomes more and more important in any move up the career ladder. The further a boss deviates from the style of management embraced by those individuals on the top executive floor, the shorter his or her tenure with the company is likely to be. For instance, a boss whose long suit is strong interpersonal skills is liable to be viewed as weak in an organization that is numbers oriented. And similarly, a boss who is only numbers oriented may be viewed as a fish out of water in a firm that puts team camaraderie before numbers.

In order to accomplish anything your boss doesn't just have to work with you; he also has to satisfy peers and superiors. Much of organizational life nowadays is run on the basis of group decisions. The group's (often called the company's) welfare takes precedence over other needs.

Even though the politics in the case you just read may turn your stomach a bit, consider this: For the university's overall good it wasn't worth losing a new student activity center that would benefit the total faculty, staff, and student body to save $15,000.

YOUR BOSS MAY NOT LIKE BEING A WHITE SLAVER

Inflationary pressure has caused many consumers to acquire goods and services through bartering. I would wager a guess that no socioeconomic group is more adept at horse trading than those bosses in middle and top management. And the items that exchange hands are diverse: computer systems, videotape equipment, parking spaces, entertainment, and more. But the trading doesn't always stop there; it also includes privileges, jobs, raises, and even people.

The horse trading that occurs in business is a far more subtle operation than takes place at a public livestock auction, where you bid so much for an animal on the hoof. Calling it a form of white slavery may be too strong, but believe me, one or both parties frequently ends up being prostituted. The amazing thing is that many employees are totally unaware of what's happening.

To illustrate, I'll recount the story of a woman named Joan who was upset that she had not received a promotion she wanted to assistant to the head of salary administration. It should be noted that the head of salary administration was a fifty-five-year-old woman who was popular among the top executives and various middle managers. If an important line manager wanted a new position created and graded at a higher level, she was more than a little obliging. She knew the value of cooperation and acted as if every wish was her command. This was also her manner in any interactions with her own boss, the director of labor relations.

Joan reported to the same man, the director of labor relations, but as his administrative assistant in the area of corporate administrative services. She had told him several times that if the job in salary administration ever opened up, she would certainly like to have a crack at it. But when it did become available, a secretary named Mary was appointed to the position.

Several weeks prior to appointing Mary, Joan's boss had received a number of calls from the executive vice-president. As it turned out, he had a problem: Mary. She reported to the vice-chairman, who had offices next to his own. Although she was very efficient and capable, the vice-chairman and Mary were not on the best of terms. There was no justification for firing her in his mind, so he asked his friend to pull a few strings. The executive vice-president never used strong-arm tactics. Nor did he order Joan's boss to hire this other woman. He didn't have to. All he had to do was imply how very pleased he'd be if Mary got the job.

Before you accuse Joan's boss of caving in, never lose sight of the fact that the boss is a human being, too. (I should also point out that Joan did not possess more technical capability than Mary. So, as far as the head of salary administration was concerned, the same amount of training would be involved with either candidate.)

Don't forget, as Joan did, that your boss has career ambitions as well as obligations to others in the department. The people in labor relations (Joan included) typically received three to five percentage points above most employees when salary review time came. This was not because Joan's boss was all-powerful. *Every* time he wanted to give a raise that was outside the guidelines set by the executive committee (spin-off of the board), he had to personally seek approval from the executive vice-president. So, maintaining rapport with this man was critical to Joan's boss, not to mention the department's budget. If Joan had been privy to these facts, it would have been unrealistic for her to expect her boss to submerge all his needs just to satisfy hers. This kind of openness rarely exists.

It may help just to be more aware that your boss has personal needs, his fair share of human foibles, and maybe even a little mush in the backbone.

YOUR BOSS MAY TRY TO WIN BY LOSING

Old fight movies invariably contain a scene in which the protagonist is offered a bribe to throw the big fight. But does he take it? No! He does a bit of fancy footwork and wins the final bout while only pretending to be on the take.

Winning may be everything in the movie fight game, but goodwill may be more important in the real business world. To build goodwill, your boss may intentionally throw a few fights along the way.

Your boss may be using the strategy of one successful woman I know. She wins selected battles deemed important by her, but lets others win smaller ones. Martha (not her real name, of course) works as the director of purchasing in a large eastern hospital.

In a recent incident Martha questioned the merits of hiring a new receptionist. Nevertheless, she didn't put up a fuss, thus letting other department heads have their own way in hiring someone. Yet several weeks before her key assistant, Jill, had been asked by Martha to check out the times when meetings were being scheduled for the conference room on their floor. As things were set up, Martha and the other managers paid for refreshments used in their meetings, which were held on alternating weeks with other departments or groups. If more meetings than their own were scheduled in the conference room during those weeks when it was the purchasing department's turn to pay, Jill's boss wanted to know it!

To Jill's way of thinking, investigating the possibility of

paying for a few extra soft drinks was small stuff, and hiring a receptionist was far more important. Jill was absolutely wrong! The receptionist's salary did not come out of her boss's budget, but all those soft drinks, which weren't so inconsiderable after all, did. Martha had to be concerned about keeping the department's budget on target, because she was held accountable by her own superiors for doing just that. Letting other department heads pick the woman of their dreams to answer the phone was of no real concern to her, even though she chose to let them think so at first by appearing to oppose it and then letting them win her over.

Jill's boss was smart enough to hit the mat when it could gain her trade-offs.

DANGERS IN MIMICKING A POWERFUL BOSS

There are a few gutsy bosses who bluster their way to the top executive floor. But as one of his or her subordinates, don't let the lack of oxygen at those heady heights affect *your* brain cells. No one's tenure of power lasts forever, and unless you plan to retire when your boss does, I would suggest not mimicking any bad behavior or style. One secretary I know is now up the creek without a paddle because she did that very thing.

Her boss is the president and chief operating officer of one of the Fortune 500 companies. He's been at the top for a long time. Recently the board of directors, dissatisfied with the last two years of earnings growth, told him they were not going to renew his contract to allow him to work until age seventy.

A gory battle ensued, because there was no love lost between the president and many of the board members. Additionally, the president was of the type who could put his own grandmother out in the street if this act would inch up profits an extra notch and keep him in power.

This style had rubbed off on his secretary. She emulated that manner in her dealings with others in the company. For example, she insisted that the secretary of the personnel department walk nearly two miles (this was a large corporate complex with several buildings spread out over a huge campus) to pick up thirteen sheets of the president's executive stationery and matching onionskin. Of course, it would have been much easier to route this stationery through the interoffice mail, but she refused to do so. It was her way to show "them" who was the boss.

Now personnel is showing the president's secretary who's boss by taking their own sweet time trying to place her elsewhere. Not one of the other executives is breaking the door down to hire her—not after she kept them on hold, waiting to speak to the president until almost closing time; not after she reduced their current secretaries to tears; not after all that!

8
Faulty Assumption Eight

IF THE BIG SHOTS GO FOR IT, IT'LL FLY

"I couldn't believe it. The V-P of operations okayed my plan, but then apparently the merchandising department was too busy with other things to cooperate. Designers are all a bunch of overrated fags, if you ask me."

Male, 33
manager, material conservation
apparel manufacturer

Even a corporate seal of approval from top management may not ensure success for a project. Singly or collectively, a lot of people farther down the line have a significant influence on the success or failure of any project. If you don't have their backing, you're dead.

BIG SHOTS PLUS LITTLE SHOTS
MAKE A BIGGER BANG

One of my clients discovered this fact the hard way. Red, as I'll call him, worked in the promotions department of a large chain of fast-food restaurants. He was fresh from a dog-and-pony show—complete with a multimedia triple-dissolve audiovis-

99

ual show and silver-embossed presentations delivered on trays to the company big shots by stunning models dressed as 1940s carhops. All the razzle-dazzle had been to introduce a sales incentive program Red had designed.

The core of his program centered on a nationwide opinion-research survey of people who frequent fast-food establishments. The findings were about what you would expect if you just thought of reasons yourself. But the cost for getting the information would keep you in hamburgers for the rest of your life. The survey showed that we go to fast-food restaurants that offer these features:

- great-tasting food
- clean eating areas and restrooms
- thick, juicy hamburgers
- the highest quality ingredients
- helpful, friendly employees
- hot items served hot and cold items served cold
- fast-moving customer lines
- consistent quality from visit to visit
- convenient locations

Red used the survey to point up the importance the store employees played in customer satisfaction. To improve their store's own quality, cleanliness, service, and friendliness, he proposed incentives to make each location compete with employees of winning stores to receive special recognition.

The voters were the customers who were induced with a free soft drink to fill out comment cards on the store's performance in those four areas of service.

Half the contest comment cards were distributed at the beginning to establish a benchmark. The remainder was held back until the end to gauge the effects of the advertising and the employees' exertions. At the end of the contest two stores out of each district, each with an average of fifteen stores, would receive special recognition on the basis of any improvements made.

Red's contest slogan was, "We gotta be better than best."

The top brass thought the concept was great and he was given a green light. However, although Red had consulted a lot of people, none of them were store employees. What did they think of all this, since they were the ones who would be most directly involved? Not very much!

Most of the lack of interest was due to the so-called incentives. You see, Red had tied up the whole budget externally in ads and production costs. When it came down to employee motivation, winning store employees would net a plastic trophy of the company's distinctive logo character mounted atop a plastic replica of a hamburger, further immortalized with the contest slogan. They would also attend a company outing valued at $300 in cash for the store with the highest number of points and $200 for second place. (Since each store was open twenty-four hours a day and had three shifts of crews, all that extra effort over an eight-week period could yield only 5¢ extra an hour per employee.) There were no cash prizes, however, because Red had read another survey that said that employees preferred group rather than individual prizes (try giving stock options sometime and see what they prefer).

Each winning crew was told the members could decide how to spend their money—but for tax reasons of great appeal to the higher-ups, they could not buy merchandise or award themselves cash or any item redeemable for cash. Store managers leaned toward spending the prize on a company outing (it's great fun to spend your free time with the same people you work with) or donating the money to charity (a big selling point with employees earning a minimum wage). Someone (certainly not one of the hourly employees) came up with the idea of going to a concert. (Employees would be given tickets only as they entered the theater, so no one could scalp them. There's a real display of employee concern for you.)

If Red thought the big shots had the last word on the success of this project, he was in for a rude awakening. When the customer survey cards were tabulated there was no improvement evident in the chain's results. If anything, their sales were more likely than ever to be far below the sales volume of their competition because their employees had really been turned off.

Part of the problem was that the big shots Red talked to were like a group of generals who have been out of the trenches too long—they hadn't wrapped a hamburger or mixed a milk shake in years. They evidently didn't know what would turn on the chain's store-level employees. I would even wager a guess that none of these executives had eaten in one of their restaurants for several years. (You may find it hard to believe, but I convinced the president of a large meat-packing firm, with ads for frankfurters on national TV, to take a walk through his own plant, something he hadn't done for seventeen years.)

LIFT-OFF TAKES BIG SHOTS BUT DEPENDS ON LITTLE SHOTS FOR AFTERBURNER THRUST

I would be the last to discount the importance of receiving top management's backing to get a major project off the launching pad and into orbit. But providing enough thrust to keep it there is another matter. If you intend your projects to soar to greater heights and not crash and burn, you'll have to rely on the support of others below and on both sides of you to get the job done.

I speak as a veteran of successful campaigns within client organizations to launch productivity improvement programs. It is important to understand that I am not an efficiency expert who comes into a company and starts telling employees how they should do their jobs differently. (I've always felt that employees would be quite justified in telling me to stuff all my recommendations if I did.) I operate from the philosophy that the best consultants are already on the payroll—you. To tap this resource to everyone's benefit, a series of workshops is held over several weeks with each participant—managers, hourly employees, technicians, and professionals—completing a plan of action to improve an aspect of his or her job.

During the initial stage of introducing a productivity or operations improvement program in a client organization, I start off talking to the big shots, but I certainly don't stop at that level. If the company has a union, I always sit down with the union's business committee, explain what I'm about, and indicate the kind of people I'm looking for. (I don't want a group packed with just "round pegs"; a few hell-raising "square pegs" are needed, too.) I ask them to give me the names of employees they feel should have the opportunity to participate in our workshops and to tell me why.

Briefing sessions for everyone in the company are held in small groups of thirty to forty individuals at a time. Volunteers are sought, and I line up a series of interviews with first-line and middle managers to get the names of individuals in their departments who they feel should participate. At the same time I'm beginning to glean important information about their perceptions of each other and the persons they recommend, which, needless to say, is quite illuminating.

From this sometimes massive list, fifteen or twenty people are selected to serve in the first work group. Those departments that have been interviewed but will not be represented in the first go-around are notified of the reasons why.

I never begin interviews until I touch base with the individual's immediate boss and ask his or her permission to invite that person to participate. Of course, the person may decline to do so; someone else is then chosen. Some individuals don't like to be the first at anything, and I respect that.

None of these steps is a waste of time. Studies find one of the reasons that men and women in top management positions (big shots) are usually far more committed to the organizations they serve is that they have considerable say or input concerning the inner workings of the business. The selection process for my groups offers this kind of opportunity to participants. I work on the premise that *people are more committed to making workable those things they have a hand in shaping or influencing in some way.*

Once I have gained as broad a base of support as possible for the program, I'm ready to research the next important areas: visibility and impact on others.

Since almost all changes and actions you take affect others, it is imperative to consider the impact of these changes. As with many of the people in my counseling groups, their actions will even affect other departments. You must remember at all times that your actions as a subordinate may adversely affect your boss's relationships with peer managers.

Before undertaking any change I recommend writing down the names of people whose assistance you will need. Your list should be pretty thorough: names of key managers or department heads and their immediate subordinates, whom they rely on to complete adequately their everyday tasks. This is not busy work; rather, it is an essential step in avoiding offending powerful people while attempting to implement change.

In general, when introducing change, I recommend you do the following.

- Develop a roster of names (big shots and little shots) with as much relevant information as possible about each person: their characters, temperaments, and dispositions, no matter how surly. (It may be wise to keep this list under lock and key.)
- Look at this list before beginning any new project and decide which individuals should be contacted in light of what needs to be accomplished.
- Involve and inform your own boss.
- Touch base with key managers and staff lower in rank in coordinating departments.
- Never move directly up the chain of command to talk to a big shot before doing all or most of the aforementioned things.

If you want to ensure a smooth implementation of a change, idea, or presentation you propose, it is vital to involve affected parties early in the process; otherwise, you may fail miserably.

Don't think for one minute that only hourly workers would

risk sabotaging a plan of your design, in spite of obtaining a big shot's backing.

HELL HATH NO FURY
LIKE A SUBORDINATE SCORNED

Though it takes a bit of tampering with the Bard's original words, I cannot stress too much that when affected managers or subordinates are totally ignored, sidestepped, or scorned you are borrowing the kind of trouble that not even the signed approval or endorsement of a big shot may allay.

Jake, the manager of material conservation for an apparel firm, learned this fact the hard way. His immediate boss was the director of inventory management who, in turn, reported to the vice-president of operations. When I first met Jake he was angry because he had written a comprehensive plan to conserve thread usage and possibly save the company something over $100,000 annually. It called for reducing the diameter of thread used to sew garments.

Before making the suggestion he had run pretests using the lighter-weight thread on work shirts and synthetic knits and women's garments. These tests had showed that the garment did not lose seam strength and turned up an additional benefit in that the lower count thread actually combated seam pucker and gave a desirably smoother look to the piece.

When Jake presented his data to his own boss, his boss pointed out that he would be creating obsolescence of thread now in use or in inventory. The company already had a problem with unused thread whenever styles were dropped from the line or there was a change in colors selected by the designers for the new lines. Returning unused thread to the vendor was largely impossible, since most refuse to accept returned goods because they cannot control how the thread is stored or how it is handled when it is shipped back. Prolonged storage of thread in environments with less than optimum requirements for temperature and moisture can affect its sewability and durability. The few firms who do accept returns charge an enormous restocking fee.

Obviously, changing to the new thread, which seemed like a simple matter, was instead going to be a major undertaking. And then there was the unsolved problem of the obsolete thread.

After more thought Jake came up with another idea. This cast-off thread could be used on the inner seams of garments, where colors did not have to match exactly. This would also solve another ongoing problem. The designers never seemed to design lines in colors that were in the company's inventory of thread, and a lot of it became obsolete because it wasn't the exact shade of a new piece of fabric. Jake's brilliant idea would use up a great deal of thread currently on hand and prevent waste in the future.

All of this was put into a formal written proposal that was reviewed by Jake's boss, the director of inventory management, and then by the vice-president of operations. Both agreed to it, and everything looked fine.

Then the director of merchandising and the associate director of design services (Jake's and his boss's counterparts, both also reporting ultimately to the vice-president of operations) got wind of Jake's proposed changes. Merchandising designed all the garments. They ordered all the original fabric. They bought the thread and other findings from the vendors. Their designers worked closely with key client accounts. A hue and cry went up from the designers: Who did the manager of material conservation think he was, using mismatched thread on the inside of their designs? The proposal would jeopardize rapport with customers.

In an effort to smooth ruffled feathers Jake agreed to submit swatches of fabric presewn with the obsolete thread, which would be close in color but would not match exactly, for merchandising and design services to inspect. Only after receiving their approval would orders be sent to the plants to use up thread inventory on the unseen seams. In actual practice, however, the director of merchandising holds on to these swatches, sometimes for months at a time, letting Jake and his people wait for a decision.

What could Jake have done differently?

- Once he had his boss's approval, he could have discussed his project in the initial stages of development with the designers. Instead, Jake let his prejudice and antagonism toward designers cloud his judgment.
- Jake could have been more aware (as Jake's boss should have been) that his plan would greatly affect others, including vendors and clients, and that these considerations should have been part of his overall planning. He could have anticipated the objections of the designers and taken steps to offset them.
- Jake and his boss placed far too much emphasis on the savings that would result. If the situation had been reversed and these two men had received orders from the top down, they might have been just as resistive and uncooperative as the director of merchandising and his designers.
- When objections were overcome (after all, the plan's basis of annual savings and solution to a longstanding waste of materials were strong), Jake could have won approval signatures of not only his boss, but those of the associate director of design services and the director of merchandising. Their signatures would have given them a stake in the plan.

On the surface it may appear that obtaining so much consensus and so many signatures is cumbersome and time consuming and apt to strangle any project with red tape. In actual practice, you risk losing more time if others don't lend their active support to you up front. Otherwise, roadblocks—often ones that can't be circumvented—will be sure to be set up in front of you when you try to implement a project or plan that doesn't have the support of those most directly affected.

In the course of my work I have examined numerous plans submitted by individuals with impressive documented cost savings or sales increase figures, such as Jake's. They promise outstanding results. They may even have won approval from higher-ups as his did. But because they don't have support from key individuals within key areas of the organizations, estimated results are far below actual ones.

Why else do you think it is that so many wonderful proposals written by those efficiency experts brought in by top management never really get off the ground?

PEOPLE ARE MORE COMMITTED TO THOSE THINGS THEY'VE HAD A HAND IN SHAPING

When attempting to introduce any change, innovation, program, or progress it is important to follow these three rules:

1. Gain as broad a base of support as possible.
2. Keep activities highly visible.
3. Consider the impact of the change on others.

Coauthorship or acceptance. There is a fourth rule that basically underlies all the others. Either signing the original copy of a plan or having *input or say-so* into various aspects of a project *gives people a stake in making a project work*. Otherwise, why should they worry about the outcome? It's your headache, not theirs.

9

Faulty Assumption Nine

NEVER PUT OFF UNTIL TOMORROW WHAT YOU CAN DO TODAY

> *"Part of my job was to keep an activity log related to a government contract for a military aircraft the company was building. I'd been there six months and so far as I could tell no one ever looked at those logs. The oldest guy in the department, who'd been filling them out for fifteen years, couldn't remember anyone looking at them. So I just stopped filling them out and nobody's complained yet.*
>
> *Male, 26*
> *employee*
> *aircraft manufacturer*

Whoever first uttered that old adage, "Never put off till tomorrow what you can do today," was no doubt assuming that the task at hand was necessary or at least made some sense. Unfortunately, most of us spend some part of our workday diligently performing activities that, if left undone, might never be missed. In fact, their omission could benefit the organization and certainly be better for our own well-being and sanity.

Let me set the record straight right up front. I am not talking about the majority of our tasks. Certainly, things will snowball or get out of hand if you put them off until tomorrow.

Writing this book is a good case in point. My editor wanted the finished manuscript in hand no longer than six months following the signing of our contract. In order to meet this contractural deadline, I mapped out a time schedule of two chapters per week. I pushed myself to stay on schedule. To get behind might jeopardize the project, and I didn't want to live with the specter of the publisher sticking hot paper clips under my fingernails to spur me to create faster, faster, faster, in order to get that final chapter turned in on time.

ASSESSING WHAT CAN BE PUT OFF

Postponement of activities or details can have dire consequences and put you in a vulnerable position. But very often, many of the things that consume our time on the job could be put off not only for another day, week, month, or year, but *permanently*—and positively, absolutely nothing bad would happen.

A young man I'll dub Slim works for a leading manufacturer of commercial and military airplanes. At the time this incident occurred, his duties included keeping a time log of all his activities throughout the day. He was in a hurry to get on to something urgent one day. As he was jotting down an entry he suddenly asked everyone within earshot, "Why do we do this? There's half a dozen ways they know what we're doing without this form."

All anyone could come up with was that it was necessary and had something to do with a requirement in the contract between the company and the federal government. On top of that, the oldest man in the department couldn't remember anyone ever asking to see the log books in which each week's set of forms were kept.

Curiosity got the better of Slim, and he read a copy of the

contract. There was no clause requiring the logs. Checking further, he found that he also was right in his belief that any information in the logs could be retrieved as easily from other sources if there was any question about what they were doing. He rigged the books and found that, indeed, over a several-week period no one had moved them—not even to dust!

He filed a formal suggestion through the company's system estimating the number of man-hours and resulting dollars that could be saved annually by every person in his job category if the logs were eliminated.

When three months passed and he heard nothing on his suggestion, Slim just stopped filling out his log to see what would happen. Three more months rolled by and Slim still heard no word concerning his suggestion. Nor, on the other hand, was any concern expressed because he penned no entries for the logbook. It was only after another two months that Slim was informed that his suggestion was approved and that he could now cease performing this task.

FERRETING OUT USELESS ACTIVITIES

My favorite story on this subject was a wire service news article that was published a number of years back about a guard at Buckingham Palace who was posted by a park bench. No one was on the bench and there was no indication why it needed guarding so far as the curious reporter could tell. Investigating why the guard was stationed at this odd post, the reporter waited and asked the sentry when he came off duty. The guard didn't know other than that he was following the orders given to him by the sergeant at arms. This person knew nothing more and the reporter was referred to the inspector general, who didn't know either! After failing to find an answer a couple of echelons higher, other than that "it has always been done," he obtained permission to search through several historic documents. On an old parchment dating back to the 1800s he found the original order. A guard had been posted at a bench in that location to prevent any lord or lady from sitting on it after it had been freshly painted. For almost a century guards had continued to be posted there to carry out an order that someone had apparently forgotten to rescind once the need had passed. Yet, as the reporter noted, incredible as it may seem, no one in all that time had dared—or bothered—to question why he was ordered to guard a park bench.

Many of us, like those poor guards, perform numerous duties without really knowing why we do them, what function they serve, and whether or not anything dire would happen if we just stopped doing it.

Questioning the standards and duties to which people cling, however, can cause them to feel very uncomfortable—and protective—when asked why they are doing this or that task.

In my workshops, each participant is expected to think of two or three things he or she might change on the job. Some look at me with puzzled expressions, initially at a loss for words. Others begin to put up slight resistance—scooting in chairs, beginning to feel downright uncomfortable. At least one or two will muster up the courage to tell me, "We don't have any problems."

This is not really an attempt on anyone's part to get off the hook. Ironically, it is often these very employees who are scrupulously and painstakingly thorough in the performance of their duties. Unfortunately, it just so happens that many of the duties that consume their time are unproductive, out of touch with present needs, or standing in the way of better ideas.

By way of illustration, in a recent group session I conducted within an insurance company, three participants were having great difficulty thinking of anything to change on their jobs. These individuals were the vice-president of marketing, a secretary in the training department, and a clerk in group underwriting and administration.

To jar the V-P into action, I asked him, "Why don't you eliminate the tests you give all men and women applying for selling positions in your field offices?" These tests were distributed by a large trade association that charged $5 a crack to grade each one. When you considered the firm's turnover rate, this was quite costly. On top of this grading expense, hours of time were expended by the firm's regional managers and staff to administer the tests. Then more hours were spent by a raft of clerks at headquarters whose duty it was to keep track of which applicants passed or failed. As a further complication, since the regional sales manager could not make a final decision on individuals tentatively hired until the test scores were in hand, these clerks were constantly trying to get the test scores to the field offices by using the phone in order to speed up the process. This frequently tied up the WATS line when there was more pressing business at hand.

As I had expected, the V-P was beside himself at my question about eliminating these tests:

Him: "You can't do that! We need those tests."
Me: "Why?"
Him: "Because they show us who's cut out to be a salesman and who's not."
Me: "How can you be sure they will be any good?"
Him: "By how long they stick around. If they don't sell much, they leave."
Me: "How many leave?"
Him: "About 25 percent."
Me: "And how many left before you started testing all applicants applying for sales jobs?" [This procedure had been adopted some eight years before.]
Him: "About 25 percent." [This after an interminably long pause.]

Since this 25 percent amounted to nearly 900 persons a year, we were talking about several thousand dollars expended for the same results experienced without the test.

Next I turned my attention to the secretary of the training department and asked her, "Why don't you stop sending letters of congratulation to employees who pass correspondence courses?"

Her: "We can't do that! Those letters are important to employees."

Me: "Why?"

Her: "Because everyone likes to receive a pat on the back."

Me: "But don't you type the same standard paragraphs every time, so that a person could conceivably get the very same letter over and over? Or notice that it's the same letter everyone else gets?"

Her: "Well, yes, but every letter is freshly typed."

It was my purpose to stir thought, and she began to see that most of her hard work probably ended up in the wastebasket along with all the recipients' other form letters.

The last participant to be questioned was an eighteen-year-old clerk who had started with the firm six months before in group underwriting and administration. She had been advanced to lead assistant and was in charge of updating file folders, with such information as personnel changes, termination, or death of an employee reported by client companies affecting their group policies. Because of the short time she had been employed there, this time I asked the group to help her think of something that might be changed in her job. The V-P piped up (it is always easier to know what other people should do than it is to know for oneself):

Him: "Why do you receive all those overdue notices for incomplete files?

Her: "We're supposed to keep the turnaround time down to four days to update a folder and send back adjustment sheets to the group policy holder. If we get behind the notices are to remind us that we're falling behind."

Him: "Do you often get far behind in your work?"

Her: "Oh, no, usually I've finished with the folders and already handed them over to the typist before the overdue notice arrives."

Him: "Isn't that a little like getting an overdue notice from the library on a book you've already turned in?"

Her: "I guess it is in my case, but some of the clerks do get behind."

Him: "Does getting these slips speed them up?"

Her: "No, you can only work so fast, and if you are already inundated with file folders on your desk, as we are, all you need is one more slip of paper."

Him: "Don't most of the clerks immediately dump those slips in the trash out of sheer frustration?"

Her: "Some do, but only when the supervisor's back is turned."

Him: "If that's the case, and the overdue notice doesn't help anything, why not eliminate them?"

At this point the clerk's responses indicated a number of other absurdities existing in the department—enough to fill another chapter.

HOW SOME HAVE MADE
PUTTING OFF UNTIL TOMORROW PAY OFF

It is easy to see that one must take heart, use one's brains, and have the courage to assess and begin to systematically fight to eliminate deadwood activities on the job. Some of the troops in my workshops have acted with just such courage and boldness in battle. Here are some examples.

Soldier number one. A computer operator working for a bank spent several hours each week preparing a report on taxes paid. A monthly report was made summarizing the weekly information. Copies of all these reports were sent to the departments of exchange, marketing, and analysis.

The operator discovered the marketing and analysis departments made no use of the reports and merely filed them. Only the exchange department reviewed them—and then only the monthly summaries. Consequently, she eliminated the others and sent the exchange department only a monthly summary.

Soldier number two. A nineteen-year-old control clerk within the raw materials department of an apparel manufacturer found a way to throw out an archaic procedure started by the company prior to wide use of copy machines that was never revised.

The system called for a copy of each purchase order to be sent from the merchandising department to control clerks in the raw materials department. They were to transfer the purchase order information onto a white master card. The copied-over data included: material symbol, purchase order number, yards ordered, vendor due date, vendor name, date of purchase, contract payment terms upon invoicing, price per yard, and a technical description of the material in mill terminology. Once transferred, the purchase order was returned to the merchandising department.

Later, duplicate copies of vendors' invoices were sent to the clerks. The clerks were to transfer the invoice information onto the master cards and route one copy of the invoices to accounts payable—and throw the other one away!

The control clerk initiated a system whereby a copy machine facsimile was made of the purchase order sent to the clerks by the merchandising department and the card system eliminated altogether. The duplicate vendors' invoice was then stapled to it.

This procedure saved 400 hours of clerical time, and because the accounts payable department no longer had to wait for the information to be copied, it could process invoices more quickly. This gained a return of $10,000 in cash discounts for payment to vendors within ten days.

The clerk, now twenty-three years old, has been promoted to supervisor of inventory control.

Soldier number three. A crew member spray-painting electric-drive irrigation systems during their manufacture fretted at the practice of having to tape the ends of the drive shafts to prevent paint buildup. The procedure was time consuming and ineffective. To overcome objections of the engineers, the crew demonstrated that (a) the paint got under the tape anyway, (b) the tape was far more difficult to remove than the excess paint, and (c) paint buildup had little effect on the fit of the drive shaft (the only real objection). It was decided that the tape would be eliminated. While the tape amounted to only about 2¢ per unit, the manpower to apply and remove it cost about 45¢ per unit. Since the crew processed 50,000 units a year, the bottom line improvement was $23,500.

Soldier number four. A foreman at a sawmill noted that wood chips, which fell to the ground as logs were transferred from railroad cars by chains and a rubber belt, were actually beneficial in terms of wear and tear on the belt. A yard man was stopped from sweeping them up—told to put off until tomorrow what he could do today.

Most people would be wise to memorize the words of the philosopher Heraclitus, *"There is nothing permanent except change,"* and to heed the thinker, Thomas Carlyle: *"Today is not yesterday. We ourselves change. How then can our works and thoughts, if they are always to be the fittest, continue to be the same?"*

PUT OFF AN IDEA NOBODY WANTS—PARTICULARLY IF THAT PERSON IS YOUR BOSS

One of several principles reportedly developed by Thomas Edison about ideas was never to work on an idea that nobody wants. This principle grew out of a costly lesson. As the story goes, though Thomas Edison had more than 1,100 patents to his name, even he didn't win all the time. For instance, Edison was unsuccessful in his attempts to convince members of Congress to buy an automatic vote counter machine he had invented and apparently built a test model of. They wanted to use the very time his invention would save to trade votes behind closed doors.

Edison was so enthused about the concept of an automatic vote counter that he built one before checking out whether anyone needed or wanted it. Unfortunately, he wasted his time. Edison's primary objective, the reduction of tallying time, remained unacceptable to the practice of the politicians, who would have been more favorably disposed to an invention to *lengthen* the time it took to count their votes.

A word to the wise: Consider what goals or objectives are uppermost in your boss's mind before spending a lot of time developing some brainchild of your own.

At this point you may think I am contradicting myself. After all, I just summarized four cases of people who were successful at eliminating facets of their jobs and have spent a great deal of space harping about the importance of asking *why,* not asking the boss.

Each one of those soldiers in the foregoing case histories *was required to seek initial approval from the immediate boss and any other affected department heads prior to acting on the idea.*

For example, the control clerk (Soldier Number Two) gained verbal approval from her boss on the basis of this actual statement of her goal:

> I would like to reduce the processing time associated with preparing all the necessary information required by accounts payable so the company can obtain the maximum allowable discounts on raw materials purchased.

Whether you state your goal in one sentence or have to use several to get the point across to your boss doesn't matter. What does matter is approval from your boss *up front* concerning what you are trying to accomplish.

I often use the Edison example in my workshops to demonstrate why each participant should gain initial approval from his or her boss and other parties that will be affected by that idea prior to putting anything in motion. The importance of taking this precautionary step—one more form of delaying until tomorrow what could be done today—is well illustrated by a story I heard from an attorney with an insurance firm. I'll refer to him by the fictitious name of James.

Due to changes in a law by the state in which the firm was located, the upper limits were raised on the amount of transfer fees and interest rates adjustments lenders could charge in connection with loan assumptions. James thought the company should take advantage of some increased flexibility under this new law to generate additional revenue on residential and commercial loan assumptions when property ownership changed hands. (The company charged a very slight transfer fee amounting to less than $30 and made no adjustment in interest rates in connection with the assumptions of loans being serviced by the mortgage loan department.) He calculated the company could nearly double its income just by charging the minimum that this new law set out.

His goal to increase revenue seemed so obviously advantageous that James charged full steam ahead before touching base with his boss. James took it upon himself to map out a series of procedures whereby his department would note alternative fees the mortgage loan area could choose between and the manner, when needed, in which the legal department would proceed to prepare a loan modification agreement.

If James had talked to his boss (the senior vice-president) ahead of time, he would have learned that there was word on Capitol Hill (where the senior V-P frequently spent up to eight hours a day) of a possible class action suit to rescind this bill. The suit was being brought by several irate residential homeowners. So, increasing revenue generated from commercial and residential loans was not the only consideration and would certainly not be a key goal so far as the senior V-P was concerned.

Uppermost in James's boss's mind was the specter of bad press associated with being named as an organization taking advantage of consumers through this new law. During the six months since this bill had been in effect, several banks and savings and loan associations had done just what James proposed and had upped their transfer fees and interest rates. In their case, handling loan assumptions was a big hunk of their business. On the other hand, servicing loan assumptions was *not* critical to James's company. Selling life and group insurance policies was its primary business and brought in millions of dollars. The money James planned to bring in through changing the policies and procedures for servicing loan assumptions was a mere drop in the bucket. James's company had other objectives that were all more important to his boss. As a lawyer, James was sadly deficient in his knowledge of the laws of real-world business: *goals must not conflict with those of the boss.*

PICK THE RIGHT TIME TO SEE THE BOSS

Let's assume you are going to stand trial for rape. Your lawyer would be quite justified in asking for a postponement if the local papers in your town were suddenly filled with case after case of the trauma suffered by rape victims. *Lawyers believe timing is everything and endeavor to schedule trial dates most beneficial to their clients.*

In your enthusiasm over a concept or an idea you've thought of today, stop and reconsider before rushing into your boss's office. It might be better to put off discussions until tomorrow or the next day or even the next week. I am constantly amazed at the vast number of subordinates who decide to share their recommendations at the worst possible times:

- Just before their boss is going to place a long-distance call, after having waited all morning for a WATS line to become available.
- As their boss makes a beeline to the restroom following a four-hour "briefing" session.
- When their boss is eating lunch in the company cafeteria with another employee—the company president.
- The same morning their boss discovers that the bonus check thought to be missing in the mail was in actual fact never issued.

In fact, there are certain types of employees who, regardless of how good their ideas may be, are never going to get approval from the boss. These are some of them.

Harassers: The ones who put their boss under virtual seige until they get in their two cents' worth.

Whiners: Those who refuse to see that the boss has other subordinates and whine like five-year-olds about never getting any attention.

Interrupters: Ones who fail to notice that the boss is talking to someone else or is otherwise occupied.

Sermonizers: The ones who, when they talk to the boss, keep making their point over and over and never know when to put a lid on it.

Bargers: The ones who never learn the value of an appointment, but just barge through the boss's door.

Employees who fall into any of the above or similar categories almost assuredly will find their ideas falling on deaf ears. They may even stir up feelings of anger and resentment.

Putting off until tomorrow, when the time is right, is better than doing something wrong today in the heat of the moment.

In summary, don't be overly eager to share your idea with your boss. What may seem like a hot idea today may cool down considerably in the clear, hard light of reason and investigation. Also, show that you value your boss's time when you at last offer your suggestion. Make an appointment. When keeping it, it never hurts to preface the meeting by asking "if this is a good time."

10
Faulty Assumption Ten

THE BOSS IS ALL TALK AND NO ACTION

"The suggestion I have for their suggestion box you couldn't print. It's just more of management's garbage to suck you into thinking they give a damn. You can put ideas in there till you're blue in the face and they won't do anything. I know. One idea I even signed because I was so proud of it. My foreman never even so much as acknowledged it."

Male, 49
union business committee
member
electrical equipment
manufacturer

One of the toughest jobs I ever had was facing a group of union business committee leaders who were sick of hearing management *talk* about how important workers' ideas are to the company, while never taking action on any worker's suggestions.

It had been decided by the powers that be at corporate headquarters that I begin my consulting work for the company at this upstate (eastern seaboard) plant. It is fairly typical in the consulting business to be given the hardest nuts to crack first on the theory that, if any positive results ensue, success in other divisions is almost insured.

My job was to get union members within this plant to attend workshops (when many of them didn't even bother to show up for work) and to fire them up to make productivity improvements in their jobs (when this plant had the lowest performance of any within the company).

The company had three divisions with a total of 1,000 employees. It produced electric signals and signs, sirens, parking meters, light poles, and other security equipment.

Shortly before I came to the plant, the vice-president and general manager of the security products division had renewed a campaign to fill the company's suggestion boxes. Posters throughout the plant urged, "We want your ideas." The boxes themselves were painted bright red and installed conveniently near the personnel office and the cafeteria. Stacks of forms were printed and made available bearing the headline, "My suggestion is . . ." Substantial ideas were sought on ways to lower operating costs on materials and equipment and to prevent downtime, improve distribution, and the like.

The pot was sweetened by the company's offer to employees of 10 percent (but not to exceed $10,000) of any savings realized by the company in the first year as a result of a suggestion. Since this reward was limited to the first person to make the suggestion—in the case of duplication—it was hoped that there would be quick response.

SOME REASONS WHY
THE BOSS DOESN'T ACT ON SUGGESTIONS

The campaign, however, fizzled because the union had previously given its all-out endorsement of an earlier suggestion campaign that had been a total washout. It was not about to do so again.

The reason for the initial failure was simple: "The company didn't do anything with the suggestions. Last time, the foremen just ended up stashing stacks of suggestion forms in their desk drawers." This complaint was thrown up to me on my first meeting with several of the company's union officials—a business committee made up of nine men and one woman. They cornered me and asked whether my program would produce the same result as most of the others brought in by management—a lot of hot air. In a nutshell, the union was hesitant to recommend that any of its members participate in my workshops if the end result was likely to be as disappointing as the suggestion box.

In this case the union had a legitimate complaint. The suggestions its members had submitted for action by the company had an implementation rate of only about 7 percent. This represented a mere handful out of the hundreds of suggestions received.

The problem with this company's suggestion program, as with those of many companies, was that employees *had* heeded management's call for ideas—so much so that *none of the bosses could keep up with them.*

The way the system worked, the personnel manager would send all suggestions directly to the appropriate boss or manager with an evaluation form that this person was expected to fill out for each and every suggestion. This form then was routed back to the personnel manager, who was to check back to verify savings derived from the suggestion so the employee could be awarded the cash percentage.

The form was no simple matter. It had several parts and called for the boss to get together information as follows:

> *Part A:* Estimate possible tangible results or savings in forms, furniture, materials, equipment, space, data processing time, overtime, downtime, or increased sales and income. A special space was allotted to highlight any *intangible* benefits that might accrue from implementing the suggestion as well.
>
> *Part B:* Calculate any possible costs connected with the implementation of the employee's suggestion.
>
> *Part C:* State whether the suggestion should be rejected

and give the reasons why; or, if the suggestion could benefit the company if it were modified, indicate how. [It seemed strange that the rejection question was posed first!]

Things were out of control because the bosses—not the suggesters—were expected to perform all the legwork to determine whether the consequences of implementing a suggestion were positive or negative.

To drive home this point with the union officials, we analyzed during our first meeting one of the actual suggestions submitted. It read:

> A lot of waste is caused by guys who don't clean their welding cones or use protective jelly so they get clogged up due to weld splatter. These young guys got no pride in their work. They just get angry and end up hitting the cone against the walls or some other object to clear the cone which damages them. I only have to replace cones on my unit once every two to three weeks while everyone else must use two or three cones a week. This costs the company money and in the end money out of the other workers' paychecks.
>
> Therefore I suggest welders be made to check out a cone for their use, and when they need another one to replace it they should be made to show the old one to the foreman on the shift. That way the men will be more careful.
>
> I also think we ought to use another liner produced by_____ [brand name omitted]. These cones would save the company lots of money and are better built and work just as good [*sic*].

Sounds pretty good, doesn't it? Well, put yourself in the shoes of this man's boss upon receiving the suggestion. It was his responsibility to find the answers to questions such as:

- What number of welding cones are actually used per week per man?

- Are the other workers really abusing equipment, or, in the rush of a production run, is it possible to stop to clean the cones and apply protective jelly?
- Would excessive downtime be caused by requiring welders to locate their shift foreman to have another cone issued to them?
- How does the life expectancy and durability of this cheaper liner compare to the one the company currently uses?

MAKING SUGGESTIONS INTO WORKABLE IDEAS

These questions are only openers. But it is clear that before putting this suggestion into action the boss would have to take quite a bit of time to gather the data and make the evaluation.

No smart boss acts on the basis of supposition. I asked the people sitting around our table to estimate how long they felt it would take them to gather all the information necessary to answer only the five questions I had posed about the sample suggestion. It was quickly apparent to these union officials that most bosses wouldn't be able to keep on top of all these suggestions without spending 100 percent of their time just to gather the necessary information for the evaluation forms.

The essence of an idea in two to three paragraphs is normally not sufficient documentation to get your boss to take action. I assured the union committee that the people who do participate in these workshops learn how to package their thoughts in a manner that makes their boss's decision making easier. And the implementation rate of those ideas for change proposed by participants in the workshops would be a far cry from the average suggestion box ratio.

HOW TO KEEP YOUR IDEAS
FROM DYING ON THE VINE

Ideas must be nurtured. And if we expect our ideas to take root and grow in the often fallow ground characterizing corporate turf, we must take on the drudgery of spadework—getting down to digging out the support data for our ideas ourselves. Here are some pointers for laying the foundation.

1. The more spadework you do, the easier it will be for your boss to evaluate your idea or suggestion and make the favorable decision you want. And remember, the boss is not necessarily a wellspring of information and may not be able to fill in the gaps for you.

2. If your ideas never come to fruition, the fault probably lies more with you than the boss. If you are expecting him or her to take action on your say-so alone with no supporting data or facts, forget it. Bosses can't (and don't!) act on blind faith. Neither are they about to take action when there isn't a clear understanding of what is involved in doing so.

3. A complete picture of the pluses and pitfalls involved for your boss and others in the department is critical if you expect to have your ideas implemented.

4. Whether you are reporting your idea on paper or presenting it verbally, never take your boss's knowledge—or interest—for granted. An idea's relevancy or appropriateness is important.

5. If you simply throw out ideas and are too lazy to do necessary data gathering or spadework, you run the risk of being labeled a lamebrain, and it is less likely that you will get any kind of hearing from the boss even if you have a fantastic idea.

6. Instead of shoveling dirt on your boss for being too slow or never acting on your ideas, next time get off your duff and dig for a few facts and supporting evidence to shore up your suggestion. Dig deep to turn up enough to prove to your boss—and yourself—what you propose will truly benefit the department. As the old saying goes, "Put up or shut up."

7. The more radical your idea, or the more divergent it is from the way things are usually done, the more digging and supporting you will have to do if your idea is to withstand winds of criticism and doubt, or the withering reluctance of the boss or department.

8. Your spadework just may convince you that your idea isn't so hot after all and could have negative impact on others in the

department. Better to find out before the fruits of your labor end up in your own bushel basket, gathering the scornful reproach and contempt of your boss and peers.

HOW TO DIG FOR FACTS AND AVOID PITFALLS

Step One

When you wish to change anything—forms, machinery, procedures, *et al*—find out who designed or was responsible for it in the first place. If possible, seek an opportunity to chat with the originator.

Rationale. How can you pose a compelling argument for change unless you have a firm grasp of what is going on now and why?

Pitfall one. Locating someone with the straight scoop concerning the whys and wherefores of the current operation can often be as difficult and time consuming as trying to uncover a pharaoh's tomb in Egypt. Sometimes things have been buried with good reason!

A former participant in one of my workshops, named Ron, found this out the hard way. He was a shift foreman in a tire department of a midwestern company manufacturing farm irrigation systems. The tires were used mostly on mobile units in fields and in certain areas of the country, often on rocky and uneven terrain. The systems were heavy and required that tires, purchased from a regular tire manufacturer, be strengthened with special rods and given additional tread as a precaution against tire failure. This operation was carried out by Ron's department.

During our first meeting, I asked the group members to answer this question: "Where does the greatest opportunity lie to reduce cost within the company?"

Ron nearly shouted out, "Stop putting tubes in tubeless tires."

After the laughter died down, he was asked why this procedure was done, and he answered, "There may be a logical answer as to why we put tubes in tubeless tires, but I doubt it."

Others in the room agreed with Ron that it didn't seem to

make much sense once you thought about it. Furthermore, Ron pointed out, their leading competitor, which built similar irrigation equipment, did not insert tubes. Everyone in the room was well aware that the competitor was cutting into the company's market share. The group began to feel that Ron was onto something and that the potential savings from eliminating the tubes could be tremendous, with real impact on competitiveness.

No one seemed to know why or to remember who had set the procedure—*or perhaps no one was brave enough to own up to it.*

A secretary from marketing who was in the workshop group remembered a special list of farmers that had something to do with tires, which she had typed some time ago. After the meeting she hunted back through department files and found the original. The list was titled, "Special test group—farmers receiving systems mounted on tubeless tires." She immediately touched base with a marketing executive who had been with the company since its doors first opened and was told, "Oh, yeah, I remember that survey. We gave engineering a special list of customers who were to be shipped systems mounted with tubeless tires. Engineering was in charge of coordinating everything. I guess things didn't pan out because as far as I know we never did hear anything more about it."

Ron could not turn up any evidence of production or shipping records indicating that any irrigation systems mounted with the new type of tire had ever been shipped as the marketing executive had indicated was to have been done. Evidently, whoever the phantom of the tire had been, he had felt so strongly about his baby that he assured its continued adoption by never conducting the test market or survey. However, even if the test marketing had been run, the results might have been kept from Ron.

Pitfall two. Certain records in your search for facts will be closed to you. Some are confidential. But the more common problem you will experience is the diplomatic lie, "Those records were lost or destroyed." (Translation: "The information in those records is damaging to my position.")

Strategy. Talk to others as Ron did. Test your idea on others.

Gain support through fact finding. But be on your guard at all times.

Step Two

Consider carefully the position or history of any individuals whose opinions you seek on the current system. Try to discover what stake they may have in it or any interest they may have in maintaining it.

Interview a broad cross section of individuals. Obtain divergent opinions. Ask yourself what the interviewee stands to gain from the facts as he presents them to you. Consider each person's neutrality or lack thereof.

Pitfall one. People have been known to falsify information, lie, withhold certain data, conveniently forget important facts, embellish or completely ignore pertinent recollections. Do not be at all surprised if you end up getting the runaround as you attempt to discover the real reason that things are the way they are.

This point can be illustrated by recounting my experience with another work group at a client company in which I had asked the participants where the greatest opportunities lay to improve the performance of employees within the organization.

At the top of the list of responses was, "Feed us better!" Now, bitching about the food in the company cafeteria has to be the one single unifying bond of brotherhood and sisterhood among working Americans. But having felt queasy more than a few times eating in their cafeteria, I found myself agreeing with the sentiments of the participants. Some of the appetizing luncheon dishes one had the privilege to encounter *and* pay for included:

- green peppers stuffed with bologna
- chow mein with a combination of stewed vegetables and mystery meat that was Greek to all of us
- greased chicken that slid off the plate at the first encounter with knife and fork
- tacos filled with a mixture that looked suspiciously like canned dog food

- spaghetti so al dente it could be mistaken for straws
- roast beef sliced thin enough to be able to allow you to read the company's logo on the plate
- lima beans reheated often enough to turn from green to gray

On a historical note, the top executives of this company had decided several years ago that it was not efficient to run the company's cafeteria internally. Consequently a long-term contract was entered into with the owner of a chain of cafeterias in the city.

One young woman in the group, whom I'll call Nancy, made a specific suggestion to have a salad bar again. When I asked the group if anyone knew the reason for the salad bar being removed, Nancy piped up, "Who knows! I tried to find out but had to play twenty questions with one of the cafeteria's employees."

From the way she recounted her experience, I imagined the conversation went something like this:

Nancy:	"What happened to the salad bar?"
* *Road Runner:*	"What salad bar?"
Nancy:	"The one that was here yesterday."
Road Runner:	"Where?"
Nancy:	"Over there. You had a cart with a salad bowl and a tray with mushrooms, beets, celery, carrots, croutons, and tomatoes."
Road Runner:	"Tomatoes? You want tomatoes?"
Nancy:	"No, I want to make a salad."
Road Runner:	"You applying for a job?"

*Road Runner: One of those people whose mouth runs circles around his brain.

Later, Nancy fared little better in trying to get a satisfactory explanation out of the manager. He would say only that the salad bar had been removed because employees were being too wasteful and not eating all their greens.

Unfortunately, Nancy was far too direct in her approach. *Quite often you have to be circumspect to hit upon the truth.* I opted to talk to someone with more brains than Road Runner and more neutrality than the cafeteria manager.

One of the cashiers happened to take her break every day in the middle of the morning. I arranged to be downstairs at the same time and asked her to join me for a cup of coffee. Now I did not come flat out and ask her why the salad bar was removed because she might very well answer, "I don't know." Besides, it is my thought that people possess far more knowledge than they give themselves credit for as a rule. So, initially we talked about my work, since I felt she might be curious about a new face in the cafeteria. The conversation went something like this:

Me: "More people ought to have a say in their work, don't you agree?"

Cashier: "Sure do, but I'm more fortunate than some around here. The boss listens to me. It was my idea to put all the desserts up front by the trays and silverware for the customers to see the first thing as they come in. Before doing that we didn't sell hardly any cakes and pies. I figured people usually feel they shouldn't buy desserts after their trays are loaded down with other food."

Me: "I would imagine it's real important to turn over cakes and pies quickly or they might get stale."

Cashier: "Oh, no, that's not a problem. We just freeze them. About the only thing we can't freeze are fresh vegetables. You just can't freeze lettuce." [Bingo! Cafeterias usually have a staple menu, meaning you as a customer can always count on liver and onions to be served on Tuesday, and I mean every Tuesday throughout the year. Thus, cafeterias can freeze and reheat what didn't sell from the week prior. On the other hand, when fresh items turn brown, they have to be dumped.]

Me:	"Sure is unfortunate you can't freeze produce. I sure get sick of having to throw out lettuce."
Cashier:	"'Waste not, want not,' that's what the big boss always reminds us."
Me:	"You mean the owner?"
Cashier:	"Uh-huh. He comes up here in his black Rolls Royce and has the manager dump trash bags filled with old potato skins and other produce in the trunk of the car."
Me:	"What on earth for?"
Cashier:	"I hear he's got a farm. I guess he feeds his animals this stuff." [Bingo! Could it be that this particular manager was concerned about the big boss picking up too many trash bags filled with produce from this cafeteria, for fear the big boss might start thinking he was being wasteful or not managing well? A large percentage of the waste was caused by natural deterioration or browning of the fresh vegetables and not from customers who failed to clean their plates.]
Me:	"Talk about cheap!"
Cashier:	"Did you ever see it fail? People with lots of money are always concerned about making more of it." [Bingo! Perhaps there was an even more obvious reason for removal of the salad bar. The average entrée on the weekly menu ran 70¢ more than the salad bar, and customers could not sneak back for more as they did with the salad bar. Thus, there was the distinct possibility that the cafeteria's gross sales figures were slipping, and doing so on an item that was costly to maintain. "You just can't freeze lettuce."]

When I shared the essence of this conversation with the group, we came up with a major pitfall.

Pitfall two. Much as the cafeteria manager did with Nancy, people frequently will give you a reason for an action. It just might not happen, as in this case, to be the *real* reason. People often use this type of camouflage because it is not in their best interest to be totally honest and frank.

Strategy. As in the conversation with the cashier, look for hidden meaning beneath casual remarks. To quote a few words of wisdom by Carl Jung: "We should not pretend to understand the world only by the intellect; we apprehend it just as much by feeling."

Step Three

Make it a practice to question and analyze all information you gather through either talks with people or a review of written documents. Information must be accurate, current, and thorough. What holds true in one particular environment and at one point in time may not in another.

Pitfall one. If your information is inaccurate or the conclusions you reach are faulty, the actions you propose to the boss could be dead wrong.

While even a well-documented proposal may not be taken on blind faith by the boss, for heaven's sake make sure the facts you do present are indeed accurate. Learn to question the data you have gathered or been handed. Never make a recommendation to your boss on the basis of inconclusive evidence.

Strategy. Don't expect your boss to sit back and soak up every word you say as gospel. Imagine instead that you're on the witness stand. The attorney for the defense—your boss—will be defending the way things are currently done. You can expect a tough grilling and cross-examination. The reliability of your "witnesses"—the names and background of the individuals who provided you with the data—will be checked and evaluated just as a real-life attorney for the defense might question the shady past of a witness for the prosecution. Be sure of your case; prepare well; present clearly. You have a lot to lose. If your analysis crumbles under the boss's probing, your credibility will go right along with it.

Don, after a year of instructing high school students in music, decided to go back to school for an MBA. He liked teaching music, but didn't like what he called the "subsistence pay."

Shortly before he was to receive his degree, a recruiter from a large consumer products firm lined up a job interview with the brand manager of a cereal product you may have purchased at your local supermarket. This firm had several brand managers, and under each one was an assistant brand manager and a brand specialist. Don was hired as a brand specialist. Despite having an MBA, Don did not have any hands-on business experience. As a brand specialist, he was not directly responsible for making decisions. Don executed the marketing strategy developed by the two men above him. He monitored sales and figures from computer reports generated by data processing in a manner that could be used by his bosses to make promotional and advertising decisions.

Don began to feel put upon and underutilized—after all, he had a master's degree. Instead of analyzing the figures on these reports and trying to understand what they meant or attempting to study the reasoning behind certain advertising and promotions, Don spent his time developing a grand scheme to increase sales. He proposed that the company sponsor a label-saving program (from box tops of their products) to be called, "Give the Band a Hand."

After a year of teaching experience Don remembered that high school principals were making financial cutbacks in such extracurricular activities as the arts and music. Therefore, he decided that many principals would be greatly in favor of sponsoring a program aimed at acquiring musical instruments, books, and sheet music and would push for parents and students to buy their product for the rewarding box-top label.

The only problem was that he had based his analysis on the success a leading manufacturer of *soup* had year after year with a label-saving campaign for schools, qualifying them for sports equipment. Both these men viewed the conclusions Don had reached as foolish to say the least, and bombarded him with numerous questions:

- Since cereal is mainly viewed as a breakfast item, how could he assume sales would increase at the same rate as for a versatile item like soup, used for lunches, dinners, sauces, and more?
- Why hadn't Don studied historical results on previous campaigns to increase the use of their cereal in everyday cooking? If Don had done so, he would have discovered that attempts had been made to increase cereal consumption by issuing a cookbook filled with recipes using this cereal brand. He would have seen that few extra sales resulted from this extra effort. Consumers ate their cereal only at breakfast. Period.
- Did Don consider the shorter shelf life and deterioration of cereal versus soup when he made his sales projections? How likely is it that a parent will stock up on cereal even for a good cause if it may have to be thrown out? Soup, on the other hand, will taste just fine a year or two or three or four years hence.
- Since the manufacturer of soup has had a label-saving campaign for several years now, what made Don think school principals and PTAs would want to devote their time, money, and energy to yet another campaign? How important is having a band decked out properly for the games versus getting new football jerseys?

Pitfall two. It is dangerous to look at things from our own personal viewpoints. We are all biased and prejudiced to some extent, whether we like to admit it or not, and this may limit our objectivity in fact finding and analysis.

11
Faulty Assumption Eleven

WHAT'S RIGHT IS MORE IMPORTANT
THAN WHO'S RIGHT

> *"So it is exploitation. So it is*
> *nothing but a media event. So*
> *you don't want to participate.*
> *Our chairman and CEO wants*
> *you to participate. You want to*
> *participate. You're going to*
> *participate. Right? Right."*

> *Male, 47*
> *vice-president*
> *Fortune 500 company*

If you grew up watching "Fury" or a lot of westerns on television or at the movies, you may have an idealized concept of ranch life as pastoral and trouble free. Well, as one who grew up on a real one, let me tell you that living on a ranch can be hazardous to your health. We lived by the edict, "When you're told to jump, just ask how high!" Numerous situations occur in ranch life when you need to jump, and I mean jump fast and hold all your questions until later. So when one of the foremen or my mother used a certain tone of voice and said, "Jump," my brothers and I knew we had better do it or we might be bitten by a snake, buried under an avalanche of moldy hay, or kicked by a horse.

This childhood training certainly helped me immensely when I entered the corporate world and found that chairmen (they invariably are men) of large corporations also expect everyone to jump when they issue an order. It came as a bit more of a surprise to me that a lot of other pretty high-up people more often than not respond with "How high?" rather than "Why?"

If you've been led to believe in graduate-level business courses that decisions in the corporate world are made solely on the basis of quantitative analysis and a hard look at the facts, you'd better wise up. You are much more apt to find your boss—and you—kowtowing and carrying out orders from on high.

The central issue in the real world is more often *who's* right, not *what's* right. When we start out in business, we figure that since the chairman, or president, or CEO, or whoever is at the top of the heap wound up there, he must somehow be more right, more often, than most people, or he wouldn't have gotten where he is. By the time we realize that being "right" may not have as much to do with anything as having and keeping a position of power—and that the top man sometimes can be very, very wrong in his decisions or orders—we also know we had better keep this knowledge to ourselves most of the time.

Catering to the caprice and vagaries of the chairman's or other big chief's ego is a big part of organizational life, whether you work in a for-profit corporation or a not-for-profit institution.

CAPRICE GOETH WITH THE CHAIRMAN'S JOB

The man—and, upon occasion, the woman—who holds the chairman's office or its equivalent has the power to inconvenience any number of people and get away with it. I know one chairman of a large corporation that holds an annual management conference. Most years he chooses a place somewhere off in the boondocks too remote to be accessible by commercial aircraft.

One year attendees had to fly into a major port, take boats inland, and, when they docked, travel for several hours in land rovers, finally making the last leg of the trip on pack mules. It was very close to Christmas, to boot.

Did any of these managers rebel? They did not. It would have been much worse not to have been asked at all! So they perform this kind of ritualistic trek into the wilderness each year to keep on the good side of the chairman. Worse yet, many of these managers mimic the chairman's style in dealing with their own subordinates. They are impatient, unwilling to listen to advice, feel their opinions are always right, and make capricious demands.

Unfortunately, the boss who will not move heaven and earth for you (no matter how right you are), most definitely will for the chairman. As part of your boss's team, don't be shocked if you're asked to move it with him. Doing so may go against your grain, but you may have little choice. The queen of England is not the only one who can command a performance.

I remember a good example of this; it happened several years ago to a woman I'll call Sarah. She was employed in a so-called Fortune 500 company.

At the age of twenty-seven Sarah was manager of training and development. She was also something of a pioneer in that corporation since she was one of the few females to occupy any position other than clerical in scope while young enough not to wear orthopedic shoes or a twenty-year service pin.

What happened to her while with that company is something she dubs Operation Vanguard. It seems that the local newspaper, which had national prestige, had just run a highly critical article on the manner in which the company pictured women in its annual report. Not one had been shown in a position of authority. The publicity came at a time when the board was critical of the CEO about depressed earnings, and the sniping at him over the newspaper article became intense.

The chairman, herein referred to by the fictitious name of Stan, wasn't about to take these jabs lying down. He ordered the head of public relations to come up with something to disprove the newspaper's claims and to help the chairman save face. The face-saving idea—purported to be Stan's, of course—was a media event that would highlight and recognize twelve up-and-coming women within the organization and gain favorable newspaper and TV coverage.

To get the ball rolling and perhaps to show how easy it was to find these qualified women, Stan picked the first three. One was Sarah. The others were an assistant brand manager at corporate headquarters and an associate director of federal affairs for the company, who was based in Washington, D.C. As Sarah put it, "Now all that was left was to find *nine* more women out of a corporation with 45,000 employees worldwide. And believe me, it was no easy task."

A decree went out from Stan that his managers should bring to him a list of females who would fit the specifications. Sarah said she never saw so many vice-presidents scurrying around and holding meetings, all to come up with the single name of a qualifying female who could represent their areas.

The key event was a dinner at which each of the women was to give a short speech to a blue-ribbon assembly. The guest list included the chairman and five top officers of the corporation and members of the board of directors—numbering among its ranks various presidents and chairmen of Fortune 500 companies.

Sarah predicted a fiasco when she questioned her boss and found out who the other honorees were to be. She was not a snob, but she knew that most of the women were in grade levels where their only exposure to top-level executives was to take orders or to receive a prefunctory "ugh" when passing one of these chieftains in the hall. In addition, most of them had no experience in public speaking. Sarah told her boss that she simply refused to participate because the whole event was nothing but exploitation and that she was going to decline her invitation.

Sarah's boss was vehement. He told Sarah, "So it is exploitation. So it is nothing but a media event. So you don't want to participate. Our chairman and CEO wants you to participate.

You *want* to participate. You're going to participate. Right? Right."

ESPOUSING THE PARTY LINE

On the ranch, for many years we couldn't get a private telephone line for love or money; lines shared with at least one other party were the only thing available. If someone else was on the line, you simply had to wait to place your own calls, and you could be sure that ears were listening in on any call you received. If we had anything confidential to say, we had to get into the car and drive to town to use a pay telephone—or risk its being repeated all around.

You may find that in business your boss follows much the same system when it comes to communicating with others inside the company. Many play it safe by saying only what's acceptable, what could be heard by anyone and safely attributed to the speaker. Few risk speaking freely in almost any company.

Espousing the party line is sometimes a substitute for original thinking. Many first-line supervisors, managers, directors, and vice-presidents go to great lengths to prove that they know the right things to think and to say in order to prove that they fit in.

One manager became so caught up in company "hosannas" that he wrote for a company publication, "This writer is deeply humbled and indeed fortunate to be associated with developing this legacy to highlight the fine management practices of this company." The booklet contained numerous quotes from the chairman espousing party line but having little to do with reality:

"I like to be in the thick of things—right down on the firing line." In actual fact, he was sometimes driven through the plant in an enclosed, air-conditioned electric golf cart.

"I like to roam around a lot and stay in touch with people at all levels." He did not carry this to the extreme of the company cafeteria. And although he had one secretary type numerous community project communications for his wife, he never seemed to know her when they passed in the hall.

"I would like to be in on major projects from the very beginning all the way through to the final decision-making process." In actual practice he told his product managers that he didn't want to hear their excuses, only their results.

"You gotta know your people well enough to smell trouble ahead of time." A sixteen-week strike hit the plant while the chairman was in Europe on vacation.

Many of the activities and a lot of the nonsense in the work world is the result of people who spend all their time and energy convincing themselves and others that they are right.

THE LOYAL OPPOSITION: HOW TO TELL THE BOSS HE'S WRONG

At the close of even the bitterest of national elections, the Republicans and Democrats bury the hatchet and get down to the business of running the country. Despite our differences and political nuances, both parties subscribe basically to the same document: the Constitution. Essentially, the two parties have far more similarities than differences. The losing side is always known as the loyal opposition. If it were not for this, we would not enjoy stability of government while at the same time having the honest give-and-take of the two-party system. This concept of the loyal opposition can be effective in business as well.

To return to Sarah for a moment, Stan had recommended her for the V-Day list even though (or perhaps because) she had made him angry a time or two. The first time Stan lost his temper with Sarah was shortly after she joined the company. She had had a big buildup about the job and was part of a team (ten men and two women) selected and assigned to various departments in the corporation to give them an intense learning experience. In actual practice in department after department, Sarah found several weeks of assigned work could be finished in only a couple of days. She was soon bored beyond belief.

At their first progress meeting, Stan opened with a long spiel about the glorious opportunity they were getting. Sarah was sitting on pins and needles to give her report, to say that she was getting nothing but busy work to do. When Stan asked for any problems Sarah waited for others to speak up—she knew some had even greater problems and complaints—but all remained mute. Throwing caution to the wind, Sarah committed the unpardonable sin: *she told Stan what he didn't want to hear.*

Stan blew his stack, all right. But after Sarah had taken the brunt of Stan's wrath, several of the people around the table piped up to reconfirm that she wasn't alone in being given mindless tasks to do. As a result, word did go out to the vice-presidents to get off their collective duffs and cut out assigning busy work to the men and women in this select group.

Whether she knew it or not, Sarah played the role of the loyal opposition. While Stan blustered and bellowed at her in the process, he let her get away with telling him the truth and didn't fire her.

During interaction with your superiors and particularly your own boss, it is sometimes necessary to flag to his attention that you are the dissenting but loyal opposition. Not every decision your boss makes will be right, particularly when your boss is pressured by time and moves too fast. It is often up to you to protect your boss from his or her own power and the possible abuse of it.

In some cases, if you think something is wrong, say so. *But check out your facts beforehand so you can explain why.* Nobody likes to be told he is wrong. Many will defend their ideas or opinions by telling you that they were right, that you were simply wrong in the execution or implementation of them. There are many subtle ways of disagreeing or getting around telling the boss that it was his fault and not yours. No one has to go to the extreme of telling the boss, "You are really off the wall."

You will be a much more valuable resource to your boss if you don't mindlessly say, "Yes, ma'am" or "Yes, sir" all the time.

In summary, sometimes you can serve your boss best by acting in the capacity of the loyal opposition and telling him that he or the situation is wrong. The rules call for knowing your facts, being on firm ground, and being sensitive and tactful. And remember, on occasion your boss may not be free to share certain information that went into making the final decision. No matter how much you disagree, you may have but one recourse. You have to say, "How high?" when your boss says, "Jump."

WHEN THE BOSS ISN'T ON THE UP AND UP

The problem of an irresponsible, unethical, or immoral boss was brought home in a situation involving a person I'll call Tina. She worked six months for a nonprofit drug and alcohol rehabilitation center that took on patients that others had given up on. The charismatic director, whom I'll call Dr. Humes, was a psychiatrist who had won some national recognition in his specialty. Committed to him and the work, many of Dr. Humes's staff were working at half salary at sacrifice of their careers and families.

As it turned out, Dr. Humes was fiscally irresponsible. Tina's position as business manager, which means fund raising and going after grants, had been created by two board members who had pumped a lot of funds into the center and were worried about the debts they saw escalating each month. Confidentially, these two board members were most concerned because Dr. Humes's wife kept the center's books.

Tina, too, noted serious deficiency in accounting knowledge on the part of Dr. Humes's wife. As business manager, she asked to have a look at the books herself. Dr. Humes's wife flatly refused.

At about this time Tina received her first anonymous note from some disgruntled member of Dr. Humes's staff who tipped her off to which filing cabinet the center's books were kept in.

Tina found that Dr. Humes's approach to salary administration was certainly creative. Though he, too, only drew half salary, his salary had been increased in the last year to well over $60,000 (half a big loaf is better than half a small one). His wife drew $15,000 for her efforts in keeping the books.

The professional staff was another matter. Several had been asked to work at half salary until the center was more firmly established and its work better financed. In their employment interview, they were then instructed by Dr. Humes to set a figure they felt they were worth.

The humble ones who chose the $16,000–$18,000 range fared badly, and Dr. Hume gained PhDs for $8,000 a year. Nor did Tina fare very well. She had to fight for her paycheck, and on one occasion she was given three different checks. The center paid her weekly salary out of three different accounts, and Dr. Humes's wife frequently managed to shortchange the total.

Tina's list of problems in her unhealthy situation went like this:

First, open warfare developed over Tina's looking at the books. Dr. Humes's wife would not even relinquish a pair of scissors to Tina so she could cut typed paragraphs from an old grant proposal and paste up a new one for photocopying. She had no secretary and had to resort to all kinds of time-saving methods, even though the new grant application, if successful, might have netted the center $25,000. Before Tina left the center she was even bringing her own paper clips from home.

Second, Tina was constantly going toe to toe with Dr. Humes about money and his profligate spending habits.

Third, despite her warnings of financial disaster, Dr. Humes would sneak around and spend money they didn't have. He hired new people whose monthly salaries the center couldn't meet.

Fourth, the IRS was after the center, and several grant applications were in jeopardy if they didn't clean up their act. Tina's position was such that one of the first federal grants she was able to gain approval for had to cover her own salary.

By now you must be asking why in the world Tina stayed at her job for even one week, let alone six months. Aside from her obligation to the board members who had hired her, Dr. Humes made a compelling case for a treatment method he had developed that was gaining success with people no one else had been able to reach. Tina saw the good the center would accomplish if only it could become and remain solvent.

The final straw was applied when Tina worked her tail off to set up a grant that would have brought in thousands of dollars a year in tuition from medical students selected to intern at the center. Dr. Humes flatly refused to approve the program but offered no better reason than that he would not have outsiders within the hallowed walls of his center.

Tina suspected his decision had more to do with the close financial monitoring that would be involved. Something snapped in her head when she learned that Dr. Humes wouldn't cooperate. "You know I actually threatened to kill him, if he didn't sign that grant! It would have saved the center. I knew I had to quit. Two more weeks in that place and I'd have become one of the patients," Tina said.

Before she left she drafted twenty-five steps that must be taken to get the center back on sound financial ground. It took the board more than a year and a half to start to implement her suggestions, which was done only after Dr. Humes had driven the center to the point of bankruptcy.

The fact that Tina was right all along carried far less weight, as you can see, than did Dr. Humes's high sounding but empty promises.

To sum up, there may come a time when you have a boss who is not right, ethically or morally. The options must fit the situation, but you can follow these tips:

- Exhaust every means to try to get the boss to see reason or change the situation before real trouble erupts.
- Protect yourself.
- Extricate yourself by quitting.

12
Faulty Assumption Twelve

IT'S BETTER TO GIVE THAN TO RECEIVE

> *"When I asked for a salary raise,*
> *the director kept going on about*
> *how great the company is, how*
> *it treats its employees like*
> *human beings and how that*
> *works to make every member of*
> *the team give 100 percent. While*
> *he was telling me that some*
> *things are more important than*
> *money, I kept in mind that he*
> *made better than three times my*
> *salary a year."*
>
> *Male, 27*
> *sales representative*
> *giant chemical company*

A friend of mine once lassoed me into attending a huge evangelist meeting. Just as we were seated, the preacher began shouting warnings about hell's fire and damnation, and the heat generated from all those tightly packed bodies came as uncomfortably close as I want to get to experiencing the real thing, particularly when I'm paying for the pleasure.

As the preacher sweated and stomped and shouted, a troupe of "disciples" passed the hat and then the choir broke into that good ole gospel hymn, "It's Better to Give Than to Receive."

Everyone but me (reasoning that hot air rises, I decided to stay low) jumped up and started clapping and singing:

It's better to give than to receive.
It's better to give than to receive.
If you want to be forgiven,
And find the joy of living,
It's better to give than to receive.

Although I could understand why people got swept up in the emotion of tent show religion and gave up their hard-earned money, it is more difficult to understand why this happens in the business arena. Too many people give away their career growth and paychecks almost as if they were, indeed, blessed more by giving than receiving. Consequently, too many people wind up receiving little credit for their ideas because they essentially give them away or fail to take steps to keep someone else from stealing them. And too many achieve little recognition and paltry pay raises all their working lives, despite all their hard work, because they give up rather than fight for their due.

Brothers and sisters, repent those ways before it is too late; all giving and no taking will leave you in a sorry state—as the following case history illustrates.

DUPED BY CASTING PEARLS BEFORE SWINE

Anyone who saw the movie *Nine to Five* was incensed when the character played by actress Lily Tomlin had her brilliant plan stolen out from under her by her swine of a boss, who then passed it off as his own.

Well, that's what you get for casting your pearls, but it isn't necessary. Consider what happened to another Lily, who was office manager in a small company whose owner wanted it to go big.

The firm was in the process of expanding its services into several other cities. Basically, the company leased office space within its own quarters (what might be called an office boarding-house) on a one-month to one-year lease to firms with short-term or temporary office space needs. They provided furniture, a central coffee station, and a wide variety of services performed by a clerical pool that all the "tenants" shared. Setting up the branches would require training new employees not only in operation of equipment but in procedures and the costing out of the firm's services.

Lily knew she would be spread too thin to try to do all the hiring and training. She decided a training manual was needed and went to work on it—much of the work done at home on her own time. She didn't even bother to ask for input from her boss, Doug the Dim (as she called him privately), who was vice-president of the firm but little more than a pretty face in Lily's estimation. She decided just to present him with the finished product so the project didn't get bogged down by his dilly-dallying.

In her usual thorough fashion, Lily set down everything in such detail and in such easy-to-understand language that the product was a virtual blueprint. She submitted the training manual to Doug for review. Ten days later, on a Friday afternoon (with the president away on vacation) he called her into his office and fired her—her services were no longer needed. Doug might not have known anything about setting up the clerical service centers before Lily drafted this manual, but now he did.

Stunned, Lily called me. What went wrong? How could she have protected herself? Had I known in time I would have advised her to take the following steps.

1. Publicize Your Efforts

Nobody knew that Lily was working on the manual. This made it all the easier for Doug to steal it. She should have run the idea up the flagpole with others—particularly the president, since he was accessible in such a small company and because his key goal was to speed up the expansion of branch offices. (Lily had hoped to present it to him as a surprise, knowing how pleased he would be.)

Rule number one: Be sure to talk to several individuals about the project. Get their input. Even mention their names as sources for certain information in your report, plan, or idea documentation. This kind of name dropping will insure that your boss, or someone else in the firm, will not try any monkey business. If no one but you knows that you're working on a project, it might be a your-word-against-his situation.

2. Give a Wider Review

By limiting the manual's distribution to her boss, Lily increased the risk of pirating. Though this is tricky in many settings, Lily might have waited until after the president had returned from vacation to present her work, or she could have taken advantage of his being gone to send a copy for his catch-up file. Her own boss might have been angry, but she could have apologized sweetly and promised never to let it happen again.

Rule number two: Don't give away all your chances for proper credit by making only one person aware of your work, even if all you can do is alert the boss that you may be causing a typing overload because the secretary is handling *this project* you've completed. The best bet is to find a way to get a copy to someone else for review.

3. Obfuscate through Language

Lily's simplified, comprehensive manual literally wrote her out of a job. She might have used that old maneuver of wording everything in jargon or technical terms so that no one but the originator can decode it. This frequently serves to keep others off balance. Many subordinates then obtain proper credit when it comes to the presentation of their work by playing on the boss's fear of stumbling through something he or she doesn't understand very well in front of his or her superiors. However, since Lily's whole purpose was to make instructions clear enough to get her out of a round of training, she might have simply held back some of the information—just enough so that Doug couldn't have proceeded as he did.

Rule number three: Keep yourself an integral part of your work.

4. Copyright; It's Easier than You Think

Lily was in such utter shock when she was fired that she left without even getting a copy of her manual. That manual, which was put into use by the firm's staff and was later out in plain view at a secretarial station, had Doug's name on it. This could not have happened if Lily had registered it (for a small fee) as an unpublished work. A simple request for a form and instructions can be made to the copyright office at the Library of Congress in Washington, D.C. Once an unpublished work is copyrighted, you can, in fact, submit unlimited revised copies of a single manuscript without any problem. Lily could have gotten around any criticism of disloyalty to the company on the basis that her preliminary registration simplified matters until an approved version was accepted by the company. And it certainly would protect the company from having the manual fall into hands of other companies or competitors, which, in this case, might have been an on-premise tenant.

Rule number four: About the only time it becomes necessary to let others, including your boss, know that you have taken steps to protect your work is when someone is about to steal it!

5. Share the Credit

It never occurred to Lily that she was most likely viewed as a threat to her boss by virtue of her own intelligence and initiative. If Doug had been on top of his job, he should have known that the manual or something similar was needed.

One of the most obvious tactics to employ with a boss who is prone (or in a good position) to take credit for your ideas is to share or seem to share the spotlight with him or her. Lily could have offered to Doug the possibility of submitting a case history article on the manual and its use by their company to any number of trade publications dealing with office systems and procedures, with him as coauthor. In large organizations, the company magazine or newsletters offer some of the same possibilities.

Getting into Trade Publications

1. Your local library has indexes listing weekly, monthly, bimonthly, and quarterly publications that cover a wide assortment of trades and industries, along with information about what kinds of things the magazine accepts, the editor's name, the address, and so forth.

2. Check by telephone to make sure the information is current. Even directories for the current year are often dated, since the information is gathered months before publication and there is another lapse of time before it reaches the local library. Psychologically, it never helps to send information to an editor who just left or was fired.

3. Query by letter, highlighting the idea and offering your credentials as author and indicating that you will be following up by telephone after a specified duration of time.

4. Offer to write the article; don't ask to be paid. Many editors of trade publications are short on writing staffs and welcome this kind of contribution.

5. If you get an OK—or even a qualified, "Let me see something"—present the article long in advance of the publication's deadline. Pay strict attention to the publication's specifications on length, tone, and content. Keep the amount of company fluff and "free advertising" to a minimum.

6. Be prepared for the article to be turned down. Be willing to reslant it and try again with different publications.

CAST YOUR BREAD UPON THE WATERS: SMART BOSSES PRAISE THEIR SUBORDINATES

When was the last time you praised one of your subordinates in front of your own boss? If you can't think of any time during the last six months that you've put in a good word about a subordinate's performance to your own boss, consider how that looks.

Keeping your subordinate's accomplishments under wraps may do harm to yourself. Your boss might reasonably assume that you have a bunch of deadheads working for you. And if you hired them, how does that make you look? The boss may also wonder why you need such a large salary budget if the performance of people reporting to you is so iffy that it isn't worth mentioning.

Ask yourself, would a football coach try to keep the owner of the team (his own boss) from knowing that the players are doing well? No, of course not. Yet thousands of bosses stupidly misdirect their energies by attempting to do just that.

Never downplay the work of your subordinates—talk it up. *Their good works directly reflect on you and your skills as a boss.*

Hearing this advice, you may think I have had a change of heart and that it is truly better to give than to receive. Nonsense! Giving public praise to a subordinate, with a little modest mention of your role in the matter, frequently results in your own boss in turn praising you to peers or to those at the next level up.

If this motivation sounds more like personal aggrandizement than Christian charity, so what? It is not as if you were setting out to hurt the other person.

To give a brief example of how this works, several years ago in a consumer products plant an operator on one of six production lines frequently had to replace suction cups used to grip cents-off coupons from metal trays and release them into open boxes of cereal before they were sealed up. He was so disgusted at the shoddy equipment provided through the corporate purchasing department that he bought and installed some better (and cheaper) suction cups from a local hardware store. They turned out to have a much longer life span. This operator's foreman bragged about the improvement to the night shift supervisor, who bragged to the production foreman, who bragged to the plant manager. He, in turn, shipped off samples of these suction cups to every other plant manager in the division and to his own boss, the divisional V-P, who turned around and told his own boss, the executive vice-president. When he visited this plant a short time later, he went out on the production floor in order to meet this operator personally and shake his hand. In a roundabout way, everybody received a pat on the back.

PRAISE THE LORD AND PASS THE AMMUNITION

That bit of military advice gives credit where credit is due—to the Lord—but faces up squarely to the fact that survival and success also depend on continuing to put up a good fight. Yet you have probably read this phrase in the guide on management style published by your company (if it's one of the Fortune 500): *"There is no end to what can be accomplished as long as you don't care who gets the credit."* Or, if you work in a smaller organization, you probably have heard similar sentiments spewed forth with conviction by a top executive who doesn't live by this guideline himself.

I don't wish to appear snide, just factual. *Anybody who has reached the top has been acutely concerned every step of the way about who got the credit—and it isn't the Lord.* You can be certain that those very individuals take great pains to be sure they receive all that is due them and then some in the form of bonuses, pay raises, promotions, and accolades for their work.

HOW TO GO ABOUT
GETTING YOUR PRAYERS ANSWERED

A young man, whom I'll call David, has had four promotions in his five years with a big chemical company. David's secrets are very simple:

- well-placed initiative
- the ability to take risks
- belief in himself and his capabilities

- the knowledge that you have to give the boss solid reasons to promote you

CAREER MOVE NUMBER ONE

David's first position with the company was as a customer service representative. Unlike his peers, David took to heart the part about service to the customer. Most of the reps went no further than to enter customers' orders in the system and automatically tell them they would have whatever they ordered in a week, whether or not this was the case.

This created a problem for David's boss, the product manager. Typically, the distribution department had to call David's boss back to straighten out orders, particularly unusual requests such as large quantity orders that might require multiple sourcing to locate or the juggling of production runs to avoid delays in shipment.

Recognizing the problem as one of inventory conditions, David started asking his boss how certain orders should be handled *before* they were keyed into the computer so that the distribution staff would not have to call back. The results:

- Customers, usually the purchasing agents of the companies, began asking for David by name.
- Because he and his boss had frequent powwows on how to handle orders, David learned his boss's concerns and could attune his recommendations to the boss's way of thinking. Thus his recommendations to the boss were more consistently accepted.
- David was able to get a handle on the real cause of the department's problem—two major warehouse operations in different states.

Almost without fail, when David called either one of these operations to verify the amount of products they had on hand, the answer came back that they couldn't find it. David found it pretty hard to believe that they didn't know where 200,000 pounds of raw product used for the manufacture of a protective inner layer in windshields was!

A risky undertaking. David spent his own money and vacation time to check out several warehouses that stored these raw materials for his company's customers to see how well organized and equipped they really were. This included inspection of the two rotten-apple facilities, one of which was located in Alabama and one in Kansas.

On a pretext that he never did disclose, David took photos in the various facilities he visited, including new ones which he thought offered superior advantages. Upon his return to work, he showed these pictures to his boss and recommended canceling the contracts held by the two troublemaking warehousers. David knew that someone—probably his boss's boss—had signed the original contracts with these firms. He was careful to indicate that the internal procedures of the facilities had simply gone downhill, though in actual fact neither facility was ever up to standard. But he was too smart to rub anyone's nose in that particular truth. He also was armed with a list of the warehousers he believed were better, along with documentation of his reasons. The result:

- David's boss had a meeting with the head of distribution, and in short order the company entered into two contracts with warehouses from his list.
- Despite turfdoms, the distribution department that funneled back customer complaints was delighted to be out from under the gun.
- Service was improved.
- David was offered a pay raise and a higher position as a sales representative in the Northeast. He packed his bags and moved on.

Lesson 1: Stand out; do something noteworthy.

Don't expect your boss to praise your work if the most that can be said of you is that you show up for work on time.

Documenting achievements. David increased his chances of getting the raise and promotion by documenting his own achievements; he did not count on potentially unreliable co-workers to bring his performance to the attention of influential people. He did this by monitoring the results and consequences of his work. Many subordinates make a mistake in not doing so. David made it a practice to follow up with customers who placed their orders through him. He used a rating card system. His "survey" showed 60 percent of the customers rating his service as "excellent" with none of the remaining responses falling below "good." He routinely routed these cards to his boss along with letters he had received from purchasing agents commending the company for its fine service, indirectly shining a spotlight on David's own performance.

Lesson 2: Manufacture your own limelight.

Take time to monitor the end results or consequences of your work. Never fail to arm your boss with your accomplishments. Too many things may be forgotten, taken for granted, or never given proper importance.

You may have to use some ingenuity and creativity to measure your performance so that specific improvements and accomplishments can be highlighted. Not all situations are as dramatic as David's. If David had been selling insurance policies, he could have measured his performance, for example, in terms of policies sold, in number of applications canceled by customers within six months of issue, by the average time it took to close a sale, and so forth.

If David had been a secretary, he could have set any number of standards—the maximum number of times a phone should ring before being answered, limits on personal calls, letters typed with no visible corrections, etc.

If David had been a guidance counselor, he could have talked about the number of people he had placed in full-time jobs, the turnaround time to place them there, and how long those individuals he placed stayed on, etc.

Assessing the promotion. Many people might feel that David was unwise to accept a position away from corporate headquarters. It's always risky to go to the smaller office or plant. But I have seen few who make it to the top who do not have broad experience in the company, having spent a lot of time in various field locations.

David knew that to achieve his career goals he needed broad hands-on experience in how the company's products were made and sold. He also needed direct knowledge in the money-making nuts and bolts end of the business—and a chance to be on the firing line.

Think about it. Who would be willing to promote to general a soldier who had refused to set foot on the battlefield?

Lesson 3: Be prepared to move out to move up.

Most company presidents and divisional vice-presidents have spent a lot of time in various field locations.

CAREER MOVE NUMBER TWO

In his new job, David had his work cut out for him. The market for the company's products in the New England area was quite mature. The company had 50 to 80 percent of the business from purchasing agents representing area manufacturers. But these buyers wanted at least two sources of supply for raw materials to avoid coming up on the short end, and made it a practice to play off one supplier (David's company) against the other (David's competition).

Historically, David's company met the lowest bid submitted by any competitors to these purchasing agents—a procedure known as *down deviation*. But David became aware that quite often their competitor would bid higher than his company. He reasoned that instead of trying to increase total sales dollars building market share, he could accomplish the same thing by *increasing* his price, matching that of the competition. Thus

David introduced an innovative procedure known as *up deviation.*

David wangled the competitor's price from the purchasing agent most of the time by way of a consummate acting job— holding back on price and poor-mouthing to the agent to discover the other company's quote. If, by way of example, David was initially prepared to make an offer of $1 a pound for a quantity of 100,000 pounds of raw product delivered FOB at the buyer's plant and he found out the competitor's bid was 10¢ a pound higher, David would gain approval to match the higher price.

David then laid the increase in cost over the last purchase to a differential in freight cost, letting the buyer think the product was coming from a more distant plant—usually in the area from which the competition was shipping its orders. Most of the time the source was closer to home.

Seizing new opportunities. In the meantime David had received little credit for his performance. He bided his time and kept alert.

He began to assist a customer in designing new products using a combination of resin and wood flour—raw materials sold by David's company. The client company already manufactured molded products such as coffee table tops and shuffleboard pucks. After a great deal of input from David, this company combined two molds already in use to come up with a new product line, a houseware item known as a *lazy Susan.* Sales to this customer, which were already substantial, increased some 20 percent.

David got his chance to crow at a sales review meeting attended by an entourage from corporate headquarters that included the field sales director, director of marketing, and the vice-president and general manager of the division. While the other bigwigs were aware of David's concept of the up deviation, the biggest wig was not.

When his turn on the program rolled around, David presented figures that showed a sizable gain in money brought into the firm through the up deviation concept. But his *tour de force* was the new lazy Susan product line, which at first view drew chuckles from the crowd.

However, the increase in sales to the manufacturer and David's initiative in working with the client in the new product's development got the attention of the proper people.

A month after this presentation David received a merit increase of approximately 10 percent of his base salary and moved up one notch on the career ladder.

Lesson 4: Save your crowing for those individuals who can give your career a boost; be selective about when, where, and how you present your triumphs.

CAREER MOVE NUMBER THREE

In spite of all this extra effort, David was beginning to feel as if his career was moving at a snail's pace. If he expected to reach his life's goal of the company presidency he had better take more radical action.

He approached his boss, the regional manager. He told him that he had received several job offers from a number of their customers. (The next time you say nix to a sales career, remember the number of contacts that can be built in such a profession.) He disclosed that he had three firm offers and that the starting salaries being dangled in front of him were in the range of $10,000 to $12,000 more than his present salary. (Actually, David had two such offers and the increases were more in the neighborhood of $5,000 to $8,000.)

Lesson 5: It is generally advisable to pad your salary range requests as long as they are reasonable, and you have good, documented reasons for approaching that level.

Always make sure you have received at least one firm offer to work elsewhere in case the powers that be call your bluff.

Higher salaries take higher approval. A typical complaint made by first-line and middle managers—and often as high as the director level—is the limited salary incentive budget they receive and the rigamarole they have to go through to get increases for their staff.

David's boss was no exception. While he wanted desperately to keep David with the company, and he sympathized with his wishing to further his career, he had no power to approve such a significant salary increase. He suggested that David write a letter to him and carbon the field sales director and the director of marketing, outlining all the information they had discussed.

David's letter hit just the right mix of fact and humility. With only a few changes made for anonymity, this is the letter he wrote:

Dear Chet:

This letter confirms our recent conversation regarding my current salary level with the company.

As I indicated to you, three firms have made overtures to me. These offers were unsolicited on my part and presumably reflect the positive benefits each organization has gained through the manner in which its account was managed.

One offer is in the area of technical sales, the second in sales management, and the third position in production control. These firms are offering salaries in the $35,000 range.

It has been a rich and rewarding experience to work for _____. I would never seriously consider leaving if there was not such a disparity between my current salary level and these offers.

The sales gains that have been achieved in several key accounts reflect the pride with which I perform my job and also the receptive climate created by the management of this company to new and innovative ideas.

In short, I have enjoyed my career with the company and hope that a considerable salary adjustment can be made approaching these outside offers. I would appreciate any help you can provide to resolve this matter and look forward to the pursuit of many promising and fruitful years of work with this company.

Sincerely,

David

cc: (Name of field sales director)
(Name of director of marketing)
(Name of divisional vice-president and general manager)

The experience he gained with purchasing agents while developing the concept of the up deviation had made David a fine actor. He was a master of the mournful stare. This skill made it easier to get through all the poor-mouthing he had to listen to as a result of his letter.

First the field sales director called him in and gave him a verbal browbeating. David was told he needed to gain more experience before making such outlandish demands. He called David's letter a veiled threat.

In face of this hot air, David replied, "Look, I got three offers which caused me to question why I'm paid less here. What would you have done in my place?"

Within a matter of days David was summoned to corporate headquarters by the director of marketing—a meeting arranged by David's boss. But David was on his own to do his own talking and was on guard.

The red carpet was rolled out—a first-class flight and a luncheon meeting at a prestigious country club. In buddy-buddy fashion, the director told of offers he'd had and turned down and painted the glories of working for the company even if

David might never become wealthy doing so. David found this amusing when the company's chairman's salary was more than $400,000 a year along with handsome stock options.

David didn't back down. He again stated his concerns about the divergent salary level. But he carefully suggested that he would like to be considered for the position of area sales supervisor. This position was five grades above the one he held now and carried a salary in the range of David's dreams.

David knew he was talking to a man who understood ambition. Before the lunch was over the director told him, "I'll see what can be done, but I'm not making any promises about when. It may be a week from now or it may be six months." It took almost five months, but David got the job.

Lesson 6: Even in these inflationary times, you should recognize that most companies restrict managers to giving merit raises within a given interval, usually with an upper limit of 12 percent.

To obtain an increase beyond that upper ceiling level takes matters completely out of your own boss's hands.

Lesson 7: Winning significant salary increases often takes nerves of steel and more than a little brashness.

Two or three months before your anniversary date (the usual benchmark for salary review), begin to compile a letter or memorandum appraising past performance and making note of the current year's accomplishments. Note plans for the upcoming year.

If you have a formalized appraisal system, writing out your own appraisal has several advantages. Psychologically, you can see how you really do stack up. Typically, in organizations with formal appraisals, you don't get to see what the boss says about your performance or have a chance to debate it. So don't use appraisal for vanity alone. If you get the boss to sign or initial the appraisal you draft about yourself, at least these letters can be some form of proof of performance if the boss later has it in for you, or you need something to show a prospective new employer.

Lesson 8: You should have a track record of some note before applying this technique.

Usually you will not have attained a high batting average on the job in less than two years. Don't jump the gun.

Lesson 9: Never bluff about having a job offer from another organization.

The boss may call your hand and you'll be out of the game. But remember, in the hiring policies of many companies the law of supply and demand applies.

On the same theory that a man's wife often looks better to him when she attracts the attentions of other men, the reality of an employee being lured away by another firm or competitor inflates his worth in the company's eyes. If possible, however, let the offer be backed up or corroborated by a third party, even if you have to leak the information to someone who has the boss's ear.

Lesson 10: Don't let yourself be pressured by fear or guilt.

Higher-ups will try to lay guilt on you for having the temerity to seek an "unreasonable" request for money. The boss may threaten first that you will have to go to a much higher-up, perhaps even to the president, for such a salary increase. Fine. Welcome this as an opportunity to get your accomplishments mentioned in high places.

Realize that your boss is obligated and pressured by his own boss to discourage you and try to get you to back down. But remember that the very people who are making you feel guilty about a salary increase request may well be pulling in tens of thousands more than you do over the course of any given year.

Learn to handle the tormented sighs exorcised from your boss and the higher-ups by your request for a raise. (Shortly after winning a considerable increase for myself, my boss said, "You know, there are very few men in this entire building who make that amount of money." I was indeed touched by all those on the floors above me who felt it was better to give than to receive.)

Lesson 11: Keep in mind that ambition is no stranger to the people from whom you seek your increase or they wouldn't be in their current positions.

However, be specific about what you want. Be firm in your resolve to get ahead. Like David, you might consider going after a job that represents a quantum leap forward in your career. Don't be wishy-washy or indecisive about where you wish to be or what you want. That sort of individual is scarcely the type to warrant a 50- to 60-percent increase in pay and responsibilities.

Lesson 12: Generally, the worst thing that happens to you when a request is made for more money is to be turned down.

CONTINUING CAREER STEPS

The last time I talked to David he was moving back to the corporate compound at a hefty jump in pay to fill the duties of director of marketing for his division. He's still going places. He attributes much of his success to the negotiating experience he gained in selling. *If you don't ask, you probably won't receive.*

PART III

13
Faulty Assumption Thirteen

YOU MUST CLIMB THE PROMOTIONAL LADDER RUNG BY RUNG

*"In our company there was no
conventional way a staff
professional could break into
line management. But in effect I
did just that by parlaying my
credentials and connections into
the directorship of a special
research institute."*

*Male, 44
scientist
Fortune 500 corporation*

Getting ahead in your job often hinges on where the boss is going. It is a misconception, though, to think you have to take your immediate boss's job in order to move up the promotional ladder in an organization. In fact, in numerous cases individuals have progressed to high levels in their organizations without ever taking over their bosses' jobs.

At least a couple of bosses I've observed get one promotion and then immediately start planning moves to get promoted again in a kind of leapfrog pattern up the promotional ladder. In the process they may sweep subordinates right along with them. But these types are in short supply. There are more of the

166

other kind, the ones who saw off the rungs as they go, leaving others in the lurch.

If you're like a lot of people, the boss's job will never be available. This is the boss who could be described as the great immovable object—the type who seems to have no ambitions at all (except, perhaps, to retain the *status quo*). Like great stone Buddhas, they appear planted in their jobs.

There are many reasons why individuals don't move up through organizations, and if you are a subordinate in one of them, you had better understand them so you can assess your own future.

- Has your boss been passed over for a promotion?
- Has the boss turned down a promotion?
- Does your boss face other constraints, such as lack of talent, training, or general promotability?

Any of the above will make it very tough for you.

I have a friend whose boss recently received a terrific offer and turned it down. The job required a transfer. The guy's wife drew the line. She wanted to seed a lawn and, for once, be around to mow it. And the man refused to take the job and commute six hours to work eight. Now my friend is really frustrated. He counted on being promoted to his boss's slot.

When your boss isn't promoted—or promotable—it is important that you regroup. Analyze other departments or areas within the organization to determine potential opportunities open to you. *You may have to make your own way.*

You may have to:

- Create your own job.
- Eliminate your own job.

CREATE YOUR OWN JOB

Impossible? That's exactly what one young man did. I will call him Jim. He worked in the public relations department of a large southern manufacturer that produced all sorts of camping and sports equipment. After only a couple of years he was beginning to feel boxed in by going-nowhere bosses. He was ready for drastic action but not as drastic as creating his own job.

It is unfortunate that vast numbers of employees think all jobs are created by the personnel department. This is utter nonsense. Personnel recruits individuals to fill positions that have been created by someone else. Positions are created by people who are smart enough to identify needs that are not currently being met by anyone within the organization.

Jim had good reason to feel boxed in, frustrated, and desperate. The first time we talked he described his department. Besides the usual clerical staff support, he and two other men made up the core of the department.

At the top was Lynn, a sixty-year-old, twenty-five-year veteran with the company. Basically, he got this position because personnel couldn't figure out where else to put him. In addition, Lynn had developed powerful connections in the company that kept him comfortably insulated from being fired (other old heads didn't want to set a precedent). He spent a large share of his day planning (mostly where and with whom he would have lunch) or reading "to keep on top of things." And he had set routines for subordinates and insisted on lots of meetings, at which he sometimes chewed up as much as two hours writing and rewriting a two-line, ten- to 15-word title on a news release in order to make the lines come out the same length.

In the middle was Jim's boss, Bruce. He had been with the company almost ten years. Jim found Bruce to be only a fair implementer but not much of an initiator, and dreaded the thought of continuing as his subordinate. Bruce was biding his time until Lynn retired and did little to justify his existence except shuffle and reshuffle papers while letting Jim actually do most of the work. He affected the intellectual, drawing pensively on a pipe all day and occasionally performing his smoke-ring blowing prowess for the secretaries.

As Jim and I talked in our counseling session, he began to analyze his situation. Together we began to develop an escape plan. From his experience emerged a system of logical steps to take.

Step 1:
Let Others Point Out Your Faults

Since the true mission or purpose of the department had never been defined, Jim started there. (If he was to know where he was going and why, he had to know where he *was*.) He first set up a series of interviews with several managers at different levels. At these meetings he asked for an honest critique of his department's services to them. Since he was doing the bulk of the work, it was something of a performance appraisal of himself.

Although some people will be hesitant to criticize, most won't. And, while it is always easier to see faults in others than it is to see them in ourselves, most of what Jim found out was constructive and illuminating. It is also fairly typical for managers to question the benefits to them of certain staff support functions like public relations, so they were glad to have the chance to blow off steam.

In any interview session you have to think on your feet and seat. However, you might try something along the lines of these questions, posed by Jim.

1. Please tell me your reaction to our current newsletter. What comments have you heard subordinates make about the newsletter? If you were the editor tomorrow, what changes would you make to improve the readership? (Many employees never read the newsletter, as was apparent from the number which wound up in the wastebasket shortly after they were distributed.)
2. What do you perceive is the key role public relations should play in the company?
3. How could PR be of further service to the company and, in particular, to your department?

It is critical to gather such information in a face-to-face

interview. Jim was, of course, careful to gain Bruce's permission ahead of time. (Some bosses might not readily give it.) If your boss is the insecure or paranoid type, you may have to show how the information gathered may be of use to him in order to vanquish all his imaginary enemies. Later you can bemoan the fact that the information was useless because people weren't on the up-and-up with what they told you. If your boss turns thumbs down on the interview approach, you may have to use the informal approach to getting this information, such as happening to run into people in the cafeteria. Of course, with the newsletter Jim was writing he could have scheduled the interviews by using his editorial prerogative to run a series of articles on certain executives. The point is, where there's a will there's a way.

Step 2:
Lose Your Misery in Corrective Action

Jim immediately began to analyze the data he'd gathered. Unlike so many other survey takers, who put such information in bright-colored folders to store on the shelf, Jim vowed to meet the needs expressed by the individuals he interviewed.

Apparently, one of the main reasons employees didn't read the weekly newsletter was that it read like a report from Dun and Bradstreet. People like to read about other people. Consequently, Jim began to run a whole series about employees, with features on everyone from the janitor to the executive vice-president, describing what they did on and off the job. He found one employee who had hitchhiked to work every day for twenty-five years and ran pictures of him thumbing a ride to work. One of the operators on the line turned out to be a jazz musician with two albums to his credit. A special question-and-answer column featuring executives answering questions of concern to employees was also created.

During the interviews Jim conducted, more than a few

managers were concerned about the future direction of the company and felt their subordinates were, too. This column gave them a chance to speak out and to be answered in return. Writing this column also gave Jim an inside track to the concerns of the top brass.

He had also found out another startling fact: Many managers really felt strongly that it did not do the company's image much good to be located in a run-down section of the city marked by high crime and decaying buildings. When Jim shared this bit of information with his own boss, Bruce, his attitude was, "Well, we certainly can't do anything about that."

Fortunately, Jim didn't let this stop him. He felt he was on to something. He felt the company would have to address this concern by either moving or upgrading the neighborhood around them. Jim opted for the latter.

Soon Jim was spending weekends and evenings at the library reading volumes of material on what other cities were doing to upgrade blighted areas. He contacted the historic preservation society in town to find out whether federal grant money might be obtained to rehabilitate the buildings in the area and turn them into livable housing stock. He contacted city agencies to see whether any support was ever available for these kinds of projects. He talked at length with a developer, and together they took several tours of the area to look at the delapidated homes and still surviving small businesses that surrounded the company headquarters. Under the mantle of newsletter editor, Jim visited with aldermen and local residents to gain additional insights without raising questions or hopes.

Gradually a game plan with two phases evolved. Phase one encompassed the restoration of several blocks of homes and area businesses, with special provisions to leave period architecture intact. Phase two involved an effort to reduce area crime (the executive vice-president had actually been conked on the head going for an afternoon stroll to work off a heavy lunch). Since most of these crimes were perpetrated by teenagers in the area, Jim's recommendation was for the company to sponsor a summer work program with other businesses for these youths.

Step 3:
Pick the Right Time to Make Your Move

Don't think for one minute that Jim rushed up to the president to share his glorious plan. He waited until the right time.

You see, the company's leader had made plans to triple sales over a ten-year period. (These goals might never have come to light if they had not surfaced in the newsletter's question-and-answer column.)

It dawned on Jim (Bruce only blew smoke rings when Jim mentioned it) that the company would eventually have to increase administrative white-collar jobs to process orders, since tripling sales creates a lot of paperwork. Within a short time Jim knew the critical decision—whether to expand where it was or pick up stakes and move elsewhere—would have to be made by the company.

At the right time Jim presented his ideas and plan to the chief. He made a strong argument for simultaneously keeping the company's facility where it was and becoming a leader in community commitment. He stressed the prestige (not lost on the president) that would flow from such a decision. He also made a compelling argument for hands-on supervision from the top.

Jim subsequently was appointed as assistant to the president to begin implementation of the plan once it had won approval. The president thought he had created the job, but you and I know better. He created the title, but Jim created the job.

Step 4:
Play Close to the Vest in a Big Stakes Game

Jim was careful to unveil his plan to no one but the president. Although Bruce had been flippant when Jim had tried to interest him, now that Jim had the president's ear, things might be different.

The best way to protect all your hard work in a similar situation is to keep your mouth shut until the right time. Always remember that your boss can't steal what isn't in sight or hasn't been placed in his or her hands. I am not an advocate of going around the boss because it usually gets subordinates into a lot of trouble, but in a case like Jim's, situations sometimes justify taking this gamble.

REAPING THE REWARDS OF YOUR OWN CREATION

Leapfrog is a game in which one player usually kneels or just bends over while someone next in line jumps over him. In the military it is a maneuver to advance two military units by engaging one with the enemy while the other moves to a forward position.

Job leapfrogging—moving forward or progressing as if by alternating leaps—has all the elements of a game and a military maneuver because the back you leap is that of your boss. You generally get where you are by winning out over him or her, or someone else, and this creates enemies and even open warfare.

But when you leapfrog by creating your own job, you may provoke jealousy but not the same hurt feelings produced when you get what someone else wanted. (Bruce was probably secretly pleased to see Jim leave, because he certainly was a threat to him when and if Lynn's job became available.)

Creating a job for yourself is also a strategy for rapidly getting to the top, or at least within very close proximity. Take Jim's case. In only a few years after he became assistant to the president for the special project, a subsidiary was formed to handle the redevelopment activities. Guess who was appointed its president and guess where Lynn and Bruce remain.

People occupying mid-management positions in their late thirties and early forties often come to an uncomfortable crossroads. They feel their careers are finished. Often there is just cause for this feeling. At this level you must take advantage of all job-creating potentials for all they are worth.

MILK ALL JOB-CREATING POTENTIAL
IN YOUR PRESENT POSITION

One scientist I knew, named George, made giant strides by using this strategy. Although George was a brilliant and innovative employee, he was struck by the fact that many managers with less glitter or talent were getting quite a bit more pay. He decided to break into management. In his company that was a little like a general in the army fraternizing with staff sergeants— the line management and staff professionals simply did not mix. George was determined to buck the trend and set his own precedent.

As a member of a large, national, professional organization, which I will call the Society of Chinese Scientists and Technologists, he was struck by the fact that most members were in need of more labs to run important tests, while George's own company had excess capacity. On his own time he analyzed these laboratory facilities carefully and drafted a proposal for his boss, a vice-president who had never held a test tube in his hand but knew a good business deal when he saw it.

Basically, George's plan could net a substantial amount of revenue for the company by selling its research expertise and excess facility capacity outside. His boss approved the plan and George was put in charge of a special subgroup to bring on board new customers. As its director, he could now be regarded as management.

Starting up this new venture was a little slow at first, but then demand for the new services began to go through the roof. Clients also were beginning to ask for more complicated tests. The company didn't have facilities for these.

George read the handwriting on the wall and immediately developed another plan. This time he came up with a recommendation to acquire a research institute in another state. A special section was enclosed highlighting important new trends in governmental protection for consumers, which he predicted would require substantial numbers of organizations to run toxicological studies on their products.

George's boss presented the plan to top management for their approval. I was at that meeting and watched George in action. He appeared to take a back seat and defer to his boss. But he was there to bail out his boss, quietly answering the tough questions that were asked.

Before you yell "Unfair" or "Foul," let me assure you that George had an ace in the hole in the event of a double cross by his boss. It so happens that among the best-selling tools a research lab has are the credentials of its scientists. George's boss did not have connections to the scientific community. The names of countless scientists, as well as how to lure them away from other jobs and yet hold on to them once they say yes, were all safely tucked away in George's head. Consequently, George, and not his boss, was picked to head this research institute as its president after the company acquired it.

ELIMINATE YOUR OWN JOB

Another way to get a leg up on the promotion ladder may be to *eliminate* your own job. Your eyes may have blinked just then, but you saw right. I said, *eliminate your own job.* That's one sure way to get noticed.

I know one woman who used this technique with excellent results. For purposes of confidentiality I'll use the name Betty. She was in a nowhere job in the personnel department of a state university. If you've been around, you know that such a job is certainly a thankless one at best.

Betty decided it was time to regroup after five years on the job. During this time she had added an assistant and a secretary to her immediate staff. Her boss, the director of personnel, was quite happy with her work and was more than shocked when she proposed that her job be eliminated. She further proposed that a portion of her salary go to her assistant and the secretary upon her departure. She had trained both well and they were now carrying out most of the work. Betty, a black woman, had been hired to get the equal employment opportunity program rolling. The university had made excellent progress under her leadership. Most of the staff and faculty liked Betty's style, but it was obvious to Betty that her services were really no longer required.

Until then Betty had met the chancellor at a few social functions, but that was the extent of their interaction. Hearing of her proposal to eliminate her job was like flashing her name in front of him in neon lights. He requested a meeting with her. (Note how Betty got the chancellor's attention without going around her boss to seek an appointment. She counted on the grapevine, and she was right.)

When they met at last they started out with the usual amenities regarding what a good job she'd done. The chancellor assured Betty that it would be a shame to lose someone as valuable as she. At that point Betty took another risk and put in her two cents. The chancellor obviously hoped that Betty would stay on at the university, so Betty outlined how that could be accomplished. She shared her thoughts concerning the need to build more rapport with outside businesses to bring in more endowment money. She outlined how she would like to try her hand at sponsoring a special conference mixing businessmen and businesswomen with students. She already had a name in mind—"Business Today." She suggested bringing speakers and several government officials to get a cross section of views. Besides, it couldn't hurt to build more rapport with some of the individuals who approved the university's budget and who checked up on its adherence to new regulations. (At the time the university was under scrutiny regarding program accessibility to the handicapped.)

Then Betty flatly stated that she wanted to be on assignment to get the job she had just outlined done. The chancellor took her up on the offer. For several months she didn't even have a title and was paid out of the chancellor's own discretionary funds. After her business conference turned into a great success she not only received an increase in pay, but the title of director of university relations.

REFUSE TO STAY BURIED

If you're low man or woman on the totem pole, the fastest way to get noticed and move up is to define the full scope of your job. This certainly will separate you from the rest of the herd.

You would be surprised at the number of men and women in many corporations who have no idea what's going on in their own department, much less beyond it. No wonder it's easy to get buried. If you refuse to stay buried, there are some sure ways to get out.

Step 1:
Discover Where You Fit Into the Organization

Get a copy of your firm's organizational charts. This is the best way to determine where your department or division fits into the total scheme of things and the chain of command (i.e., the name of your boss's boss and so on). Looking at these charts will give you the big picture. If you're a small fry (and we may as well be honest with ourselves), you need to go several steps further.

Draft your own organizational chart. Take a piece of paper and put yourself in the middle. Draw a box and put your name on it. (Now you know what it's like to be one of the big shots.) Next, draw a box on each side of you, to the left and to the right of you. The box on the left represents the department and people that send you work to do. The box on the right represents the department that receives your work.

People you rely on	You, Inc.	People who rely on you

Step 2:
Find Out Where Your Work Ends Up

Your next mission, should you decide to accept it (and you must if you want to get ahead), is to gather the following information:

- From what group of individuals (name names) come the materials, forms, parts with which you work?
- Who are the people responsible for getting material to your department and, more specifically, into your very own hands?
- Where do these materials go after you process them?
- Which departments and individuals in those departments depend on you to get scheduled work out right and on time?

After you finish, you will know:

Where your work comes from	What you do with it and why	Where your work goes, what they do with it, and why

Going through this process does take time, but the rewards are worth it, as those who've been through it will attest. Sally, for instance, started out as a secretary in the treasurer's department in a large insurance company somewhere up in the snow belt. She is now several grades up from there in general accounting. She started her career as one of three secretaries in the treasurer's office. Her analysis of their organization charts revealed her department to be under the investments division along with mortgage loans, real estate, and others. General accounting, on the other hand, was a subsection of the accounting and control function reporting through the operations division.

As one of the treasurer's secretaries, Sally had oh-so-many exciting chores to perform—handling check requisitions from other departments, typing the checks delegated to their department, making vouchers, and so on. But Sally didn't mind. In fact, she always volunteered to take the pink voucher copies over to accounting each day. It was not unusual for them to type out hundreds of checks a week. This necessitated that Sally make at least one visit there a day. She soon knew that department almost as well as her own.

Unlike her predecessors, Sally did not dump the voucher copies on just anybody's desk and make a fast getaway. She inquired for the name of the individual who should be given these check copies. She smiled a lot and kept giving the quite logical excuse that it would save everyone a great deal of time and keep her out of trouble with her boss. Shortly, she introduced herself to the assistant manager, who directed her to his head bookkeeper.

Over the course of several weeks Sally made note of what the bookkeeper did with these check copies. As it turned out, the woman spent a good twenty hours a week transferring information from these voucher copies onto a special coding sheet so the information on the top of the checks was formatted properly for the data entry department. (For those of you who are only used to writing your own personal checks, I must give a bit more explanation. Voucher checks are twice as big in size as the ordinary checks you carry. This additional space is used to provide an adequate explanation of who got the money and why.)

In essence, the bookkeeper was recopying by hand what was already on the voucher copy and what had already been done once by Sally and other secretaries like her. Performing this tedious chore took two to three minutes per check copy. What a waste of time. What a bottleneck. There had to be a better way!

Sally took a copy of the coding sheet to the print shop and had one of the artists draw in special columns on the check for the explanation, the account number, the bank code, and other information. After a few sample checks were made up she decided to practice typing on them to see if the new format slowed her down. Then she tested the other women she worked with. They clocked each other, comparing their speed at filling in the old checks versus the new check. They discovered the new columns and lines on the checks actually helped them *reduce* their typing time an average of twenty seconds per check.

Next, Sally tested these checks on the late-night data entry clerks and experienced similar success. She then presented the results of these tests in a memo to her own boss (the treasurer), the assistant manager of accounting, and the data processing manager. With her current skills she obviously was not bucking for her boss's job, though, with a base in accounting she might eventually do so. The fact that Sally contacted several people ahead of time was not breaking the chain of command. None of these people were managers. All were paid on the hourly scale. Since her boss was a big shot, she salved his ego by pointing out in the memo that it was imperative to gather this data before occupying his valuable time.

Sally made another smart move. She shared the by-line with the bookkeeper, even though that person had done none of the work. Her name was placed right at the top of the memorandum next to Sally's.

This was the second time in recent months that the management in accounting had been made favorably aware of Sally's existence. Prior to this project, Sally came up with a unique way of cutting down on rubber band and paper clip purchases. What I'm about to share with you may very well cause a run on the banks of America—not for deposits but for paper clips and rubber bands. Anyone who has worked in a large bank knows that such institutions accumulate these items literally by the hundreds of thousands. The bank next door to the company where Sally worked, which was also a major depositor, was no exception. On a daily basis bags full of perfectly good rubber bands and paper clips were picked up for discard by the trash men (something Sally had noticed on midday walks around the block). Sally had them make deliveries across the street instead. This drew several chuckles from many who knew Sally, but none from the treasurer or the controller in accounting. They both were keeping an eye on this bright young woman. When an opening for a trainee was created through a corporate development program, Sally was tapped for the job and shortly was auditing expenses in the field offices, working in property accounting, as well as learning duties in general accounting such as consolidating monthly financial statements.

A short time ago we talked on the phone. I wasn't surprised to learn that she had begun to coordinate a lot of reports and requests from tax administration. Could that be her next move up the career ladder?

NEVER FIGHT WHEN YOU CAN SWITCH

It may seem odd to you that a mere secretary would be given such an opportunity. If you're wondering why they offered Sally the job, the answer should be obvious. She had demonstrated that she had a good mind and was not afraid to innovate or take responsibility.

Creative placement goes on all the time in business. I know of one large firm that placed a *lawyer* in charge of its poultry division. Previous to this promotion his experience with chickens had been limited to eating them. But talents he demonstrated in other positions made him the logical choice.

In recent years several studies have shown that many top executives hold an MBA degree. Consequently, the business schools of many colleges and universities are bulging at the seams. Yet in several interviews I've had with high-ranking managers they place zip weight (translation: next to none) on their degrees as the key to getting ahead. Most attribute their success to the broad base of experience they gained by working in several divisions of their respective companies. In fact, many feel it's often far better to be a generalist and have a good grasp of what makes a business run—how to produce a product, how to market it, how to mobilize people. So it seems that many of the individuals whose noses are buried in their school textbooks might do well to spend at least an equal amount of time and energy studying their own companies.

Most of the executives I interview are in their fifties and sixties; some are in their forties; *rarely* are they in their thirties. By these age ranges you can tell that these individuals did not get ahead through the benefit of the latest personnel vogue, the human resource job bank. Today's successful hard hitters didn't sit back and wait for opportunity to tap them on the shoulder or fall out of a computer readout. Instead, they took their future into their own hands and forged their own way.

WHAT A PERSONNEL RESOURCE BANK CAN AND CANNOT DO FOR YOU

Before every member of the industrial relations profession throws this book out the window, I should elaborate. I am not opposed to what backers and designers of personnel resource banks are trying to accomplish. I am against all employees tying all their hopes and dreams to a computer data bank or, for that matter, to any *one* system or approach to move themselves ahead. This includes riding the boss's coattails. To resurrect an old directive, never put all your eggs in one basket.

Having your name on a computer resource system may be useless if your name never gets pulled because a supervisor or manager doesn't have to or want to tap that source when a job opens up. Even if it's corporate policy that all supervisors and managers must call for a search of the computer bank to find possible applicants among the company's employees, there is no way that personnel can force a boss to choose you or anyone else. That prospective boss can still go outside to hire someone. If the boss already has someone in mind, you aren't any more likely to get the job than you would have been before the day of the computer.

There is also the matter of your current boss. He or she is not compelled to let you know that someone else wants you. It would be breaking the chain of command for any prospective boss to approach you with an offer before getting the go-ahead from your current boss. And most computer resource systems still observe the chain of command.

Some companies try to mix a form of job posting in the systems they design, but many jobs are never advertised on these firms' bulletin boards. Again, even if corporate policy dictates that all jobs be posted in thirty point type on the bathroom wall, this won't guarantee you a job if that prospective boss already has been impressed by someone of his or her own choosing and has made a decision to have that someone.

If you work in one of America's large corporations and don't get along with your boss, perhaps your only hope of escape is to be noticed by another *division*. The majority of large corporations let their divisions more or less do their own thing, at least when it comes to their personnel function.

In the event that another division wants you, but for various reasons your boss won't stand for it, pull your trump card. *Quit*. The division that wants you can then hire you. Unfortunately, this usually jams up the company computer or causes someone important somewhere to ask questions. Usually the mere hint of this kind of notoriety will cause your current boss to back down. So consider this a last-resort tactic. But remember, being buried is forever.

14

Faulty Assumption Fourteen

LOYALTY IS OLD-FASHIONED

*"Paul brought me into the
company and gave me my first
real break. Now they want me to
put the screws to him. The sad
truth is, he should step down.
The philospher Hegel once said
something to the effect that the
greatest tragedy of mankind is
not the struggle between right
and wrong, but between right
and right. Which do I choose?
Loyalty to which right?"*

*Male, 53
chief corporate legal counsel
giant food processing company*

When I went to grade school we started off each day by saying
the pledge of allegiance to the flag. I must admit, at age six and
seven those words really didn't have much meaning. But later
the exercise took on an unexpected value. Acceptance of the
idea of allegiance proved to be excellent training for my
entrance into the business world. There bosses at all levels place
a high value on displays of allegiance and loyalty. Of course, the
primary reason is that the only way to the throne room (AKA

184

the board room) is by building through this virtue of profound personal commitment a cadre of loyal supporters who will stick with you through thick and thin.

In this age of "me first," ideas about allegiance and loyalty may at first appear outworn or irrelevant. But loyalty is at work in many levels of our business lives, whether we recognize it or not. For example, there is an exchange of value (meaning that there is something in it for both of you) in being openly loyal to your boss, particularly when he or she is in the hot seat. In addition, the demonstration of lack of loyalty seems to brand you as unworthy of trust—sometimes for as long as forever.

Let me recount a high-level power game which I think demonstrates these principles.

LOYALTY IS SOMETIMES BEING BETWEEN A ROCK AND A HARD PLACE

In the 1960s two factions were struggling within an organization in the food processing business. For nearly half a century this firm had been managed conservatively by members of the founding father's family. In fact, the founding father had been fond of leading the employees in a mid-morning round of calisthenics, followed by a few bars of the company's "national anthem" (changed here ever so slightly from the real thing, and that's the God's truth).

Fight, fight, fight for old Acme
Push forward with great speed
Never whine and never slack
Keep our company in the black
Fight to keep good old Acme in the lead.

Fight, fight, fight for old Acme
Let's all meet our customer's needs
Never whine and never slack
Keep our company in the black
Fight to keep good old Acme in the lead.

Upon the death of the founder, his eldest son, Paul, inherited the presidency. Although Paul no longer asked employees to do things like deep knee bends at their desks, he was nonetheless not what I'd call forward thinking in his approach to management. What was good enough for dear old Dad was good enough for him, too. Unfortunately, the board didn't hold sacred these same deep and abiding beliefs.

The board had never tried to buck the founding father, mainly because he carried real clout, namely controlling interest in the company. But following his death hundreds of thousands of shares wound up in other hands from their sale by relatives of the old man, who were panicked into unloading the stock.

Furthermore, some of the managers wanted a change. They had invested several years in the company and were growing tired of the traditional way in which the business was run. The prospect of now having to outlive Paul in order to change the firm's antiquated policies was too much for many of them.

The spokesman for this group of managers was the vice-president of marketing. Let's call him Mark. Mark felt strongly that the firm could triple its sales and earnings over the next decade through diversification of its product line. He wanted to reshape management along product lines instead of categories of specialized functions like production or his own job, marketing.

Paul, in the meantime, began to gird himself for a real fight to the finish against this group of managers. He enlisted the aid of one of his subordinates, named Harry, who served as chief legal counsel and secretary to the board, to gain needed support of various stockholders. Now Harry knew that the odds of stockholder approval were not in his boss's favor. The market price of the shares had dropped since Paul took office and had remained at a low level.

But Harry took every step possible to support Paul and to gain the majority of votes needed to insure Paul's position on the board. In light of the promises Mark and the manager's group made for future earnings growth, however, they easily won out over Paul. After all, shareholders are nothing if not self-serving, and they were smart enough to figure out how that would increase the market price of their shares and the dividend checks they would deposit. Even some of Paul's own relatives voted against him for the competition, a fact Harry kept from Paul. Why rub salt into an open wound?

TO THINE OWN SELF BE TRUE

Enough about Paul. What happened to Harry after this display of loyalty and apparent sacrifice?

Harry lived by a saying, "Look for the man in the catbird seat. Imagine that you see what he sees and you'll be OK."

That sounds pretty much like a riddle, but if you apply it, it begins to make sense.

Mark, having won out over Paul, was in the catbird seat (defined as a position of great prominence or advantage). But what did he see? Here is a rundown of the situation:

1. The age of the consumer and of environmental protection was just beginning to get into full swing. As a result, the federal government was starting to issue widespread regulations affecting the food industry that would require, among other things, sound legal assessment for a good many years to come. Harry was already something of an expert in this field.
2. Mark was of that new breed of management who, when they know they lack certain types of expertise, get it rather than fake it.
3. Mark was able to see that Harry possessed a lot of other experience and expertise that would be of benefit to Mark, including valuable insights into the politics of the company.
4. Mark won the battle but not the war. Now he must deliver on his "campaign promises." Although he now had the majority of stockholders' blessings, more than a few were uneasy and could swing things the other way pretty quickly. Basically, this powerful minority had voted for

Paul and liked his more conservative approach to running the business. Furthermore, Mark knew that Harry had the support of this group of shareholders.

After analyzing the situation, Harry made what appeared to be the ultimate gesture of loyalty to his deposed boss: he submitted his letter of resignation to Mark. In this letter, however, he was careful to point out certain upcoming trends that Mark might not be aware of, which would have impact on the future of the company.

Having done what he thought was right and true to himself, Harry set back to play the waiting game. He didn't have to wait long. In short order, Mark appeared in his office to talk things over. He wanted Harry to stay.

Surprisingly, even to Harry, Mark's reasons had less to do with Harry's expertise and more to do with his character. He told Harry up front that he recognized him to be a man who could be trusted and whose loyalty could be depended on and that he appreciated the value of having such a man working for him. In short, Harry had won Mark's respect. If Harry had not backed his former boss, Mark could quite logically have assumed that he could not be trusted in future situations.

It is easy to back a boss who is not under the gun. But it takes real guts and integrity to give all-out support when there's trouble.

The degree of support is important. In fact, to paraphrase another gem of wisdom, you can be damned by faint loyalty. If Harry had supported Paul in a halfhearted manner, he would still be finished in the organization. Mark quite logically could have assumed that Harry would be just as halfhearted in *his* behalf if the going again got rough.

WHAT TO DO WHEN THE BOSS IS DOWN
BUT NOT OUT

Unfortunately, too many subordinates shy away when their boss is in trouble. They don't want to get involved, like certain individuals who refuse to risk even calling the police when they see a crime in progress. Don't think your bosses won't remember who backed them and who didn't when they were under fire.

No one should minimize the risk involved in loyalty. You could end up on the wrong side.

In the business world there are a few basic rules for remaining loyal. After all, misplaced loyalty may help no one.

- Find out the facts; don't act irrationally or on the basis of emotion alone.
- Analyze what's going on and who's doing what in much the same way you would approach a game of chess.
- Look for hidden agendas, the reasons behind the reasons someone gives.
- Consider a person's overall record. If the current situation seems out of character, have second thoughts before acting. Chance are that there's more to what's going on than meets the eye.
- Scrutinize carefully why you are being pulled in by either side. You may be the only one who can really help (as with Harry); on the other hand, you may be drawn in as a patsy.
- Avoid putting in your two cents' worth unless you have to become directly involved. Many people who fail to follow this rule get themselves embroiled and suffer consequences unnecessarily.
- Realize that all of the above may have to be dealt with in an instant. Frequently, in the heat of loyalty issues, your first reaction must come immediately. This is especially true if it is your boss who is in trouble.

Regardless of the Risks, Significant Gains Can Be Realized from Loyalty

These go beyond being able to live with yourself or having the satisfaction of knowing you did the right thing.

A subordinate who assists the boss when he or she is looking down the barrel of a shotgun, figuratively speaking, may gain special consideration during review time as well as a definite competitive edge over peers vying for the same promotion. This certainly was borne out by the recent experience of a middle-aged woman who beat out a couple of younger, more aggressive males for a job they wanted badly. For the purposes of this story, I'll call the woman Kathryn. Kathryn currently is a program director for a large life care facility that is a subsidiary of a large hospital. In case you don't know, a life care facility permits an independent style of living with medical and nursing care available for people in their retirement years (provided, of course, that they can afford the five-figure endowment it takes to get in).

For many years Kathryn has reported to the chief administrator and chairman of a large hospital complex in the role of director of volunteers. Of course, she is only one of several subordinates he has; among others are his two administrative assistants. These two men in turn have such departments reporting to them as transportation, safety, dietetics, security, and the like. In other words, the administrative assistants had all the paid staff reporting through them, while Kathryn had all the volunteers and the hospital auxiliary to deal with. It never occurred to them that she would be considered for the job of program director when the chief announced plans to build a life care facility.

After all, they reasoned, Kathryn held only a high school diploma and they had been to graduate school. Furthermore, they had key operating responsibilities, while Kathryn only managed a bunch of housewives and retirees who didn't have anything else to occupy their time. (Never mind that it's harder to mobilize people you can't order around or command to come to work for fear of losing their paychecks.)

Since these two guys totally discounted Kathryn, they only competed with each other. Both went back to school to get their nursing administrator's certificate. But then so did Kathryn. Nevertheless, they were shocked to hear that she had been chosen over them.

Kathryn credits her personal loyalty to the chief over the years as both a volunteer and a paid employee as an important factor leading to his decision to appoint her to this position over the others.

At one point, for instance, the chief's own secretary had accused him of using hospital funds improperly. This secretary deliberately falsified or misclassified his expenses so it looked like the chief was using hospital funds for personal business. (Rumor had it that the secretary was really in league with the vice-president of finance, who was after the chief's job.) Regardless of the cause, the grapevine had it that the chief was headed for a showdown with the board.

Everybody suddenly started fading into the woodwork, with the exception of Kathryn. One day, during a meeting with the chief she noticed that he was preoccupied and asked the all-important question, "Do you want to talk about it?" He then shared with her all he knew about the matter and showed her a stack of his requests for reimbursement which he apparently was to be questioned about by the board following the allegation brought by his secretary. A quick study of the documents revealed to Kathryn that there was no way he would be so obvious if he had really been using funds improperly. (The secretary had, for instance, falsely classified a $15 lunch receipt as a motel expense, which was obviously ridiculous; even a single room at that motel ran at least three times that amount.)

It was apparent that the records had been tampered with. Unlike his other subordinates, who shied away and waited to hear what decision the board would make, Kathryn offered to speak in his behalf at the hearing. The chief declined her offer but made a list of some of the points Kathryn thought should be brought out. At the hearing his "loyal" secretary got blown clear out of the water.

LOYALTY PROVIDES A COMPETITIVE EDGE

Kathryn's loyalty alone would not have ensured she would be appointed to her new position if she had not performed—and performed well—in her old ones. The loyalty she displayed for the chief did give her a competitive edge over the administrative assistants vying for the job. In Kathryn's own words, "If I hadn't accomplished much in my previous jobs with this hospital, the chief would have seen to it that I continued to have a job. It just never would have been one with this much responsibility."

If you are considering running into the office Monday morning to pledge allegiance to the boss or throw yourself at the supervisor's feet with promises of loyalty, think twice. Remember these facts.

- In business the issue of loyalty is an important one.
- Loyalty will not get you anywhere unless accompanied by other accomplishments on the job.
- Loyalty may give you a competitive edge with the boss over equally qualified peers if it comes down to a choice between you and them.
- If a position you want comes up and your boss has serious doubts about your ability to handle it, all the loyalty in the world won't get the job for you.

All this points up a major and cardinal rule: **Be loyal, but be aware that it can only take you so far in your career. You must also produce.**

BEWARE THE SERPENT'S TOOTH OF DISLOYALTY

Shakespeare wrote, "How sharper than a serpent's tooth it is to have a thankless child." Thanklessness or ungratefulness is a form of disloyalty. And unfortunately, disloyalty runs so rampant that most of us will be hurt directly by it at some time in our work or career. (Justice triumphs, though not often enough, which explains why so many legions of miserable, rotten people wind up at the top of the heap.)

Being disloyal to your boss will usually get you the shaft. Sometimes not. Where disloyalty is noted by others, you probably will at least lose their trust and respect, even if you should squeak by without the boss finding out.

But there are even those who use disloyalty and never get caught. You may in your career fall victim to someone like this. It behooves us to recognize and be able to protect ourselves from this venomous type.

An excellent example is a young man who has carved through people like a buzz saw (none of them his immediate boss, or at least not yet) to get to the top. He has the con man's charm, the ready answer, and the disarming ability to make others feel guilty for questioning anything he does. Under this facade, he is very, very ruthless. For purposes of this illustration, I will call him Bill.

Over the course of five short years he has gone from making about $14,000 a year to a base salary of $75,000 plus an additional $10,000 year-end bonus. Bill works for a large trucking outfit carrying whole loads or LTLs (less than a truckload) for large consumer products firms. Some of their clients make soap, while others ship toys and use Bill's company's fleet of trucks. Their fleet travels over half the country and is growing fast.

Bill was hired by the chairman of the board himself, who goes by the initials J.B. and whose father had started the company prior to World War II. Father expected J.B. and another son, Sam, to put in seven days a week on the job. If you work for a family-owned firm, expect to work your tail off or expect to get shot down, but hopefully not like J.B.'s brother, Sam. Shortly before his death the patriarch got madder than hell at him one day for slacking off and shot at him with a .45, hitting him in the shoulder.

J.B. was immediately impressed with Bill. Since his own son, who became president of the company at age thirty, had graduated from the very same school, he had confidence in Bill's ability to assume a new position as marketing trainee.

Bill, now a senior vice-president reporting directly to the president, started out as a subordinate to the executive vice-president, who accepted J.B.'s confidence in Bill. The executive vice-president was in his late fifties and had been lured away from one of J.B.'s leading competitors. What J.B. wanted (he had more than a touch of his father's ruthlessness) he got—and what he wanted was the executive vice-president to watch over Bill. Initially, Bill was hired to analyze which runs were profitable and which were not and to spotlight new locations to set up terminals. To meet this key objective of J.B.'s, the executive vice-president took Bill under his wing, making sure he met the right people to fulfill the requirements of this new job.

The executive V-P was a tough customer, but he related to Bill's keen mind and drive to get ahead. Bill had come up the hard way (the only member of his family ever to hold a college degree), something the executive V-P could relate to in the extreme. This man had been an orphan since the age of eight when his parents died in the German extermination camp at Auschwitz. He viewed Bill as a diamond in the rough who, with the right guidance, would become a priceless gem. Unfortunately, the executive V-P was totally unaware of the price he might personally pay, as I well knew through comments Bill made to me soon after becoming one of his subordinates. To wit, "Initially, marketing reports to sales, but historically, as a company grows, things are reversed; sales reports to marketing." Translation: "You may be my boss now, but just you wait—soon you'll report to me."

On his way to the attainment of this goal Bill went through a series of drinking "buddies" whom he used in one way or another.

Case A. In an effort to learn more about the operations, Bill started getting to know the district manager, John. John also had been hired into the company personally by J.B. John had been a quarterback on the football team of J.B.'s alma mater. First, John served as a salesman, then as a terminal manager, before promotion to district manager.

Yet within three months of meeting Bill for drinks at a local bar, John was demoted to terminal manager. John had been

Bill's closest competition for manager of marketing, an appointment that would come through the executive vice-president. Now, people do a lot of talking when they are drinking. Bill was able to ferret out in their bar sessions John's professional weak points and his personal vulnerability to the executive V-P. It was then just a simple matter for Bill to work out a campaign that made chasms out of tiny cracks in that relationship.

Case B. Next, Bill built rapport with the head of data processing. Together they founded the company's baseball team, which was looked upon favorably by its sports-minded chairman. This required spending a lot of time together, including having after-game beers. Bill found out enough about the data processing department to see the advantages of its reporting to him. The executive V-P bought the idea. Six months later Bill had the whole data processing department reporting to him. In one fell swoop Bill had more than tripled the number of people reporting to him. This gave Bill much more status in the eyes of upper management (after all, he didn't want to report to the executive V-P forever).

Case C. Bill started traveling a lot for his boss. While on the road down South he ran across the controller of one of the nation's largest trucking fleets in the motel bar. From the way this man shot off his mouth to Bill, it became apparent to him that the controller's company was ripe for a takeover attempt. Bill easily won his confidence. Then he asked for the controller's cooperation in the acquisition in exchange for a promise of a fatter paycheck with Bill's company. (This was one of the few promises Bill ever kept.) However, after the man had cut bait and moved up North, Bill started to leak some of the controller's remarks to the president, such as the controller thinking he was a lot smarter and better able to run the company than the president was. These statements, made over several Scotches at get-togethers at Bill's club, were conveniently made in earshot of people who could corroborate Bill's story. As a matter of fact, the controller was one of these big guys with a lot of Southern charm who might just have been a contender for the spot which, of course, Bill wanted eventually. Bill set out behind the scenes to make top management aware of the controller's "disloyalty" and to remind them that the controller had, after all, leaked information about his former employer, from which he then personally benefited, as his paychecks showed. And what would keep him from doing the same thing to them?

The fact that every one of Bill's drinking buddies somehow ended up getting hurt never seems to have entered anyone's mind.

The best way to protect yourself from people like Bill is to keep your guard up.

- Analyze the hidden meaning behind their comments.
- Keep not only your ears open but your eyes as well. Ascertain what happens to those individuals who become their "friends." Do those who get too chummy end up being demoted or fired?

Being a team player is fine as long as your own neck remains intact.

15
Faulty Assumption Fifteen

IT'S WHO YOU KNOW,
NOT WHAT YOU KNOW, THAT COUNTS

*"I had to give myself a
competitive edge. As far as my
boss was concerned, I wasn't
even in the running for a
promotion. There was no way to
demonstrate my management
ability, just pushing a pencil like
the rest of the herd. I knew I
had to get myself noticed."*

*Male, 59
top official
federal government agency*

What do alcoholics and frustrated job holders have in common? Individuals in both groups often take the geographic cure for what ails them. The alcoholic moves away, leaving behind people he knows. It is as if former friends and relations, the place and job, are the cause of this disease. The great beyond, the grass on the other side of the fence, Mecca, Shangri-la, Walden beckon with the promise of starting afresh.

Bored employees switch jobs and jump over to a different organization, often claiming that company politics was holding them back in their former jobs. In spite of an extra degree

197

earned, or experience, or time on the job, their opinion is that all that matters is who you know, not what you know.

Both groups hold high hopes that their futures and fortunes will be brighter with a change of scenery. Unfortunately, quite often the alcoholic starts drinking just as heavily, and the job switcher soon becomes dissatisfied again. Why?

Everyone's frustrations on the job, coupled with lack of upward mobility, can't be attributed to politics—to not knowing people with pull. For the alcoholic there is one thing he can't escape in San Francisco any more than he could in Poughkeepsie—himself.

There are exceptions. Sure, the nephew of the chairman of the board gets hired. So does the cutie sleeping with the boss or the guy wearing the right school tie. But for the vast majority of us, what we know is more important than who we know.

"THEY MOVE ON; THEN THEY ALWAYS WANT TO COME BACK"

I respect the perceptions of a man I'll call Gene. He is the director of industrial relations for a large consumer products firm located in the Midwest. One of his favorite phrases is, "They always seem to want to come back again."

As we talked, Gene told me that the day before a former subordinate called to ask for her old job back. Her name was Donna. She was floundering in New York, working as the equal opportunity (EEOC) director of a large and very well-known newspaper. She had gone there to take the exact same job— same title and duties, only a slightly higher salary—she had held when she was reporting to Gene.

As Gene talked about her I discovered several mistakes Donna had made.

Critical mistake number one. Donna logged a lot of hours to earn a degree before checking out what she'd be getting and what she'd end up knowing. She believed that her MBA was the ticket to fame and fortune. But as far as Gene was concerned, she had wasted her time taking lightweight courses in a college that did not have the best reputation within the business community for academic excellence. In Gene's words, "Buy the best in its class. If you can't buy the best mink, buy the best rabbit—go after the quality degree, not the quick degree."

Donna's approach to earning her master's degree was to get it over with as quickly as possible. You may not agree with Gene, but don't think his attitude is unusual among employers. With so many people going back to school to gain an MBA degree, more and more bosses and personnel managers are going to look closely at grades, activities, and the course content the individual completed.

Companies are similarly concerned about whether or not you graduate with an MBA accredited by the American Assembly of Collegiate Schools of Business (AACSB). Of the estimated 500 MBA programs offered in this country, reportedly fewer than one-third meet the standards set forth by this body.

Donna would have been better off if she had spent more of her time performing community work and gaining exposure with business leaders through serving such not-for-profit groups as Junior Achievement. The skills to be gained and the accomplishments realized in service organizatons carry weight on a résumé and would have helped Donna in view of her lightweight academic credentials, according to Gene.

Critical mistake number two. Donna didn't give her first job a real chance. She became impatient before she had time to find her niche.

Donna took the job in New York because she found the town so much fun while there on a vacation. Then she began crying to Gene that she found New York cold and impersonal, particularly the people at her office. In her words, "Nobody seems to pay much attention to me on or off the job." In her first job she had made some valuable contacts. Except for Gene, she had burned these bridges behind her by the move.

Donna didn't take into consideration that the job she was going to wasn't going to be any different from the one she was leaving. She had exactly the same duties. The things she didn't like about the first job she also deplores in the new one. By this time, had she stayed put, she might have been closer to improving her situation.

She was gaining no exceptional expertise.

Even the bigger salary that came with the new job was a trade-off, since the cost of living in the Big Apple was considerably higher than in the city she left.

Critical mistake number three. Donna took a lateral transfer to another company. Unless she could gain new skills and experience, she just took a going-nowhere step on the career ladder.

Donna made a common mistake of many people who get their first big job, particularly in a big corporation. The job just may not fully engage one's mind or talents. She looked to the job alone to give her all the challenge, experience, and outlet for her energies, according to Gene. He advised her to get involved in community work to gain skills and contacts that might begin to make the job take the shape she had hoped it would at the beginning.

She didn't realize it often takes more time in a large corporation to find one's niche. Gene tried to help by exposing her to others to see if she might be more interested in different areas of the company's work. He said, "I lined up several interviews with marketing people at various times to see if Donna was interested in other types of work. But she didn't know what she wanted and I couldn't make up her mind for her!"

Critical mistake number four. Donna had no clear idea about what she wanted from her job or career. Donna's biggest problem is Donna. She doesn't know what she wants now any more than she did on the job with Gene.

None of the interviews with the marketing people turned out positively because she wasn't sure what she wanted. Since she wasn't sure, they couldn't be sure, and no one risks training someone who might decide he or she doesn't want the job after all.

Bosses hire people who seem genuinely interested and committed, not those who can't make a decision.

At one point Donna thought Gene's own job looked pretty nice. She had four years of experience as the EEOC director. To set her sights on director of industrial relations she needed to add skills and experience in personnel, labor law, safety, benefits, salary administration, and other key areas. Instead, she took a job that gave her no opportunity to gain these skills.

It should be apparent that Gene could have introduced Donna to a stadium filled with the right people—*who* to know—and nothing would have come of it because she had too many deficits in *what* she knew.

Don't fall into the same trap as Donna. Where do you want to go? What do you want to be? Do you want your boss's job? Something like it in another firm? To be president of the company? *Decide,* then do the following.

- Plot out the moves and steps that must be taken to wind up where you want to be, even if it's the top spot in the company.
- Determine the skills and experience that must be acquired and how best to develop them.
- Cultivate influential friendships and contacts in as wide a circle as you can manage. Include professional and civic connections.

You can't count on doors opening for you just on the basis of *who* you know, however helpful these contacts are. What you know about yourself, your credentials, and what you know in the way of skills and experience count for more.

"ANYTHING WOULD BE BETTER THAN DOING THIS FOR A LIVING"

Donna's position has been filled by a woman I'll call Shirley. Gene introduced us after filling me in on how she came to have the job. She almost didn't have it because, like Donna, she hadn't come to terms with herself or her temperament enough to know what she wanted.

While Donna was there Shirley was the department's administrative assistant. She had been in the job for quite a while and had reached that fork in the road that most of us encounter at one time or another—anything would be better than doing this for a living. She was feeling put upon and abused.

Shirley wanted to be director of EEOC. While she didn't have a master's degree, she had trained Donna and, for that matter, the man who held the job before. But since Donna was still there at the time, she applied for an open position in the personnel department to get away from her job.

She instantly hated it. She knew the move had been a big mistake. The paper shuffling was driving her batty. She had to read an average of 1,000 résumés a week and answer them all.

Then Donna left. Shirley knew that Gene was aware that she was interested in the position and that he liked her. When he didn't offer her the job she reacted like a woman scorned and huffed around the office, giving him the silent treatment for weeks and glowering heavily at applicants he interviewed.

Finally, she marched into Gene's office. "I was going to ask for my old job back, but I really don't want that. I think I can handle the duties of the director of EEOC. After all, I've trained the last two people who've held the job."

That was all Gene needed to hear. He knew she was capable, but in his words, "She needed to be more assertive." That flash of courage to ask for the job showed that she had what it would take to deal with some of the first-line executives who were dragging their heels when it came to hiring minorities.

"THAT DEPARTMENT'S TOO INBRED; I NEED SOME FRESH IDEAS"

Before I left Gene introduced me to his new manager of training and development, whom he'd hired from the outside rather than promoting from within when the former manager left the company.

Gene got right to the point when I inquired why he'd bucked company policy to do that. "That department's too inbred. I want some fresh ideas. I knew I'd never get anything new or innovative out of the staff that was left."

Making this allegation was serious, because I knew Gene was open-minded and never put a muzzle on new ideas. What amazed me was that Gene had been able to go around a thirty-two-year company veteran with enough service award pins to fill a bread box and who even addressed the president by his first name.

This only goes to show that, if *who* you know is really more important than *what* you know, bosses would never hire outsiders and companies would always promote from within!

"SHE GAVE THE JOB TO HER FAVORITE, EVEN THOUGH I'VE BEEN THERE LONGER"

The first person who was ever passed over for a promotion— one he thought should have been offered to him—was probably the originator of that "it's who you know, not what you know, that counts" philosophy. In most cases there are more sour grapes than truth involved.

The office manager in a small firm went on maternity leave. An acting manager was to be named during her absence. The choice was between two women in the office—Judy and Martha—who each coveted the job. Both were about the same age and had approximately the same basic level of skills. Judy had been with the company eight months longer than Martha. But Martha was selected.

Judy angrily accused the firm's partner who handled employee relations and personnel duties of playing favorites since she, Judy, had longer tenure. The partner minced no words but asked Judy to recall the three discussions they'd had over the last six months. The first was a reprimand for dressing in clothing more suitable for a disco than an office. The second involved Judy's greeting the president on his return to the office with an exuberant, "There's the bum now." The third concerned Judy's developing habit of getting to work late.

Judy's boss told her, "You weren't passed over. You weren't

really in the running. You have demonstrated that you aren't office manager material."

If you want a promotion or a particular job, analyze what your chances are of being offered the position when it becomes available.

- Who is the competition?
- How strong is each competitor?
- How do I stack up in comparison?

It is amazing how few people take into consideration that if they are looking at a job—particularly a juicy plum of a job—other's mouths may be watering for it, too. So a little preparation is in order. List the competition to the best of your ability. Itemize their good points. Compare your own. Take steps to make yourself a better candidate.

On the other hand, what if there is no competition for a particular job? The position may be a dud or may have hidden drawbacks. Analyze it.

What happened to the person who had the job? Did he toil in it for twenty years with no promotion? If so, what does that mean? Does the position have little visibility? Or did the former holder of that job title just lack zip?

Is the position open frequently? If so, did those who formerly held the job get promoted or booted? If the latter, could the boss be an ogre in disguise?

Does the job look like an open road to success or a dead-end street? It often helps to put yourself in the boss's place to see what you would do if you had the power to determine who gets the position. Would you select you? Objectively speaking, would you be your own first choice?

In order to push yourself to analyze your deficiencies and to get a handle on your strengths, don't answer those two questions until you do the following.

1. Write down all your shortcomings and defects. What skills must you sharpen? What behavior should be modified? What correctable gaps have you in education or capabilities?

2. Write down all your strengths and good points. How can you get more mileage out of what you do well? What improvements can be made? How might you better sell yourself and your strengths?

"I HAD TO MAKE MYSELF PROMOTABLE TO BE CONSIDERED FOR A PROMOTION"

If I had to give just one piece of advice to those who are always whining and placing the blame on others for their lack of promotion, I would say:

- Make yourself more promotable.
- Put yourself in the running.
- Give yourself a competitive edge.

This is a difficult task in some settings and nowhere more difficult than in governmental agencies, where people can feel pretty boxed in.

At age forty-six, Peter made a conscious decision to break out of the dead-end job he held. As he so aptly put it, "My job was so unique, I was doing the same thing as 200 other people!" Some fifteen years later he holds a high level position with truly unique responsibilities. Because of the nature of his work, that title cannot be divulged.

Peter works in an agency of the Department of Defense that produces geodesic products, which is an elaborate way of saying that they draw maps. Produced through applied mathematics, exact (and I mean exact) points on the surface of the earth are determined. The government uses these products for strategic defense.

Like Rip Van Winkle, Peter woke up one day to find the world about to pass him by. He was in a rut, just drifting along. He had never even thought much about what he wanted.

Peter took hold. In his own words, "I had to give myself a competitive edge. As far as my boss was concerned, I wasn't even in the running for a promotion. There was no way to demonstrate my management ability in my job, just pushing a pencil like the rest of the herd. I knew I had to get myself noticed."

The principal tactic he used was to volunteer for community service activities. A major volunteer duty involved handling the agency's United Way fund-raising drive, which encompassed organizing task teams for five departments and several hundred employees. At the end of the campaign Peter had achieved two goals: the monetary target established at the beginning of the fund-raising drive and a personal one. Peter demonstrated to his boss that he could mobilize and effectively manage people.

Along the way, Peter had several talks with his own boss and indicated that he was interested in taking on more responsibility. This time Peter volunteered to tackle a tough operating problem. A center-wide computer system had been installed, but few middle managers knew the scope of the system. Peter knew that many managers had clerical staff consuming hundreds of man hours monthly preparing certain statistical records, which could be generated by the computer. He steeped himself in the capabilities of the system and got the go-ahead to design a training program to educate managers in its uses.

It is important to know that Peter held no degree in computer science. He is only a high school graduate. Also, he became an expert in the process of studying the system. And finally, he took some specific courses to assist him in communicating effectively to the line managers the different applications and uses they could make of the system. In doing the latter, Peter isolated deficiencies or problem areas that programmers should tackle to improve the system's service to various department heads.

Peter also gained a great deal of knowledge about the computer system and middle management's misconceptions or problems in using it by interviewing a number of managers. He sought their counsel and advice as well.

Peter has used the same tactics in the Air Force Reserve. He is what they call a *mustang,* an enlisted man who becomes a commissioned officer. (Since it might give a clue to his identity, his rank is not given here.)

He attributes his rise to the top to "doing a thankless job and doing it well." Some of the "pages" from Peter's book follow:

Maneuver Number One

If you are in a dead-end job or out of the promotional lineup, volunteer for active duty with a community service sponsored by the management of your organization.

Combat gain. A chance to show what you can do. A way to stand out among the troups.

Other tactics. Two young women I know even went so far as to create their own not-for-profit organizations and thus gained notice. One woman started a special center to counsel rape victims. The other was instrumental in obtaining financing for shelters to care for runaway girls. They both received a great deal of publicity through these efforts and experienced increased attention from their employers and personal career growth.

Maneuver Number Two

Don't stay stuck in a job; ask for what you want. Don't be afraid to identify problems that need solution.

Combat gain. New territory.

Other tactics. A man who today is vice-president of administrative services had been stuck in the accounting department of his company for twenty years. He finally mustered up the courage to write a letter to the president pointing out the problems involved with no overall coordination of the company's service center functions. He was put in charge of solving the problem. His success eventually resulted in his appointment to vice-president.

Maneuver Number Three

Sticking with the same old routine in a safe job will never get you noticed. Taking on hard jobs results in new areas of expertise. Possessing new expertise gets you noticed by people who have never heard of you before.

Combat gain. The more successful you are in helping your employer make money, save time, or just basically improve, the more *visible* you become. Bigger and better offers will come your way.

Other tactics. A medical center director a few years back could have stayed in a cushy research job. On the management board he saw that the hospitals and the medical school were losing money. He entered that fray and is now on his way to gaining a national reputation.

Maneuver Number Four

As you move up the promotional ladder of most organizations you'll find more of the individuals at each successful rung who will talk about their work and offer counsel, information, and other help.

Combat gain. The development of powerful allies.

Other tactics. Sometimes people on the line are a source of information that can't be gained or isn't available from any other source. A recent MBA graduate needed information for long-range market planning. Even though this person had specialized in this field in college, it was soon apparent to her that what was in the textbooks missed the mark by a long shot compared to what was actually done by this company. (Executives aren't apt to broadcast strategic planning techniques to a professor who might not so absentmindedly print the information in an article or book.)

She sought a series of interviews with a brand manager. Though there was nothing in it for him—no financial gain or accomplishment of any of his key goals—he spent a great deal of time and became an invaluable resource. This tactic was employed time after time as she advanced in her career. She is grateful that she stumbled on to an interesting fact: even such powerful people as CEOs and company presidents will take time from their busy schedules to talk to you, provided your motivation is to learn more about their life's work, the problems uppermost in their minds, and their perspectives on the future of the organizations they head.

WHO YOU GET TO KNOW DETERMINES TO A LARGE EXTENT WHAT YOU KNOW

You are probably thinking that the company president wouldn't give you the time of day, let alone time to see him. Now I've thrown you a curve and said that who you get to know determines to a large extent what you know. If this is the case, you may say, that lets me out of the running. This fear is particularly acute in people who may be outside the "walls" of the corporation with no access to the powers that be and who are looking and wondering how to get inside.

Even when you are a total stranger, I've found it is possible to get in to see powerful people you've never been formally introduced to—or who have no reason to want you to contact them—if you use the right approach.

First, never call to arrange an appointment. The person on the other end may have the same negative reaction as with any solicitor who interrupts his busy schedule. Besides, it lacks class.

Second, write a letter of introduction. Include some reason why a meeting will benefit both of you.

Following is a letter I sent that won me a very important interview with the vice-president and general manager of a large firm. It should be considered only as an example.

Dear _____:

Although we have never been formally introduced, please allow me a few minutes of your time to explain who I am and the purpose of this inquiry. I am president of Operations Improvement, Inc., a consulting firm. Currently I am perfecting a marketing plan to determine whether my firm should offer its services to firms producing various medical products. Several hospital administrators have told me about the high-quality products and services your division provides. Therefore, I would like to ask you a few questions concerning your business and key concerns facing this industry in the future.

Information from this meeting would assist me in determining whether my firm's services could be of benefit to your industry and what changes and adaptations must be made to insure that we produce desired results. I would need only thirty or so minutes of your time. Our conversation would be kept in strictest confidence.

To familiarize you with my firm, I have taken the liberty to enclose a brief write-up concerning the work we performed for the (client's name inserted) here in town. In a few weeks, I will be phoning to inquire whether a meeting can be scheduled.

Any assistance you can provide would be greatly appreciated. My best to you.

Sincerely,

Kay K. Wallace

I recommend keeping letters straightforward and free of gamesmanship. At the time I wrote this letter I knew someone in the firm. I did not include his name in the letter, because I was unsure how this particular vice-president viewed my friend.

Rules for Playing It Safe

1. *Unless you are sure your inside contact is viewed with respect by the individual to whom you've addressed the letter, don't make reference to the person.*

This school-of-hard-knocks advice grows out of a terrible experience I had. A few years back a client of mine told me to use his name in contacting an executive within a different company. ("Sure, I know Joe; tell him you're a friend of mine.") When I mentioned this client's name and the fact that I had worked for him, this executive said, "Really, I never put too much stock in his judgment."

Now that's a hard line to follow. It took some fast thinking and talking to line up the appointment.

Note in the sample letter that I left the door open for follow-up, but by me.

2. *Never end letters with the sentence, "May I hear from you soon?" You won't! Leave the ball in your own court and get the first serve.*

You have to keep in mind that the people you are contacting are busy people. If you leave the task of following up to a busy executive, the chances are that your phone won't be ringing.

When you do call back, don't get overly anxious. I followed up in the case of the sample letter two weeks after sending it. Use judgment, of course, not to err on the other side and wait too long.

3. *When you phone, don't ask the secretary, "Is Mr. So-and-so in?" You are far too professional for that, right? Don't force the secretary on the other end of the line to say, "May I ask who's calling?"*

An introduction that I've found works well goes something like this: "Good morning. My name is Kay Wallace. I represent a firm called Operations Improvement, Inc. Approximately ten days ago I sent a letter to Mr. So-and-so in which I indicated I would be following up by phone to inquire whether a meeting could possibly be arranged. That's why I'm calling. Is he available?"

If you're the type who mumbles and gets flustered over the

phone when talking to a stranger, write out what you're going to say and "talk-read" it. Inject an energetic tone in your voice. Purposely try to lower your voice tone and enunciate clearly. Remember, you are simply acting like a professional in calling back. After all, you said you intended to follow-up in your letter. Not to do so would most definitely be unprofessional.

If Mr. So-and-so isn't available, ask for the secretary's name and inquire when it might be more appropriate to phone back. Or you could say, "Possibly you could inquire whether Mr. So-and-so or Ms. So-and-so could fit me into his(her) busy schedule this month. I would certainly appreciate your help in this regard."

4. *Never try to circumvent someone's secretary. It is important to give the secretary the respect of another professional. The vast majority will go to bat for you with their boss.*

At higher corporate levels, executive secretaries wield great power and keep their bosses' schedule of activities. There have been times when my letters have been lost, but I never make such a brash statement over the phone. Heaven forbid. It would infer that the secretary was at fault. Better that the good old United States mail get the blame. (I'll probably be singled out for a twenty-five-digit zip code!) I say something along the following lines: "The postal service is getting so poor nowadays in spite of all the rate hikes. May I send a duplicate set of my materials and address it directly to you?"

5. *Don't be a Trojan horse. If you said you were seeking the interview for certain information, stick to that. Don't suddenly try to sell the interviewee services or hustle a job.*

I would deserve to be thrown out if I tried to sell my consulting services after having sought an interview for general information and perspective about an industry. I make it a practice to soft-pedal my work. Even when asked direct questions, I frequently remind the person that my purpose is to obtain insight into the industry's problems and not to make a sales pitch. The most I do if they request it is to send some literature about the firm in the mail. If they call me back, then I pitch!

6. *Be prepared so that you can keep the interview to the length noted in the letter and never try for a lengthy one.*

However, often such interviews last much longer than the half hour or so granted. The end result of sending the sample letter was an interview of more than an hour and a half.

7. *Take no for an answer, but only after trying to follow up. After all, the person you are trying to see doesn't grow on park benches or street corners. A chance missed for an interview may be the only chance you have for a particular bit of information.*

In those few instances when an individual can't see me within a few days or weeks I always ask, "Would it be all right if I followed up in three months' time?" At least 95 percent of the time this inquiry gets an affirmative answer. Sometimes you may have to reschedule several appointments. But on those few occasions when you do hear a no, don't argue. Just offer your thanks for their time and say good-bye.

Applying the rules to internal interviews. Believe me, if I can get in to see vice-presidents and chief executive officers as an outsider and a consultant to boot, you can certainly accomplish as much in the company where you are a full-time employee.

8. *Just be sure that your boss knows you are gathering this information for the betterment of the department and not just for yourself.*

It is always wise to have a specific agenda. In the case of Peter and the interviews to develop information on the computer system, his boss had given a clear go-ahead to find ways to solve the problem and had approved the interview method.

In some cases the boss can pave the way for you, assuming he or she has contacts. (Many bosses don't!)

By using an adapted version of my strategy for gaining interviews—and assuming the skills you are trying to acquire are reliable—you can undoubtedly get around very well on your own steam.

WHO YOU KNOW CAN DISAPPEAR; WHAT YOU KNOW IS YOURS

If you are going to toss security to the winds and risk the choppy waters of a new job or position, at least make the decision based on what you know yourself. You are in a much better position than if you make such a decision based on someone you know. You know it is what you want and what you can handle.

If you rely on someone you know, you may wind up like the national sales manager for a major glass manufacturer who was one of several hundred middle managers laid off. He accepted a transfer into a division with sagging sales, which had caused countless sleepless nights among key executives at corporate headquarters.

He was assured by his boss, a vice-president, that his job would be protected even if attempts to turn around the division sales failed. But then his boss was transferred and the "understanding" went right along with him.

16

Faulty Assumption Sixteen

AS LONG AS YOU FOLLOW ORDERS, ANY ORDERS, YOU'LL BE OK

> *"I walked in to find their*
> *produce section completely*
> *rearranged. I'll admit I shouldn't*
> *have blown up but no one had*
> *told me anything about these*
> *changes."*
>
> *Male, 43*
> *director of merchandising*
> *large eastern seaboard*
> * supermarket chain*

Stubborn as stubborn can be is nowhere better portrayed than in the symbolic Missouri mule with its rear end on the ground and its front hooves digging into the dirt as it breaks any forward movement. It is not about to do the bidding of someone trying to lead it somewhere.

I have a great respect for mules. These so-called dumb animals often sense danger (like the glue factory truck) or know that the person holding the reins is leading them into something they know isn't right. Some humans, on the other hand, often aren't as smart. If a boss, any boss, says jump, do this, do that, change this, change that, they blindly obey. Believe me, in business, there are times when something is demanded of you or you're given an order, and you should refuse to budge and you should dig in your heels and balk.

Don't, for one minute, think that I'm advocating rank insubordination. People are caught in the middle all the time in the cross-currents and rivalries between departments or managers. They are even counted on by the unscrupulous to act and not think and to jump to do another's bidding upon hearing any order—all without questioning reasons, motives, logic, or good sense.

There is unfortunately an all too frequent attitude of "boss awe." Those afflicted with this attitude generally carry out orders delivered by anyone calling himself a boss, when they should instead ask some questions.

- Who gave me this order and what relationship does he or she have to my own boss?
- Why didn't my own boss give me this order?
- Why does this other person want this? Is there some reason my boss's permission wasn't asked? Am I part of an end run?
- Who really is my boss? (You'd be surprised how many people don't really know.)
- Who will be blamed if there is a screw-up or something happens that displeases my boss?

THE CASE OF THE DOUBLE-DEALING MANAGER

Often well-meaning subordinates get into trouble by carrying out orders from a superior who doesn't happen to be their own boss.

Jodie, a systems analyst, was put in just such a pickle by a project manager, whom I will nickname "Snake." Snake and "Sweet Guy," Jodie's boss (also a project manager), both reported to the director of systems development.

Jodie would have fared better in the outcome if she had been aware of several things:

- Her boss was a sweetie but had enemies. (Even if your boss is a real pussycat, others in the organization may feel threatened by him or her for reasons that are not apparent to you. They then may try to discredit or undermine your boss.)
- She was too innocent to know that people even in high places may try to get at your boss through you. (And what happens to you is of absolutely no consequence to them.)
- She was awed (and perhaps a little flattered) when another important boss called her directly and entrusted her with a solemn task that had to be performed immediately, if not sooner. (Beware the rush jobs. High priority, get-this-done-immediately orders sometimes imply agreement or approval that hasn't necessarily been given.)

To help you understand the situation, Jodie's corporation was one of the forerunners in the design of packaged software systems. Jodie had been actively involved in perfecting a new system to store source program code, which would have vast appeal to their current corporate customers.

Just as Jodie and her boss were beginning to get their heads above water and seemed to be scoring real successes with the first set of clients to purchase their new system, Snake called Jodie out of the blue. He asked all sorts of questions, flattering and praising her creativity. Some of his questions required going through her own and Sweet Guy's files for all the answers. Snake urged her to call back with what he needed to know within the hour, and she promised to do so. True to her word, she did.

Even though Jodie was not suspicious about Snake's request, it soon became crystal clear what he had been up to. Sweet Guy stormed into Jodie's office, clutching a copy of a leading trade publication for the computer industry. The magazine had begun to run a series of articles on the latest developments in software systems with highlights of their work, with quotes from Snake.

The quotes were based on the information that Jodie had given him.

Even worse, Snake's being able to answer the interview questions inferred, as far as the world was concerned, that he was the real brains and driving force behind this new system. From reading the article it seemed as if Snake was actually Sweet Guy's *boss* rather than a peer.

You may ask what Snake could possibly hope to gain when there were many who knew the truth of the situation. In a word, plenty. Snake knew he was being overshadowed by Sweet Guy for · promotion. Snake wanted to build his reputation among other companies within the industry so he could move on.

Snake immediately ordered several dozen copies of the magazine, which he sent, along with copies of his résumé, to some select headhunters, in the event that a better offer from a competing company might not flow from someone reading the article. He also routed copies of the magazine to several executives, including his and Sweet Guy's boss, with a brief note. "The article on page 29 really gives the company a leg up on the competition." (Now how could Sweet Guy complain about the article, when it would be perceived as in the best interests of the company?)

Sweet Guy was sweet no longer. He had been cheated out of the credit for a real contribution to the company. In addition, his own subordinate had been the source of the information that had been responsible for this career upset.

Clue to success number one: Never blindly accept a request, directive, or order from someone other than your boss. At least, don't do so without informing him or her.

THE CASE OF TOO MANY CHIEFS
AND TOO MANY DECISIONS

When I worked on a consulting basis for a supermarket chain, I came upon a produce clerk packaging fruit and talking audibly but incoherently to no one but himself, so I interrupted. He snapped when I asked where his boss might be. "Around here, you really can't be sure who your boss is."

It so happened that this man had just received a dressing down by the director of merchandising. He had hit the roof when he found that none of the produce on display was prewrapped in "boats" (not the seafaring kind, but those plastic or cardboard containers used by stores to hold fruits and vegetables, which are then surrounded with shrink wrap so the customer can see but not touch or pick over the merchandise).

As it turned out, *the clerk was acting under orders from his own boss,* the produce manager, who was relatively new to this grocery chain. He had ordered the change because he thought displaying produce unwrapped might increase sales per man-hour expended, which was a key measure of his own department's performance. He figured that if sales per man-hour went up, he might not get as much hassle as he had been lately about the money expended on salaries. Furthermore, the manager really felt that customers like to select their own produce. And the manager took very much to heart the company public relations flyer passed out to all new employees that stressed in bold terms: THE CUSTOMER IS BOSS.

In practice top management's attitude about customers was that, if you scratch most of them, beneath the exterior you'll find great con artists.

My own observations back this up. The ones who complain loudest about high prices and not being able to squeeze the avocados are the same ones who wear oversized coats in the winter to stash goodies in the pockets or to camouflage the fact that they are waddling out of the store with a three-pound rump roast gripped between their legs. These are the same gems who were considerate enough to dispose of the empty containers of potato chips, crackers, or cookies their kids had consumed before reaching the checkout counter. They also make off with the shopping carts to make use of them at home as outdoor barbecue grills or as clothes hampers in which to wheel their soiled laundry to the laundromat. And they bring back a half-empty carton of cottage cheese with a sales receipt dated a month ago and demand a refund from the cashier because of spoilage. These popular consumers bring plastic lids and marker pens from home to change the prices on all the items ordered from the deli counter.

And finally, these people use the store's shopping carts to bash in cans of coffee and then try to get the grocery manager to lower the sticker price because the cans were dented.

What the produce manager didn't realize was that the edict to package and seal produce was to keep it from the prying fingers of customers who could wreak more havoc than the Med fly. The rule came from a hard-bitten group of top brass who all were former store managers.

However, this particular supermarket chain's basic problem was being top-heavy in terms of decision makers—too many chiefs and too few Indians. They bothered with nothing but issuing rules out of headquarters written up in "plan-o-grams" specifying such things as where merchandise was to be arranged, how much above or below eye level each brand was to be, how many inches or feet of space each brand was to occupy, and the pattern and manner of display. Though other chains do so, this group did not allow discretion in deviation from these recommendations. Going by the book was the only real rule.

When the produce manager countermanded the prewrap rule, he was gambling he could get by with it. He hoped to gather enough hard data to prove that his method of displaying produce could pay off in customer satisfaction and an increase in traffic, and thus avoid layoffs of his good people.

Normally, the director of merchandising or an assistant would visit the stores at regular intervals, always at the end of the month. But the director broke routine and came in mid-month, when he found the changes. In the produce manager's temporary absence when he went to run an errand, he reprimanded the clerk who was carrying out the manager's orders.

The clerk was justifiably bitter at the injustice. He had, after all, only been following orders from his boss.

Clue to success number two: There are people in this world who would not be thrilled if you threw a big surprise party in their honor. *Bosses* generally fall into the category of those who *do not like surprises,* particularly if they are operational ones. Inform your boss of what you're going to do before you do it— particularly when it involves change! Otherwise, you may place your own subordinates in the line of fire and lose their respect.

THE CASE OF THE IRON FIST IN THE VELVET GLOVE

Delegation of authority can be a ticking time bomb for subordinates. Most of the authors way out there in academia, writing on delegation, categorically insist that delegation is not delegation when a boss reserves the right to review decisions.

Well, while they are splitting hairs, many subordinates in the business world are getting their butts kicked for screwing up a delegated duty or happening to be in the way when their boss screws up a task delegated to him or her.

Don't think it necessarily will be any better in those organizations whose top executives espouse the virtues of participative management and advocate pushing decision making down to the lowest possible level.

Here's why. A lot of vice-presidents or directors are in a double bind. They certainly can't be caught doing nitty-gritty work because it's beneath them. It is demanded and expected that they delegate and redelegate tasks and the authority to carry them out, right on down the line to a department manager.

However, delegation of authority often does not relieve the delegator of responsibility for what happens. Upper and middle management still will be held accountable for all delegated decisions by others. A lot of companies call this policy by fancy names. One that sticks in my mind is "delegation without nullification."

How does it work? Let me paraphrase (with appropriate changes to safeguard identity) what a top executive told the editor of a national business magazine. The editor had asked,

"How do you achieve a sense of participation within your company?" The executive answered:

> One of the best ways I know to achieve it is to push decision making down to the lowest possible level. This gets a lot of interchange of ideas. But in order to tap this hidden resource inside our employees' minds, it is necessary to delegate. Delegation, however, without nullification!

When asked to explain what that meant, the executive said:

> You don't go in and hold a man's hand and do the work for him. Nor do you make his decisions for him. But you damn well better know what's going on down there and what those decisions are. And, if need be, you have to bring down the iron fist.

It is simple enough for a first-line supervisor or department manager accustomed to making hundreds of routine decisions to feel somewhat exempt from keeping his or her own boss informed. This is particularly true where there is power to make decisions and take whatever actions are necessary to get the job done.

Informing is really feedback to your immediate boss. Some of it is pretty routine. But some of it is not—at least it may not seem so in the boss's opinion.

Remember: **The success or failure of decisions you make in the performance of delegated—either original or passed along—responsibility is technically still the responsibility of your boss. In the eyes of the chairman, the executive vice-president, the president, the vice-president, the director, or anyone else in the pecking order, the buck stops with the person who initiated the delegation of duty. And pleading ignorance is no defense at all!**

So what and how do you report? Technically speaking, you may think it is a vice-president or director who is supposed to establish controls and communications to monitor responsibilities. The magic phrase is *supposed to.* Many are very lax. If that is the case, you have to pick up the ball yourself. The only way to get a reading on your range of authority is to set up some type of feedback pattern. This takes many forms, among which are:

- spot memos
- informal discussions to clarify what is to be accomplished at each step in the process
- alerts or reminders on progress or problems that might affect deadlines
- reports (regular or special)
- telephone conversations

Generally speaking, it's better to over-inform than under-inform. Whenever you take any action (this does not include trips to the bathroom) you should inform your boss. It goes without saying that you should use common sense and inform the boss with the frequency, and in the manner, that he or she finds most acceptable.

On routine matters you might hold off informing him or her until you write your usual biweekly or monthly reports or any other regularly established form.

Clue to success number three: Despite what the textbooks say about delegation, in the real world the boss who delegates reserves the right to review decisions, to change or countermand them. In spite of what top executives espouse as policy, the truth is that how you do the job reflects on or affects your boss (except in rare cases in which you're being given enough rope to hang yourself, but that's another matter).

THE CASE OF THE CLOBBERED DECISION

No matter how high up your boss may be in the corporate hierarchy, his or her actions are always subject to review by yet a bigger boss. No boss is totally independent. Even if your boss has the power to take action, your boss had better keep his or her immediate superior informed. As we have seen in the foregoing case, failure to inform cannot only get your boss into hot water but can put the heat on you, who may be an innocent bystander.

The key, then, is *to inform.* On nonroutine matters it may be wise to meet with your boss immediately. If that isn't possible and you decide to go ahead and take action, let the boss know as quickly as possible. In situations in which you aren't sure what the reaction may be to your ideas or thoughts or plans, it is better to bring a recommendation to your boss and gain his approval before taking any action.

Believe me, taking these precautionary steps sometimes is painful. *It hurts to put a lid on your ego and its needs for liberty and independence.*

Paying attention to these realities would make a lot of situations better in offices and board rooms everywhere.

THE CASE OF THE CROSSED WIRES; OR WHY YOU SHOULD STAY ON THE BOSS'S WAVELENGTH

Take the case of Margaret, a transportation assistant in a large company who reported to a regional traffic manager, Mr. Small. He, in turn, reported to the vice-president of transportation, Mr. Big.

Small gave Margaret an assignment. She was to run a survey of all their bills of lading from the company's several plants. The railroad that was handling their shipping—here called Rapid Rails—was going to raise costs 58¢ per hundredweight. Mr. Big was considering switching to trucks for transportation of their products. He considered the rail line's rate hike exorbitant, despite the carrier's protestations that it was only attempting to make a fair and reasonable profit.

The material survey Margaret was compiling was to be used by Mr. Big and higher-ups in the company at a meeting with representatives of Rapid Rails in order to negotiate a favorable contract or decide to part company.

Mr. Big had delegated the task to Mr. Small, who had

redelegated it to Margaret. Small had been told to come up with a cost breakdown on shipping by rail going back over a period of six months. Rapid Rails already had prepared a breakdown covering the last two months. Mr. Big wanted to be armed with information that he felt covered a more significant experience sample—more favorable to the company's position, of course.

At the time he received the assignment, the meeting between the company and the rail carrier was scheduled one month away. Margaret went right to work, following her boss's instructions to the letter. In two weeks' time she was well on her way to completing the survey.

Mr. Big dropped by to see how she was coming along. Margaret was able to show him the preliminary compilation, which already amounted to several pages of statistics grouped alphabetically by city and state and numerically by date, on a month-to-month basis.

To Margaret's utter surprise, Mr. Big began pounding his fist up and down on her desk and screaming, "Damn it, that's not right! Those figures should be compiled on a plant-by-plant basis with all figures lumped together over a six-month span, not broken out by month."

Margaret was mentally counting the days of overtime it would take to get the information on this new basis. Mr. Small— hearing the commotion—stepped to her defense.

Small explained and argued that the sample size was more representative, the way he had Margaret compiling the survey. Big was not about to be convinced easily and it took some time to cool him down and get him to agree.

Margaret's boss could have saved everyone a lot of grief if he had provided an explanation of the summary at the outset. You are detective enough by now to pick out the clues Small tripped over:

- The survey was not a routine task.
- The survey results were of considerable importance. They had long-range effects for the company. A lot of people would be putting their necks on the line on the basis of these statistics.

- There was a chance that Small had not understood the assignment, particularly since it covered new ground and Big was less than explicit in mapping it out. (When a boss is rather vague, it sometimes signals his or her own unsureness as to exactly what is needed or the best way to approach it.)
- The boss was tense about the meeting and his role in it.

It would have taken Small less than an hour to review with Big the way the survey was to be taken before it was started. Margaret could have run up a sample page of the survey so that nothing could be left to doubt about the kind of results to be expected. And Small probably would have had Big's blessing. He certainly would have avoided an unforgettably embarrassing experience for Margaret and for himself.

Clue to success number four: Writing memos and other boss-informing techniques are not just ass-covering procedures, as people sometimes joke. Your boss may absorb points presented in a written format better than those in an oral exchange. I'm a great believer in using both methods: following up what's been talked about in writing. Outlining in black and white what you feel your boss has agreed to is simply smart. And being a boss yourself does not mean you are allowed to do your own thing without informing your own boss.

WHY THE BOSS GOES OVER YOUR HEAD

Some of you may think I let Mr. Big completely off the hook in the foregoing case. You probably feel that he should have handled things differently. After all, Margaret was Mr. Small's subordinate. Small was the one that Big should have consulted with questions about the survey. Why did he go to Margaret directly? And if Small hadn't stepped in, wouldn't Big have demanded that Margaret redo the entire survey against Small's orders, after all?

There is a very important issue here: **When your boss goes around you to ask your subordinate questions he should be**

**asking of you, or issues directives directly to your subordinates
and bypasses or countermands you, you should analyze why.**

There usually are valid reasons a boss makes this kind of
forward pass. Now remember, the invention of the forward pass
was a great boon to football, allowing teams to make yardage
without carrying the ball on the ground the entire distance to
the goal. When your boss maneuvers with a forward pass to one
of your subordinates it may signal his fear that you aren't
carrying the ball—or worse yet, that you've dropped it.

It may be that your boss is not so subtly letting you know
that your results have not been up to par and that it is necessary
for him or her to step onto the playing field. Or is it that you
have just failed to keep the boss informed?

Out on the football field the players have the yard line, the
referee, and the cheering crowd to give them immediate feedback
about how close they are to the goal.

Your information about the goals of a project or any situation
is the closest thing to the yard line and the cheering crowd the
boss has to go on.

If your boss's forward passes are only occasional—and born
out of being in too much of an all-fired hurry or just not
stopping to think—stay cool and dust off your ego.

If nothing dire happens to the work performed in your
department, and no great damage is done to your credibility
with subordinates, just chalk it up to everyone's having their bad
days. But be careful to look for long-term negative effects from
consistent forward passes.

- Do your subordinates now verify all your instructions
  with your boss before proceeding to start work you've
  redelegated? (This may be justifiable if subordinates
  have been pulled in different directions by you both in
  the past.)
- Are there perceptible morale problems, excess frustrations, or threats to quit by subordinates?
- Is your work or the work of the department suffering
  because of the interference?

Clue to success number five: As an additional word of warning, beware of the wandering boss. In particular, if you're a first-line or middle management type who is about to take a new job, try to find out how many times your prospective subordinates interact in any given month with your soon-to-be boss. If it seems excessive, you might want to probe a bit deeper to find out the circumstances, especially if he or she seems to hang around a lot in the halls or at other people's desks. Stray bosses, like stray dogs, can be quite dangerous, perhaps even rabid.

17
Faulty Assumption Seventeen

THERE JUST AREN'T ENOUGH HOURS IN THE DAY

> *"Of course there's a committee*
> *for the service award banquet,*
> *and I've got Judy from my staff*
> *following up every day with the*
> *caterers. But you know you just*
> *can't leave these things to*
> *others—something always goes*
> *wrong. Like last night, I ended*
> *up having to hand-letter all the*
> *place cards. No one thinks about*
> *these things but me."*
>
> *Female, 45*
> *director of volunteers*
> *hospital/medical center complex*

Several years ago I toured a research facility in a large hospital complex. Lab technicians were monitoring the heart rate of a beagle called Max as he ran on a treadmill until his tongue was hanging out.

Max returns to mind often in my interviews. How frequently I hear people complain about being on a treadmill and never having enough time to do anything.

- They seem to expend tons of energy performing duties and wind up in the exact same spot.

229

- They feel guilty if they leave work before the Big Dipper is overhead.
- They are back at work at the crack of dawn; yet in spite of getting an early start they can't seem to keep up and seem to be slipping farther behind in their work.

Max's droopy-eared, worn-out look was duplicated at my office. His name was Felix and he was the property manager for a land development company with extensive real estate holdings in hotels, shopping malls, theaters, and office buildings. He was in a state of shock. He had just received word of a "restructuring" in the company, a shift that would leave him in the position of foreman for the maintenance crew. Translation: He'd been demoted.

Felix was looking for a pat on the head and someone to tell him that everything would be all right. He was looking in the wrong place, to the wrong person, for solace. I knew too much about his situation. The president and founder of the company employing Felix valued loyalty, but that was about the only reason he could find to continue to keep Felix on the payroll.

One aspect of Felix's job was to keep the merchants happy. Felix translated this as shoveling snow with his crew, keeping the sidewalks salted in the winter, and cleaning up dog excrement from the steps in the summer (a task I saw Felix do himself while twenty feet away one of the groundsmen stood ogling at and shooting the breeze with a waitress from one of the hotel restaurants). To keep the merchants content, a new position of public relations supervisor had to be created—not through Felix's foresight but by the president, whose vision of growth for the company had resulted in many new shops. The merchants needed added support to build traffic, not just a clean place for customers to walk.

Felix knew but overlooked the fact that traffic was what created sales volume and that the company received 4 percent of each shopkeeper's gross above a base sales figure set forth in the lease. The president had to hire another young man to assist in gaining zoning clearances and to expedite the necessary approvals so new, leasable space could be created. Felix neither saw the necessity for this position nor carried out any of these duties himself.

Felix's building and maintenance staff morale was low. In his inimitable management style, Felix dubbed as his favorites those employees who were conscientious, speedy, and thorough in their work. This entitled them to repeated assignments for the unpopular tasks or rush jobs and the opportunity to carry more than their share of the work load. Meanwhile, Felix let the slackers get away with murder.

As a tenant, I knew this was true. When I questioned him about why the carpets in the hall weren't vacuumed three times a week as promised, Felix replied that I was probably long gone when the work was done. Wrong. Two nights that week I had worked until 10:30 P.M. Two other nights my neighbor had worked as late. The janitor had done nothing but empty the trash and fill the paper towel dispensers. His favorite trick was to jam these so full that you ended up shredding six towels to get one full sheet out to dry your hands. They were about as soft as a brown paper sack, but tenants frequently were forced to substitute them for toilet paper. More than once the janitor, in all his wisdom, left only two or three nearly empty rolls for twelve women and visitors to make it through the day. Yet this man was never put on probation, and probably would never leave. Felix's only turnover involved the good employee.

Felix himself put in long hours. He even came in on weekends, but nothing ever seemed to be done, completed, or taken care of properly—he was a great hand wringer.

When the president's young assistant phased out the work for which he was hired he was moved to a new trouble spot— director of property management. Felix's peer had become his boss. (Actually, it is axiomatic to note that individuals who fill the role of assistant to the president—with the exception of those in some nonprofit institutions—are slotted into trouble spots and frequently assume posts that had been above them on the organizational chart.)

The first thing Felix's new boss noted was the long hours he worked. His conclusion was that Felix was in over his head and the job must be too big for him to handle.

An old familiar complaint: Hundreds of people I have spoken with think the answer to moving up each rung of the promotional ladder is to add an extra five or ten hours to their work week. "There just aren't enough hours in the day."

An old familiar reaction: The most typical stance superiors (possibly your own boss) may take is simply to bypass you when other promotional opportunities open up. *Why offer you a larger job when it's evident that you can't cope with a smaller one?*

TAKE HEART: YOU CAN FIND MORE TIME

Every time someone complains in this day and age about not having enough time or carrying too much of a work load somebody pipes up with this advice: "You simply must learn to delegate." It's a lot like being told to eat less or drink less or stop smoking.

In fact, a lot of people make a lot of money holding seminars on that one theme: learn to delegate. Just like smokers who know they need to stop smoking, these sessions are filled with people willing to part with their money and time to learn to do what they already know they should do.

I, too, have given countless seminars on the topic of effective delegation and time management to managers of large and small companies, technical and professional people who have no subordinates reporting to them at all, and to hourly employees. The feeling of not having enough hours in the day to do all your work knows no boundaries of sex, position, or type of industry.

But take heart. Advice is cheap. There are some important tools and easy techniques to help you spot your troubles and arrive at a solution.

JUST WHAT ARE YOU SUPPOSED TO BE DOING, ANYWAY?

You probably won't believe me, but a very great number of people really don't know what they are supposed to be doing on their jobs—what is expected of them and what duties form the basis on which they are paid. What's more, the employer and the subordinate often can't even agree on what is expected.

The Responsibility Test

I challenge you to run the following test.

1. Ask your boss to write out what he or she considers to be your responsibilities.
2. On your own, list the activities you feel are your responsibility to complete.

Predicted Results: You'll be doing well if you agree 20 percent of the time on a side-by-side comparison of the two lists. In some of my workshops, disagreement often runs closer to 30 or 40 and sometimes even 50 percent.

Some readers—particularly those of you employed by big corporations with huge personnel departments that are so proud of all those job descriptions—may feel inclined to doubt this high level of disparity.

How Current Is Your Job Description?

The second part of my challenge is this: When was the last time you got to look at this wonderful job description—assuming that's allowed in your company? (Some companies guard them like the crown jewels.) And even if you were to review it, would it mean anything?

Most job descriptions are not kept up to date. It is not unusual to find them averaging ten years of age, with no update in between. Consequently, looking at your original description may be like looking at that of your assistant's today.

Job descriptions are typically written when a new position is created. At that particular juncture the line manager or supervisor (that is, the boss) may not have a very clear idea of what the job will entail and therefore doesn't give personnel a complete picture of the job responsibilities to begin with.

Job descriptions are too general in scope, with few specifics in the definition of responsibilities. They also say little or nothing about how the individual should interface with the boss or others in the department.

Consider a typical example from a large corporation. This job description is for a purchasing agent who reports to a vice-president.

Description: Reviews, signs, and issues all purchase orders.
Practice: One agent could do this when the description was written twenty years before. Now there are several agents covering many different accounts.
Description: Develops and maintains good vendor relations.
Practice: The director of supplies/service would be interested to know that seven of them have been doing her work for years.
Description: Expedites delivery of purchased items.
Practice: This chore is now filled by a lower-level clerk.
Description: Reviews vendors' invoices for prices and discounts.
Practice: This is now a responsibility of general accounting.

The very capable person who holds this job title in this corporation handles responsibilities and volumes of work that would be graded higher if the job description and title were updated.

You Wonder Why You're Underpaid?

It is indeed hard to argue that you deserve more money, that you are overworked and carry weighty responsibilities when your job description—dusty document that it is—hasn't been updated for years. As inadequate as most job descriptions are, they seem enough for many companies to establish the high, midpoint, and low salary range and grade level for anyone slotted into these positions.

In the final analysis, job descriptions are salary administration tools. Is it too much to ask that these be living documents? Or does such old parchment help personnel carry out the word from the powers that be to help hold the line on salary increases?

A WAY TO GET A HANDLE ON TIME

One such living document that will help you analyze how you are distributing your time is the Responsibility Chart on page 236. Among the things it will also help you determine are:

- who does the work
- who is sloughing off
- if you are doing too much picayune stuff
- any gross misconceptions about what others around you do
- what your responsibilities are and if they are primary or secondary ones; a better fix on who takes action and to what degree
- the "slackers" in your department
- key results you are expected to produce
- priorities
- who else might be performing certain tasks
- where overloads exist
- where there is duplication of effort
- staffing or training deficiencies or the converse
- if too much responsibility rests with only one or two key people (what happens when they get hit by a truck?)
- the true scope of your job
- how you relate to others in the department
- if your salary or title is outdated

RESPONSIBILITY CHART

P = Primary
S = Secondary

ACTIVITIES	NAMES	Kay	George	Susan	Harry	Tom
E.g. Conducts assertiveness training workshop			P	S		

How to Fill Out the Responsibility Chart

The following is a checklist to help you put the chart to use. Then I will point out certain pitfalls to avoid. Finally, I will move on to uses of the chart and the benefits others have achieved by employing it.

1. Across the top, in the slanting blocks, pencil in the names of your boss, coworkers, and subordinates in your department, office, or group.
2. Down the left-hand portion of the chart, list all the activities that occur in your department. That's right. List *all* the activities you think are performed within the parameters of your department, and not just for yourself but for everyone.
   Rationale: I recommend that you take this step because a great deal of hatred and discontent occurs in departments simply because people have gross misconceptions about what others do or are supposed to do. People often feel put upon or jealous that someone is paid more than they are but doesn't seem to work harder. Once things are down in black and white, the picture often changes considerably.
3. It is critical that each individual fill out his chart on his own with no discussion among members of the group.
4. Listing all the activities that take place in a department should ideally take place over a period of several days or weeks. Don't try to fill it out all at once. It generally takes several sheets, and better lists emerge when they are done a bit at a time.

Determining Primary and Secondary Responsibilities

After you have listed all these activities, then and only then go back and, for each activity, record who you feel is primarily (P) responsible for completing it and who is secondarily (S) responsible.

What do I mean when I use these terms? As you know, the

dictionary defines *responsibility* as being answerable for one's actions or conduct. This definition doesn't go far enough.

A person who has *primary responsibility* for an activity can take action without consulting with the boss first. Shortly after taking action, this individual should inform the boss and others. Through a weekly staff meeting or a memo the boss should be informed of the end results.

A person who has *secondary responsibility* for an activity does not take action without consulting the boss first.

There is overlap, of course. Quite often a person who is secondarily responsible may be in training for a particular duty or may act as a substitute and may perform certain functions if the person with primary responsibility is sick, on vacation, or otherwise absent. Everyone may pitch in to help out on an emergency basis, whatever the reason.

These simple categories serve to overcome a major source of conflict between bosses and subordinates. Quite often a boss becomes upset because a subordinate takes action without consulting him or her in advance. Conversely, bosses can get miffed about delays in completing activities because subordinates come to them for approval when they should have gone ahead and taken action on their own.

Rationale: By designating who is responsible and at what level of action, both boss and subordinate clearly understand expectations and duties.

Let's assume for a moment that you are the manager of training and development for a large company and have five subordinates reporting to you: George, Susan, Sally, Harry, and Tom. On the sample chart the activity line says, "Conducts assertiveness training workshops." A *P* has been placed under George's name and the letter *S* under Susan's. Thus, George is primarily responsible for carrying out that activity and to act on his own. *He also will be held accountable for that activity come review time.* Susan's role is that of relief pitcher. She will pitch only if George is sick or otherwise absent.

When you are filling out these charts the first time, be honest. Tell it like it is. List all the activities that occur, then accurately put down who you think has primary or secondary responsibility for those tasks. The first series of charts you complete should reflect what is truly going on in your department. Later you will analyze these charts, realign activities, and solve problems that may well become apparent to you while completing the first set. But don't try to solve any problems yet. Jot down your thoughts on a separate piece of paper or in the margins of these charts.

In other words, you will have two sets of charts in the end, equivalent to "before" and "after" photographs of a person who's had plastic surgery. One set of charts will show with glaring, uncharitable detail every line and wrinkle in your department. The second set will reflect how smoothly your operation is running after a few alterations are made—which brings us to the uses you can make of these responsibility charts.

ARE YOU PERFORMING THE RIGHT DUTIES FOR YOUR JOB?

Considering the key results your department is expected to produce, are the types of activities on which you are expending your energies the ones you should be doing? Look over the activities you are primarily responsible for on your responsibility chart. Ask yourself two questions.

- Should this activity be performed in this department or elsewhere?
- Is this activity necessary? If so, should I be primarily responsible for it, or can someone else effectively perform this task?

Realign and shift responsibility for certain activities wherever it makes sense.

You may be as shocked as a friend of mine was when the chart revealed that a vast number of insignificant activities were consuming hours of her time each day. Marilyn is the director of volunteers for a large hospital complex and medical center. She suffers from what I call the *carry-over effect*.

Marilyn carried over duties and work she used to perform from her previous work. This syndrome affects people at many levels. Hourly or technical professionals who have been promoted often find that they bring along excess baggage in the form of duties from previous jobs they have held.

Marilyn was still performing activities such as filling out time cards and doing all the legwork involved in the annual service award banquet for volunteers—work the volunteers were to do. She might as well have moved the clock back some fifteen years when only a secretary reported to her. Now she had two assistant directors and eleven full-time paid clerical employees on her staff to monitor the work of more than two hundred volunteers. On the basis of the jolt she got from the chart, Marilyn reassigned to certain members of her clerical staff the primary responsibilities for the unnecessary activities that were draining off her time.

I am not suggesting dumping more work on subordinates who are overworked. When realigning responsibilities, always be careful not to overload other individuals.

FINDING OUT WHO'S PULLING HIS WEIGHT AND WHO ISN'T

These charts will reveal who is overloaded with work and who is not.

I feel compelled to make one quick aside. For those of you who are overworked subordinates, getting your boss to use this tool will show who's pulling his weight in the department and who's not, without bad-mouthing coworkers or creating a scene.

Because there were thirteen members on her medical center staff, Marilyn modified the chart preparation and had each member list daily all the activities he or she carried out over a three-week period. They weighed themselves as primarily or secondarily responsible for each task. A comparison of these charts revealed quite a bit.

Not only did Marilyn discover her own bad work habits in the chart analysis; she also found that one of her assistant directors was overloaded with work while another woman in the medical center office was taking it easy. Both of these assistants were paid the same salary and held the same job description, but they in fact did not do the same job.

However, shifting the load isn't as easy as taking a sack of corn from the back of one pack mule and adding it to the other to make both carry the same weight.

A word of caution seems necessary here. It is important and necessary to use a joint problem-solving approach when shifting responsibilities and making reassignments. Marilyn held a series of curative powwows with her staff in this instance. No changes were railroaded through without benefit of discussion and mutual acceptance.

As it turned out, Marilyn had formed the bad habit of overrelying on one of her assistants because she was always willing to take on more. The other assistant always seemed less sure of what she was to do and needed more instruction. Results were less reliable, so Marilyn frequently bypassed her in dishing out work. Until Marilyn looked through these charts, she hadn't realized how badly out of hand things had gotten.

Her most significant discovery was that it had become harder to track the individual contributions each of these assistants made because Marilyn held them jointly accountable. The team either pulled the wagon to the top of the hill or it didn't. Marilyn didn't stop to analyze who laid back on the traces and who pulled the hardest. This is a big mistake, but one that creeps into management philosophy.

The management style guide of a large corporation urges joint accountability, which means that individuals are collectively held accountable for successful end results, even though no single individual has total authority over all the necessary resources to accomplish the result. Since all are deemed jointly accountable for a result, performance will be judged according to whether or not the result was accomplished—not by how each performed his or her individual role.

When you make more than one person primarily responsible for a task, no one is responsible. All you do is extend an open invitation for certain people to pass the buck.

TOO MANY CHIEFS, NO INDIANS

Sometimes the responsibility chart turns up a whole string of *P*s for a single activity. One of three things is probably happening:

1. Joint accountability has been assigned for the activity or activities. Keep in mind that, if everyone is responsible, no one is! It will always be the other person's fault, if something doesn't get done.

Nine times out of ten, it's the boss who gets stabbed in the back when joint responsibility is assigned for activities, because, where no one else is responsible for failure, he is. That's a high price to pay for letting people take a free ride.

Preferred Alternatives: Assign responsibility to one individual only. Or, as in Marilyn's case, you might consider making more than one assistant primarily responsible and accountable for certain activities, but within separate and distinct areas.

Advantages: This works to distribute the work load and allows better tracking of performance. It also removes the common escape clause of some assistants who palm off work by claiming, "You're so much better at that than I am." And it keeps capable employees from being tied to the role of playing *rescuer* (a situation that frequently leads to morale problems).

2. Activities on the charts may be stated too broadly. In the sample chart George is shown as having primary responsibility for the activity "Conducts assertiveness training workshop." Susan is designated as secondarily responsible. Now consider what would have happened if this activity was listed only as "Conducts workshops." Suddenly, as imaginary manager of training and development, there would be a *P* under your name and a *P* under the names of each of your five subordinates, since all are responsible for conducting a workshop.

Preferred Alternatives: Take care in writing out the activities performed in your department. Don't be too general, or you'll wind up with a document about as helpful as a typical job description.

3. An actual duplication of effort could be occurring among your staff or by departments.

EXTENDING ADVANTAGES TO WHOLE DEPARTMENTS

In the merchandising department of an apparel company the director of merchandising analyzed charts his designers filled out and discovered a serious problem of duplication of effort. Each designer showed on his or her chart as a responsibility keeping files on individual accounts and patterns. Unless a designer could remember a design or pattern already done by someone else for something like a jacket or vest to use in sketches or sample garments to model for the customer, in all likelihood one would have to be designed all over again and another pattern made. This was wasteful duplication, since many were basics that required only a creative adaptation.

One designer volunteered to develop a central system to file all the work of each designer. This individual took on primary responsibility for keeping this file updated. Designers could at any time go to the file and determine whether or not an existing design or pattern might be used.

Consequently, many hours of design time were saved. There was also a beneficial impact on the pattern makers in the marking department. It was a real sore point among pattern makers that these workers often had to redraw and cut patterns that were exactly like ones already prepared for a previous customer when they were loaded down with work.

While I recommend the responsibility chart primarily as a tool for individual departments or staffs, you can add the names of key individuals from other departments and hash out those activities that they are responsible for completing. Frequently, this results in building communications and clearing the air between areas that must interface frequently.

CHART RESPONSIBILITIES THROW LIGHT
ON SALARY INEQUITIES

Armed with these charts, you, like Marilyn, are in a much better position to attain a grade and salary increase for yourself or your subordinates. As it turned out for Marilyn, two of her clerks were assuming primary responsibilities for activities normally performed by employees at a much higher grade level. Consequently personnel rewrote the job descriptions of these two clerks and Marilyn was able to get through substantial pay raises for them.

Marilyn also realized that the job descriptions were out of date because she hadn't brought up the issue. This is a problem in many settings. Personnel takes its cue from department heads and supervisors, so a large percentage of the blame rests squarely on the latter's shoulders.

On a personal note, I once received a substantial pay raise by filling out a set of responsibility charts to arm my boss for a series of meetings with the manager of salary administration. This administrator was a notorious penny pincher but, when faced with the documentation in black and white, he gave my boss the go-ahead—not only to approve my salary request but also to change the job title as well, so that it would reflect the true scope of my responsibilities.

This was of critical importance. My old job description contained broad descriptions of four responsibilities, whereas my boss's charts showed I had primary responsibility for *thirty-six* activities and provided support (secondary responsibility) for *eleven* others.

Key to Success: Many self-help books point out the importance of taking on responsibility as the pathway to success; but doing so does you no good if everyone else is blind to the fact!

Studying these charts may reveal staffing or training problems.

THE INDISPENSABLE EMPLOYEE—A DANGER SIGNAL

As a boss you should be concerned if you find one subordinate with primary responsibility for several critical activities and no one else in the department designated as having secondary responsibility. The chart ferrets this fact out quickly because there will be a *P* across from a listed activity on these charts but no *S*s. If indeed only one person in the department can, or does, perform critical activities, what will happen if he or she quits or is hit by a car? You have no relief pitcher.

This situation developed in an advertising agency by design of an employee who decided that the key to job security was to be indispensable. He was the bookkeeper for the firm and had been a good one when the company was just a small enterprise. But it had grown to more than sixty employees and had acquired other small companies that became operating divisions in two other states.

"Ask Paul," was a phrase heard a hundred times a day. Buried behind towers of ledgers and stacks of paper, Paul could be found at almost any hour writing out information *from his head.* As the business became more complex, Paul made more and more errors. No one else could find anything. It became a matter of choosing between going under with Paul or risking going under without him.

The agency's president decided on the latter course as the lesser of two evils. For more than ten months, with expensive accountants and professional bookkeeping help, the agency reconstructed what Paul took off with in his head.

In cases in which activities are critical or most be performed without fail, you have two workable options: *add more staff or crosstrain.*

If everyone else in the department is already carrying a heavy load, adding a new person to the payroll may be the answer. The charts can be a useful tool to visually display to superiors that your staff is already quite lean. On the other hand, it may be possible to crosstrain others to perform activities adequately or act as backup.

If you're the affected subordinate—the one primarily responsible for certain activities with no one else as backup—be likewise concerned. Your situation could be far worse than that of being overworked. As long as you are the only one who can perform certain activities, you are apt to be trapped. Your boss is unlikely to let you leave for the greener pastures of promotion if it might take you elsewhere. Indispensability can lead to job stagnation for the individual. For the boss, the loss of a "good right arm" can cripple an operation.

I ran across this situation in the policyholders' section of an insurance firm. One of the clerks in my sessions was frustrated at remaining in the same spot year after year. I told her point blank that as long as she was the only one who could perform certain work in her department, she would remain stuck. Training someone else was the only way her boss would ever let her jump the fence from the policyholders' service to another department. Her boss had been most reluctant to let her come to the sessions—even though they were spread over three months— since she was the only individual who could perform certain activities.

GAINING CLEAR-CUT RESPONSIBILITIES

If you are training an employee to take on more responsibility, or you are bringing a new person on board from the outside, the completed responsibility charts will give these individuals a much better idea of the true scope of the job and how to relate to others in the department. Regardless of the level of a position, a new person rarely can automatically step into a job and perform at peak efficiency on day one. But it follows that the more clear-cut the responsibilities and expectations, the faster one knows and gets on top of a job.

In the prevailing mood of liberation and equality, a small public relations firm with two public relations assistants (secretaries) came up against the ever-popular coffee problem. Whose responsibility was it for making coffee and, on occasion, serving it to clients?

The president made a valiant attempt at showing everyone that it was not a demeaning task by making a pot himself. Unfortunately, he forgot to place the pot under the stream and the problem became one of whose responsibility it was to mop up the floor.

When one of the assistants left the firm for a career change, a responsibility chart was drawn up for the incoming employee. The category concerning the coffee was worded as primary responsibility for "seeing that coffee is *made* and, on occasion, served," not "You make the coffee and serve it."

Because it is a close-knit, unstructured group of people, the new assistant handles her responsibility this way. (Remember, she has primary responsibility.) Anyone going in the direction of the water supply may be asked to bring back a pot of water for coffee. She has made sure everyone has been checked out on the full procedure for making coffee (including putting the pot under the stream) and the foibles of that particular machine (which sometimes won't let down its water and sometimes lets down too much). Clients who are regulars to the office are invited to stop by to pick up their own coffee (tactfully phrased as the best way to make sure that they won't get too much cream or sugar). New clients or prospective ones are given service that would grace a banquet at the White House.

Another advantage of these charts is a clearer understanding of which activities a new employee should be held primarily responsible for and which may be better to take on temporarily with secondary responsibility. This may hold true even if the person holding the job previously had primary responsibility for the same tasks.

There is no reason that certain activities could not be shifted to the shoulders of another subordinate who wants to gain new skills and meet greater challenges. In other words, just because certain activities have always been the primary responsibility of a first-line supervisor doesn't mean a clerk couldn't learn to perform the same activities adequately.

GETTING THE STRAIGHT SCOOP ON OVERCONTROL

This brings me to a final point. If you are the boss, did any of your subordinates not mark a single activity with a *P*? If not, this is a good indication that they aren't—or don't feel like they are—allowed to make a single move alone before they consult you. Or is the situation even worse than that? Do any subordinates mark you as primarily responsible for activities and themselves as secondarily responsible when it obviously should be the other way around?

One dead giveaway, even without the chart, is your office door. Does it seem to be mounted on a revolving pedestal instead of hinges, with subordinates constantly popping in and out to ask the most routine questions or directions—and asking the same things over and over?

Any one of these telltale signs may indicate *to your boss* some of the following about your management effectiveness.

Management by bluster. You may carry on and holler just because subordinates don't perform the work exactly as you would, even though the final outcome or results are positive. This makes them leery of taking any actions without first asking how you want it done.

Management by finger in the dike. You and your staff are nearly being swept away by a sea of work. It's always emergency time with you. It's your finger in the dike trying to hold everything together. You yell a lot for help, but you won't accept it.

Management by herd. You consistently make requests of your superiors for more staff. If only you had more people to shoulder the burden. They tell you that the current number of subordinates is sufficient. You probably had better learn to get organized.

Management by nose to the grindstone. Your boss may never consider giving you a promotion since your staff doesn't seem to be able to get along without you.

Marilyn has thanked me many times for the responsibility chart system and attributes to it her recent promotion to executive director. She now handles the financing, construction, and staffing of a series of health and athletic facilities for people who have had heart ailments and other serious illnesses. This was a long-time dream of the medical center's top administrator, but he had not previously been able to find anyone he considered organized enough to handle the project.

Then Marilyn showed her mettle. Her staff was carrying its own weight, and the department was functioning smoothly without Marilyn's constant supervision. Her two assistants also were promoted. The responsibility charts aren't gathering dust, but have been revised and updated more than once. The assistants—now associate directors—have lowered decision making with increased responsibility for the clerical staff. They, too, have received increases in pay and merit raises. When one clerk left, it was decided among the others to take on her work. The salary for that "position" was apportioned among them—a direct benefit attained through the better use of time.

> How many miles to Babylon?
> Three-score-miles and ten.
> Can I get there by candlelight?
> Yes—and back again!
>
> Mother Goose

PART IV

18
Faulty Assumption Eighteen

IF AT FIRST YOU DON'T SUCCEED, TRY, TRY AGAIN

"The company took on this enormous promotion in cities where there are big league baseball teams. The idea was dreamed up by two hotshots recently added to my staff—Rick and Dick. This 'dynamic' duo was in charge of pulling the whole thing together, handling a big budget, and carrying it off with very short lead time. By the time we were ready to open in the first city I knew we had a small disaster on our hands— and the V-P would have my ass in a sling."

Male, 43
director of sales and promotions
bicycle manufacturer

You may never get the chance to try again in the real world of business. That's why this honored assumption is a faulty one, and belief in it is a particular pitfall for many recent college graduates. In fact, they may not even get a chance to try in the first place.

A writer interviewing a cross section of college seniors graduating with a degree in business prior to commencement found the vast majority of them couldn't wait to get started making million-dollar decisions within the corporations that would soon be lucky enough to have them on their payrolls.

Boy, are they in for a rude awakening. Rarely, if ever, is a boss likely to risk giving an important assignment to someone who lacks experience on the job, no matter how great that person's grades may have been in college.

What many job seekers—and rookie subordinates—fail to grasp is how very different the real world is from the academic nest from which they've just been pushed. In college, if you fail a test you can often soft-soap the professor about being ill that day and take a makeup exam. Or you can decide to drop the course and try again next semester. You don't get that many second chances on the job.

School's out. No matter how many times you've heard it said, "If at first you don't succeed, try, try again," recent graduates should realize some basic facts.

When starting out in a new career you have a limited number of chances to show your boss you can cut the mustard. And if you screw up on your first assignment, you may not get a second chance. Even if you do get a second try, the boss will be watching critically. If you screw up the second time around—providing you're still employed—odds are high that you'll only get to do the small stuff for a very long time.

A high grade point average in school may get you in the door over someone with poorer grades, but it will not insure that you make the grade in your job. As far as the boss is concerned, you're starting out the game with no score at all—no hits, no home runs, but no misses, either.

The problem is that your boss wants to stay in the promotional lineup. So chances are assignments you would like to have will go to subordinates who have performed well in the past, while you virtually warm the bench.

And for a very good reason—your boss's performance "scorecard" depends on your performance. Any boss who puts a young and untried subordinate on an important and difficult assignment is putting himself way out on a limb. Lots of people will question his judgment.

If you are a new recruit fresh out of school, it is critical that you tackle any assignment with a sense of urgency. You can't afford to relax. Your boss's reputation is also on the line. Careless mistakes can prove costly to you both.

YOUR MISPLAY CAN TAKE THE BOSS
OUT OF THE GAME

The risks for the boss in putting an inexperienced employee on a big assignment are great, as the following case concerning a man named Chuck will illustrate. He was director of sales and promotions for a bicycle manufacturer.

He really got raked over the coals by two hotshot subordinates named Rick and Dick, whom he assigned to handle a campaign. Although these two sound like a comedy team, no one ended up laughing—certainly not Chuck and, more to the point, not his boss or his boss's boss. The company lost a lot of money due to the inept way this pair managed things.

Chuck dreamed up what he thought would be a traffic builder for bicycle dealerships in cities across the country that had big league baseball teams. Little League baseball players, aged seven to fourteen, would be able to win a night at a big league game for themselves, their teams, their families, and their coaches. All they had to do was come in and register for a drawing at one of the company's dealer stores. The company hoped to sell a lot of bicycles in the bargain.

The basic premise may have been sound, but Rick and Dick got so caught up and bedazzled by meeting the baseball stars, sportscasters, and celebrities involved in the promotion that they forgot that someone also has to do the real-world work.

Careless mistakes Rick and Dick made in the campaign's kickoff city included these:

- They broke full-page newspaper ads with headlines inviting Little Leaguers to "win free baseball tickets to a pro game for your entire Little League team." Unfortunately, there were virtually no such teams in this city, only Khoury League teams—the two being competing organizations. Consequently there was a lot of confusion and people weren't exactly beating a path to the dealers' doors.

- The home game date picked by Rick and Dick to start the promotion had not taken into account delays in production (caused by their poor scheduling) of the promotional material. Consequently, by the time it was ready, they had less than two weeks to get hundreds of people to register at the dealerships.

- The dealers then were pressed into service to beat the bushes for contestants. They called coaches and some of them just stopped by neighborhood ball fields to get kids signed up. The dealers were not happy about the extra work and were downright angry about the goof-ups. In the meantime, Chuck's frantic calls to Rick and Dick went largely unanswered because they were too busy wining and dining dealers, celebrities, and so forth in other promotion cities to bother with phone calls.

- With the winners finally selected, Chuck flew in to see what was going on and found that Rick and Dick had not nailed down arrangements with the dealers on where to meet. Six busloads of kids, coaches, and parents were going to converge on the stadium with no idea of where to go.

Rick and Dick were fired that night by Chuck's boss, a vice-president, who flew in to see how things were going. He was so disgusted with the haphazard way this event was handled that he came real close to firing Chuck on the spot, too, and probably would have except that the company was committed to the campaign in the rest of the cities. Although Chuck wasn't fired, he noted that future assignments often were given to others and his next "promotion" was only a horizontal one.

Recommended for promotions over Chuck were managers who had accomplished significant results for the company through their uncanny ability to appoint the right people to the right job.

If you are a rookie subordinate, don't feel put upon should your boss give you dull and menial tasks to perform. Are these duties really busy work? Or is your boss trying to increase the level of understanding you have concerning critical facets of your department's operation? Don't fall into the trap of thinking that certain work is beneath you. Don't run the risk of making careless mistakes, as Rick and Dick did.

If you are a boss, you can't afford to rest on your laurels. Superiors often forget your previous good work when there is a foul-up. You may not be out on the sidewalk, but don't expect superiors to be charitable. You may, like Chuck, be cut off from the mainstream of business activity and never be given the opportunity to try, try again.

THERE IS ALWAYS A FALL GUY
WHEN THINGS GO WRONG

Baseball's home run king, Babe Ruth, got where he did by racking up an impressive record of hits. He also struck out in key situations. When he did, fans (whose memories are notoriously short) booed him unmercifully.

Business is very similar. *There always has to be a fall guy when things go wrong,* and no matter how good your record or what you've done before, it can be wiped out with one mistake. This applies to bosses and subordinates alike.

The higher up the organizational ladder you go, the greater the risk that one mishap will bring your downfall, regardless of how many good things you've done. Just look through the business section of your local newspaper. Over the course of several months you'll probably be able to find a number of people with twenty and thirty years' experience who are being given the "boot." The report is much more likely to read "resigned" rather than "fired" or "has taken early retirement," not "asked to leave."

In one such report I read that an executive vice-president for a company producing petrochemicals had turned in his resignation at the "suggestion" of the board. It seems that he had taken a firm position in assuring the president that all was well with the company; but shortly after that conversation the earnings report belied his optimism. Since earnings actually dropped by nearly 20 percent in the third quarter, the executive vice-president wasn't allowed to stick around through the next one. He'd been with the company for thirty-three years.

Another executive I knew had been the prime mover in getting his board to approve the acquisition of a company that was in Chapter 11 bankruptcy proceedings. As with so many acquisitions, everyone gets so involved with unnecessary negotiations on areas of basic agreement that they either fail to assess or downright ignore certain facts. In this case, the fixed costs to manufacture the about-to-be-acquired company's products were way out of line. They were constantly undercut in price by small competitors. In addition, the market was nowhere near what their original forecasts had suggested. Of course, these figures were provided by the executives who had initially driven the corporation to the point of near oblivion—obviously not a sound and objective source of information.

This man managed to hang on three years after the acquisition by assuring others that all was well. He got by with it because everyone perceived him as being successful. When he could no longer juggle the figures, he was pressured to resign. Promises carry you only so far in the business world.

At a certain level in business, there is an awful finality about mistakes. Everyone is expendable.

DARWIN'S APE
WEARS A GREY FLANNEL SUIT

When it comes to survival of the fittest, Darwin's ape might well have worn a grey flannel suit. In business perhaps more routinely than anywhere else in the world, only the strong and adaptive survive; others fall by the wayside. Make no mistake. It's a harsh, cruel world out there with numerous people ready to pounce on you and take your place if you screw up. Opportunities to "try, try again" do not come automatically.

You may scream and holler, "Give me one more chance," but it's too late—you had it and botched it!

The price of success is high; so is the price of failure. There are even unwritten laws for handling failures—harsh treatment dealt to individuals who have screwed up.

The law of abandonment. It is illegal for the proposer of a project that has failed to pretend it was not his mistake alone. Those others who voted for said project will deny having raised their hands or will claim only to have been swatting flies.

The washroom law. Failures are no longer considered trustworthy to hear the privileged conversation in the executive washroom after board meetings. Such individuals will be expected to turn in their keys voluntarily. After a decent waiting period, should anyone spy the offender's shoes from under one of the stall doors, orders will be given to change the lock.

The company car law. Having fallen from the fast track, failures are expected immediately to turn in the company car, even if they have to borrow bus fare home.

The reserved parking law. Blacklisted failures shall forego using their reserved parking space or risk being towed to the free lot.

The throwing in the towel law. Some failures opt to beat the system before it beats them by handing in their resignations. If you are an executive who dissolves a relationship with your firm on these conditions, remember that the company may insist on custody of your briefcase emblazoned with the company logo, the luggage won when you accumulated 500 bonus points in the sales incentive program, and your service award certificate with the chairman's face imprinted on it.

The law of nonexistence. Nearly every company invokes severe penalties on failures who dare to join forces with their closest competitors. Tactics used to punish such traitors involve striking the executive's name from all shareholder reports remaining in the archives and clipping his pictures from all in-house newsletters.

If these seem like facetious examples, make no mistake; each and every one happened to someone I know.

19

Faulty Assumption Nineteen

IF I HAD THE BOSS'S JOB, THINGS CERTAINLY WOULD BE DIFFERENT AROUND HERE

> *"When it was suggested in our workshop that two of us trade jobs for a week and keep tabs on our experience, it seemed sort of crazy. But after this gal had to deal with what I do for just one week, she really changed her tune and even stopped complaining so much. Now if I could only get my wife in the program!"*
>
> *Male, 42*
> *production foreman*
> *medical equipment and supply*
> *manufacturer*

You have probably heard someone at your place of work declare, "If I had the boss's job, things certainly would be different around here." These persons apparently feel that their departments or sections would be better off under their command. But would they? Things could be worse, not better, with them at the helm of the departmental ship.

If, perchance, you hold similar sentiments, consider these thoughts.

- You may have the savvy to manage the department when the seas are smooth, but do you have the experience to keep the ship afloat when the waters get choppy? And what if you run into a full-fledged hurricane?
- Can you remain calm, cool, and collected when the going gets rough? Or might you panic, causing your crew to lose confidence in you or even mutiny?
- If the ship sinks, can you really take being cast adrift alone with no one to bail you out or rescue you?

Could it be that the boss's job just *appears* to be glamorous, or easy, or a lot less work for a lot more pay? Or maybe he or she just makes it *look* easy. And maybe work that's *different* from yours just looks as if it takes less exertion or even less talent.

WHAT IT'S LIKE TO WALK
IN THE OTHER GUY'S SHOES

Work means different things to different people. Work means sweat and dirt to a laborer laying asphalt on a street. To a chemist the precise notations required in countless experiments are work, even though they involve little physical exertion. Yet both jobs can be just as demanding, even exhausting, in their own way. One of the best techniques I've found to convince a sweat-soaked worker that someone in a three-piece suit sitting in an air-conditioned office could be working just as hard is to get both parties to sit down at the same table and talk to each other.

If you've ever attended typical training seminars, you know there is a uniformity about them. By that I mean that everyone sitting around the table has virtually the same title or is at the same level. The general rule of thumb followed by most seminar leaders in selecting people to participate is "no mixie." Secretaries should only be in the same room with other secretaries; similarly, accountants should only sit next to their own kind (other accountants); and so on. Consequently, such segregated meetings have a surrealistic quality, which is my high-falutin' way of saying that these get-togethers are frequently out of touch with reality. How on earth can you get people to work more effectively together when the problem may be that they hold gross misconceptions about each other's jobs and what it takes to do them?

In spite of all the organizational charts and job descriptions that clutter up the file cabinets of your company, I'll wager that most people don't have any real concept about what others actually do to warrant their paychecks. That's why I mix employees by grade level and from different departments in the counseling work I do within companies.

I remember one series of workshops we ran for a large supermarket chain. There was a cross section of attendees ranging from the vice-president of sales and merchandising to a part-time cashier. One of the participants in this meeting was a stocker who felt at the outset of the program that nobody worked as hard as he, particularly those guys from the head office. After the second meeting he made a telling comment: "You know, I get more tired in this session listening and thinking than I do stocking fifty cases an hour on the shelves." Believe me, stocking that many cases an hour would be strenuous enough to cause anyone to work up a sweat! But after hearing what others had to contend with on their jobs and all the contingencies that even the big shots had to face daily, he discovered that no job is a bed of roses. This includes even the chairman's job. Everyone has duties he or she doesn't like to perform. There's a good side and a bad side to every job, to yours as well as your boss's.

While working with one of my first clients I conducted a radical experiment. We gave someone the "opportunity" to do the boss's job for one week while the boss took over the subordinate's job. At the time I was employed by a firm manufacturing oxygen equipment, respiratory devices, and medical supplies that were purchased by several large hospitals around the country. One of my participants, whom I'll call

Nancy, worked on a large injection molding press, stamping out items such as oxygen tubes. She reported to the production foreman, who made readings after each shift change to see if the operators were hitting "standard" (the rate of production set for this task).

Nancy and her boss actually switched jobs for a week. At the end of the week, both took time to record key events in writing and submit them to the group. I use their reports of the experience in training sessions with other organizations to this day. I'd like to share them with you.

THE BOSS'S WEEK

Nancy's boss had the following story to tell:

"On Monday I checked into the plant—a process that took the better part of forty-five minutes since I had to park my car in the far lot and walk a mile. Before I could punch in on the time clock I was photographed and fingerprinted by the plant guards. When I asked a guard why he was wearing a sidearm, I was told, 'You should be glad that management is so concerned for your safety.' On Tuesday I figured the warehouse must be at least 50,000 square feet. After walking nearly every inch of it, the first time I sat down to catch my breath I was told, 'Keep slacking off and you're going to get docked!' On Wednesday I decided to wait and change into my uniform in the locker room. I found it had no soap or towels and a hole in the floor where one of the toilets used to be. When I complained the janitor just joked, 'At least there are no mirrors to steam up. This is uptown. A few years ago we had to change *inside* our lockers.'

"Good old Murphy's Law seemed to be working overtime—'If something can go wrong, it will.' Its corollary, 'When things just can't get any worse, they will,' applied to the rest of the week.

"On Thursday I found out my wife had tried repeatedly to reach me by phone to say she had checked our eldest son into the hospital with a broken leg. Each time the operator told her, 'We do not page employees on the plant floor.'

"On Friday the ventilation fans conked out, and the temperature in our wing of the plant shot up so high that the thermostat kicked off the automatic sprinklers. The guy next to me shouted, 'I didn't need to fight the kids for the bathroom this morning. I could've bathed down here!' "

THE SUBORDINATE'S WEEK

Nancy didn't fare much better at her boss's job by her own written account:

"On Monday I began with the briefing session my boss ordinarily would have had with the production superintendent and was told that one of my subordinates led a panty raid in the women's locker room, made an obscene gesture to the company nurse, and was parked in the superintendent's reserved slot. I asked him what should be done and he said, 'What do I pay *you* for?'

"On Tuesday it seemed like half the morning crew called in sick. The other half just acted that way, and one Romeo, who wanted to leave early to make a hot date, tried to speed up the cycle time on one of the presses, which cost us two hours of downtime and buckets of wasted resin. When the superintendent looked at the production sheets, I told him it wasn't my fault and he responded, 'Well, it's not mine, and you're sure as hell going to get the blame.' "

Lest you think things got better during the latter half of the week, read on.

"On Wednesday the conveyor belt snapped, the forklift truck developed a hernia, and I had to cancel a date with my boyfriend to fill out some reports. He cheerfully pointed out, 'That job'll make a man out of you.' On Thursday I was teaching a new operator how to stack finished goods in the warehouse when the load shifted. As I sat there under a pile of cases the nurse took my pulse and said, 'You're lucky. There's hardly any damage to the truck.'

"On Friday I attended a series of meetings that highlighted the upcoming estimates for sales and earnings growth. A real dog-and-pony show was put on by two guys from corporate head-quarters ("the presentation palace," Nancy later found out her boss called it). I didn't know what to do. They were threatening to slash our crew to match what they called 'our lousy standard.' That standard was set in the first place by corporate engineers who never stayed long enough to soil their pants cuffs. Every argument I made fell on deaf ears, and I thought about how many people depended on me. As I walked to my car I was thinking about what it would be like to have this kind of responsibility for real when one of my friends yelled, 'You lucky stiff. But just wait until next week; you'll have to get back to the regular grind.' "

When the laughing died down after hearing these two recount the week's events, some serious discussion followed. I asked Nancy point-blank if she wanted to keep her boss's job. Her answer was, "Although I wouldn't mind the salary, for now I think I'll pass." Both of them had pretty rough weeks, which made them aware of the hassles each faced walking in the other's shoes. Both gained enormously increased respect for the other.

PERCEPTIONS OF THE OTHER GUY'S JOB
ARE OFTEN DECEIVING

It's easy to comment about how the other fellow is not worth his salt, but it's quite another thing to step into someone else's job and do it as well. Many times we have false perceptions about another's job, based on small isolated actions, situations, or our own frustrations.

A friend I used to work with is bothered because his boss always seems to be taking it easy. Every time he walks by this manager's office he's sitting with his feet propped up on the desk, staring off into space, trying to act lost in deep thought.

Well, perceptions can be deceiving. The boss with his feet upon the desk may well be concentrating intensely on a problem. As a matter of fact, this also is a pose many bosses strike just so others will think they don't have a care in the world, when in reality they may be masking inner fear and trembling— a move like whistling in the dark.

You may have coworkers who always look busy and talk like

eager beavers but in actual fact don't get the work out, unless shuffling paper counts.

It helps to stand back sometimes and ask yourself, if you had your boss's job tomorrow, would you be able to carry out his or her duties and responsibilities as well? Could you really fill the boss's shoes? And if you could, would you really want to? Would it be worth the price?

FOLLOWING IN SOMEONE ELSE'S FOOTSTEPS

Those "lucky" few who inherit or take over a family business, willingly or unwillingly, usually find it a lot more difficult than someone on the outside may realize. This may be due to any of the following reasons.

- A number of entrepreneurs who have created vast financial or power empires from scratch find it difficult to relinquish control.
- Heirs apparent are often puppets on a string.
- Succession may require a lot of sacrifice of personal desires or ambitions.

The Case of Promises Made But Not Kept

Early in my career I worked for a large family-owned bakery run by a dynamo who made up for his lack of height (five foot two) with his energy. Jack was eighty-two. His son, who was then in his early sixties, had been slated to take over the business for forty years—just as soon as Dad retired or departed for the hereafter. In the meantime, Jack still handled all the production scheduling and business matters while the son led tours through the plant for visitors and school children.

The Case of the Stolen Inheritance

C.C. was definitely an empire builder. At seventy he was chairman of a large conglomerate that included 150 grocery stores, a bakery and ice cream company, a cannery, several farms and orchards, automobile agencies, three banks, and massive real estate holdings. Innovation was his secret of success. He started self-service and cash-and-carry in his grocery store and offered lower prices while competitors were still struggling with credit to customers and home delivery. He built traffic through giveaways of cars and mink coats—no cents-off bologna for him. His first-born son unfortunately took this giveaway philosophy to heart and got tied up in a religious group into which he tried channeling the old man's money. The very thought of losing his empire was abhorrent to C.C., so he set up a small foundation and a religious retreat for his elder son and set out to mold his second son in his image—and it was this son who, for all practical purposes, ended up inheriting everything.

The Case of the Father Vampire

Some who pass along the family business completely absorb, or live their lives over through, those who inherit or take up the reins from them. Some of them even continue to do so from the grave. This is a kind of vampirism and the results are unpleasant.

One of my good friends recently divorced her husband (whom I'll call Joseph), who had followed his father into the family business, a landscaping firm with a large nursery. Her father-in-law completely controlled her husband, and he would do nothing to displease his father, even though that meant working morning, noon and night; never having time to develop friends of their own; never having time to themselves without mama and papa tagging along; and going on "vacation" trips driving through hot dusty fields of nursery stock.

Even though the old man is dead, Joseph conducts the business in the same manner, telling himself, "This is what Papa would have done."

BEWARE THE PREDETERMINED LINE OF SUCCESSION

Predestination is that doctrine which concludes that our

destiny or fate is preordained and we have little or nothing to say about it. This pretty well describes the situation for those who are selected as the heir apparent of their boss's job. If you are one of these, beware—uneasy sets the crown, to paraphrase a little Shakespeare. Those with hiring power may fear that a long-term protégé will follow too closely in the boss's footsteps.

This kind of situation came to mind recently when I had an interview with a newspaper reporter who suddenly asked me if I was surprised ("off the record") that a particular man within a client organization was presumed to be about to step into the retiring chairman's shoes. (As an important aside, although this reporter had laid down pad and pencil, I knew she was quite capable of remembering my answer. For those of you who may have to deal with the press, remember that there is no such thing as "off the record." Even if the reporter chooses to honor it, all he or she has to do is verify what you said through another source and then feel free to publish your comment. Thus it may appear in print as follows: "An opinion by Jane Doe, former assistant to the chairman, to the effect that he is over the hill, was corroborated by a company spokesman.")

I was, therefore, at my diplomatic best (meaning I didn't answer, "Hell, no, I'm not surprised"). I pointed out the track record of the chairman's presumed successor but kept my reservations to myself. I suspected that the board of directors at this particular client company wanted to see some changes made in the company. I also thought the board members were pretty sure that no new directions or ideas would flow from anyone presently on the chairman's staff. They also seemed inclined to want anyone, except someone that might prove to be a clone of the present chairman.

My reservations were right on target. The supposed heir apparent really was a clone when you got right down to it. He spoke, walked, and talked like the chairman, having almost literally sat at his feet for ten years in preparation for the job. In the process, the man had lost his own identity. The board definitely did not want someone who would do nothing more than duplicate, duplicate, duplicate.

Somebody else got the job.

20
Faulty Assumption Twenty

THE BOSS DOESN'T NEED MY SUPPORT

> *"I could take her bitching but
> not her backstabbing. I lost my
> cool and screamed at Irene that
> everyone expected me to be Miss
> Perfect. I was expected to worry
> about her needs, expected to
> service our distributor's needs,
> and keep my own manic-
> depressive boss from taking us
> under in one of his downswings.
> What about my needs, I wanted
> to know? I'm not impervious to
> wind, weather, and storm."*
>
> *Female, 29*
> *associate director of*
> *   institutional marketing*
> *paper products division,*
> *   large corporation*

A study conducted by a leading insurance company concluded that the perils of executive stress have been blown up way out of proportion. Its survey of more than 500 industrial companies revealed a very interesting fact: presidents and vice-presidents had 40 percent fewer fatal heart attacks than did the middle managers of the same companies.

266

Your own boss, if you report to a first-line supervisor, manager, or director, is far more likely to drop dead than is the president of the firm. If top executives are at lower risk, as studies indicate, it may be because (as anyone who has worked longer than two minutes in the corporate arena knows) they have control and someone under them to dump their work on. Read "someone" as middle managers and their subordinates. This group has virtually no control over what gets heaped on them and little or no choice but to dig in and shovel their way out.

BOSS IN A FOXHOLE

On another survey answered by middle managers they cited three primary stress factors on the job with which they had to contend: interaction with superiors, the work load, and the deadlines imposed on them by their bosses.

The average boss, the category that in all likelihood includes your boss, ends up being squeezed on many fronts:

Peers: Some peers may feel threatened by his or her success and take potshots or throw up roadblocks of one kind or another to make the going rough.

Superiors: Superiors have a way of expecting prompt attention to any requests as well as reliable performance. The value of any employee to any superior is determined by the speed and quality of response, which means that promotability and sometimes jobs are frequently on the line over even relatively minor matters.

Subordinates: A boss is expected to be a tower of strength and to set a good example for subordinates.

Soldiers in combat take refuge from enemy fire in a shallow pit called a foxhole that they dig in the ground. Bosses sometimes wish they could jump into one and pull it in after them. Instead, they frequently withdraw into themselves and become cold, aloof, stiff, and uptight to gain protection from the sniping, criticism, and pressures of the daily fray.

Very often individuals around them—peers, superiors, and

subordinates alike—force them to be this way. Other bosses seem to subscribe to the "if you can't lick 'em, join 'em" approach and try being just one of the guys or gals.

PALSHIP IS A POOR SHIP TO SAIL

A food technologist I know was promoted recently, and for the first time in his life he became a boss. He wanted to be different from the bosses he'd had. He was bound and determined to have his subordinates like him. But he found out the hard way that being a pal or a friend to subordinates often ends up being a one-way street.

He had come up with the idea of a company-sponsored soccer team. Several of his own staff were on the team, and all of them were spending lots of hours together after work organizing it. This was all just great until he discovered that these same subordinates were moving a lot faster out on the old ball field than back in the lab. (Of course, many people are far more energetic in the pursuit of their hobbies than their duties at work. The office mail boy who moves like greased lightning while playing touch football moves with the speed of cold molasses in making his deliveries each day. A forklift operator who keeps his mean machine on the rugged, dirt bike course, manages at least once a week to run his truck off the loading dock in the warehouse.)

Within a matter of weeks this boss had no choice but to resign as coach. He became more aloof and started keeping his personal life separate from the office. It took some time before subordinates started taking him seriously and began to heed the assignments and deadlines he issued.

It's been my experience that most subordinates are liable to misinterpret attempts made by their boss to be a pal or a friend. They either tend to take advantage of the relationship and start slacking off or they perceive such behavior as an attempt to meddle into their personal affairs and resent it.

Be cautious about following any human relations theories that urge or even imply that to be a good boss you must be a pal or a friend to subordinates. Most people don't want such behavior from a boss. This does not mean that a boss cannot be friendly, warm, or cordial.

TRUST AND SUPPORT MUST BE A TWO-WAY STREET

Assuming that subordinates can't have what they most desire—their boss's paycheck—most will settle for trust and support from their boss. More bosses would be glad to oblige if they thought trust and support would be returned in kind. But too often, while subordinates expect these values from their bosses, they seem to feel that the boss can get along without their giving it back in return.

Trust and support are rare commodities. They must be earned. Can your boss really depend on you? Do you stand behind the boss, or do you make it a habit to complain about how he or she doesn't do enough for you. What would you answer if the question were reversed and you were asked what you do for the boss, department, office, or company? Have you ever offered the boss a sincere compliment on his handling of a problem or project? Do you really deserve your boss's trust and support?

I am reminded of the predicament of a manager in charge of clerical services within an eastern bank. Wilma, as I will call her, had a number of employees under her who typed, filed, and stored records on microfilm and microfiche. These subordinates seemed to make a lot of errors. At least Wilma was constantly getting flak from the users of their services within the company, and she frequently found herself covering for her people. She was so tense about what might happen to the department if she left for one second that she had seventeen weeks of accumulated vacation time (even though it was counter to company policy) at the time I began my counseling work with her company.

The personnel director had been lenient when her vacation came around because Wilma had pleaded that the department was in the middle of something new and she couldn't risk leaving. But the director was beginning to worry about her. She was acting as if she might come apart at the seams. Consequently, he decided she must be persuaded to take her vacation.

He knew it would not be easy, and he hit upon the idea that I should tell her.

As I approached the clerical services department, trying to figure out how best to broach the subject, I overheard the tail end of a telephone conversation Wilma was having with an obviously unhappy user of their services. From what I gathered, there were several errors in the letters one of the managers had sent over to be typed by Wilma's staff. She was apologizing profusely when I stepped into her office. She barely noticed my presence, and when she put the phone down, she rushed past me to have a little talk with one of her subordinates.

> *Wilma:* "That was Mr. Burns on the phone again! Why didn't you have the proofreader go over your copy before you sent it back to him?"
>
> *Typist:* "He was in a hurry. Besides, I proofed each line of those letters while they were in the machine."
>
> *Wilma:* "Look, you know it's virtually impossible to catch all the errors yourself on copy you've just typed. That's why we have a proofreader! *Honestly, am I the only one who cares about the work that goes out of this department?*"

Wilma continued venting her feelings to me concerning the telephone conversation she'd just had with Mr. Burns. "It's not efficient to have to send back work two or three times for corrections. Those girls wouldn't be nearly so flip if they had to contend with our irritated users over the phone like I have to do."

When she stopped to take a breath I jumped in and asked, "Why don't you let them do just that?" Wilma was taken aback, but I had her attention and as I talked, I went on to point out that she was the boss, but from the scene I had just witnessed she was actually more like her subordinates' subordinate. I also said that it was time for her to start letting the "users" demand results directly from her subordinates.

We set up a hot line system by which users would talk directly to the person who had typed a dictated letter, microfilmed a lengthy report, or retrieved a file for them.

I gave a short seminar on how to handle such calls, so users didn't wind up madder after they phoned the department to lodge a complaint than they were in the first place. To gain their support, I asked each of them to think of a case in which they had been dumped on as a customer and tell us how their complaint was handled by the other person. Each of them had to highlight what he or she felt should have been done differently.

After hearing everyone in the group recount his or her personal experiences on the receiving end as irate customers, we came up with a long list of dos and don'ts on the best way to handle complaint calls.

Wilma still needed to be able to trust her staff to know and do their jobs. So Wilma's staff wrote out their own training manual for the department with a little editorial help from me.

For you readers who head similar departments and wish to develop such a manual for your staff, use a light writing style. Training manuals are notoriously dull and quite boring. You are wasting your time in writing one if it never gets read. I have reprinted two excerpts here to help you get started:

How to File Correspondence

This department uses the alphabetical method of filing correspondence, reports, etc. The first step is to sort the correspondence according to the twenty-six letters of the alphabet. For example, if a person's name begins with Ph (which is the F sound) you should not put it in the F folder. It goes in the P folder, odd as that may seem. If at this point in reading these instructions you were amazed to discover there are twenty-six letters in the alphabet, STOP! Do not attempt to file anything.

How to Use the Dictating Equipment

First, check to see that your transcriber cassette machine is plugged in. Next, place the earphones on your head. Not everyone in the office wants to head the latest commodities quotations. Only you will be privy to this exciting information before it hits the grapevine.

Before you begin to type, place a cassette in the machine— preferably not one brought from home. Spot checks will be run to see that no one is listening to his or her favorite recording artist instead of that favorite boss.

Special Footnote: Notices have been sent to all dictators to avoid smoking or sucking on Lifesavers. Both make for particularly distasteful listening. The dictating smoker sounds like a heavy breather and the Lifesaver muncher produces noises that sound like you're transcribing in the middle of a hailstorm.

After all this up-front work, I told Wilma that the personnel director wanted to see her trip plans by the end of the month. I dropped off a copy of her staff's training manual, along with some travel brochures to read through. She actually looked relieved, as if a tremendous weight had been lifted from her shoulders.

FACE FACTS: YOUR BOSS ISN'T ATLAS

A Titan of Greek mythology, Atlas was gigantic in size and power. His word carried a lot of weight until he was overthrown by the Olympian gods and condemned to spend the rest of his days supporting the heavens on his shoulders.

Well, many modern-day bosses I know are expected to carry such a weight of responsibility on their shoulders that only a few can pull off this wondrous feat without breaking under the strain at some time. The so-called nervous breakdown only happens in extreme cases. Today's overburdened boss is likely to suffer from a string of constant illnesses or physical distress or even pill popping. I know this from personal experience. I reported to a boss who took Valium to calm his nerves. I made it a hard and fast rule never to talk to him unless his hands were shaking, which generally occurred by afternoon. Talking to him when his hands were steady as a rock (and he was practically sedated) was a complete waste of time; within an hour this man wouldn't remember a thing we'd discussed. I'd say that this former boss of mine was productive only about 60 percent of the day. He was undependable and I never knew when he might do something that would cause me problems on the job. While he happened to be fifty-plus in years, this problem afflicts very young bosses as well.

Remember that the boss under stress may be dangerous to your health. Anger unvented and turned inward is often at the root of muscle aches, insomnia, ulcers, backaches, high blood pressure, and even heart attacks. On the other hand, you may be contributing to your boss's stress.

LACK OF SUPPORT CREATES CONFLICT

One young woman I'll call Dee was feeling extremely guilty over an incident in which she had screamed at one of her subordinates. Dee was then the associate director of institutional marketing within her company's paper products division.

She unloaded on me. Her boss was in the middle of a divorce, and she had just come back from a week-long stay on the road, making speeches and drumming up sales for their distributors.

"Do you have any idea how many small towns I've had to stay in overnight? And when I'm not on the road I'm spending hours here at the office listening to my boss's problems. Evenings and weekends I have to play catch-up with all the paperwork that accumulates on my desk while I'm out of town. That was the situation," she continued, "when Irene came into my office and started to lecture me about how I needed to get out more I completely lost my cool. I know it was the wrong thing to do."

"Like hell it was," I assured her. I knew Irene's type well. She was a marketing analyst approximately fifteen years older than Dee. She was one of those who loves office gossip. In fact, Irene spent so much time roaming about the corporate compound that her salary should have been reduced to that of a part-time employee. In a word, Irene was lazy. She never failed to comment on the character flaws of people around her but seemed totally oblivious of her own.

On the occasion in which Dee blew up and shouted at Irene, Dee had asked if she would mind picking up a ham sandwich on rye on her way back from the company cafeteria. Dee was inundated with paperwork, much of which Irene should have attended to but didn't, during Dee's absence. Irene bristled at Dee and told her, "You need to get out more. Everybody talks about how stuck up you are, never going out to lunch, and how you've let your job go to your head."

Hearing this comment was the last straw. Dee let go with a few choice words about always being expected to be Miss Perfect and not being impervious to wind, weather, and storm. Then she really wound up: "My job's gone to my head, huh? Well, nobody in their right mind would have this job. It isn't enough that I have to be constantly on the road to keep the distributors happy, but I have to do handstands to please you, too. You think I ought to get out more? Well, I think that's a great idea. In fact, I'm leaving right now, and I'll bring back a sandwich for *you*. You'll need the extra time working your way through that stack of papers you so kindly left on my desk while I was gone! You're going to miss having long lunches with your friends while I do the work, because I'm sending you in my place on some of those trips you feel are so glamorous!"

Dee was more than justified, considering that she had kept her own boss from firing Irene when he was in one of his blue funks. She had also bailed Irene out more than once with distributors when she failed to let them know the hospitals and schools that wanted their "Adventures in Eating" program. On another occasion Dee had to smooth the ruffled feathers of the president of a leading trade association when Irene booked her as a speaker for their conference at the exact time she was scheduled to be in another city some 500 miles away addressing a different group. And Irene had failed to give Dee even so much as a single thank-you for bailing her out time after time and providing much, much more support.

The real issue in Dee and Irene's conflict was a common one:

lack of appreciation and support from subordinate to boss. Often I ask attendees in my seminars, "When's the last time you gave a sincere compliment to your boss, such as, 'You handled that well.'?" I always am faced with a roomful of people with blank puzzled expressions.

Spokesmen and women for union organizations trying to increase their memberships say office workers are the most abused members of the work force. I wonder. Hourly workers can vote in a union for added support if they so choose. Top executives usually have the support of a long-term contract with the respective organizations. But bosses in between remain in that uneviable position between a rock and a hard place. In spite of being surrounded by people, they often stand alone, with virtually no support or assistance from superiors or subordinates.

Regardless of the situation, or your boss's position, you can make your own life easier if you understand these facts.

- Your boss needs your support.
- The average boss is impinged on by superiors, the work load, and deadlines.
- The boss is not an unfailing tower of strength or wisdom and may have conflicting feelings about wanting to be a friend while ending up being cool or stiff in boss–subordinate relationships.
- Many subordinates complain that the boss doesn't trust them to do anything without realizing that they have yet to earn that trust.
- Sometimes a little appreciation of the boss goes a long, long way.

21
The Faultless Assumption

YOU'RE THE BOSS

You're the boss. Believe it. Use that faith in yourself to control your own career, and you will be in step with the ideals of this book.

You now have at your disposal a whole arsenal of ideas and steps that have worked for other people—who are just like you, who come from similar work settings, and who confront the same kinds of problems you do. It is important that you avoid making the same mistakes others have made. It is even more important to *learn* from their successes.

Properly applied, this new knowledge can give you influence over a wider cross section of people and events than you ever thought possible before.

You can now take a more informed look from the point of view of others—particularly the boss. You have increased your capacity to control the forces in the work environment: political, social, and organizational.

Many of the people you have met in this book are people who decided they were boss of their own careers—people who came to grips with the fact that no one else was going to do anything for them. They had guts enough to break out of the herd. They used their brains to get noticed, and took the necessary risks to come out on top.

By now you realize there are all kinds of ways to reach goals. Nonetheless, you must always begin by getting into the habit of thinking about yourself and your situation and tapping your own creativity. You can solve the problems encountered on the job and in your career. You're the boss!

Index